THE KING, McQUEEN AND THE LOVE MACHINE

THE KING, McQUEEN AND THE LOVE MACHINE

My Secret Hollywood Life with Elvis Presley, Steve McQueen and James Aubrey

Barbara Leigh with Marshall Terrill

Foreword by Joe Esposito

Copyright © 2001 by Barbara Leigh with Marshall Terrill.

Library of Congress Number:		2001119587
ISBN #:	Hardcover	1-4010-3885-9
	Softcover	1-4010-3884-0

All rights reserved. No part of this book may be reproduced or transmitted in any form or by any means, eleictronic or mechanical, including photocopying, recording, or by any information storage and retrieval system, without permission in writing from the copyright owner.

This book was printed in the United States of America.

To order additional copies of this book, contact:
Xlibris Corporation
1-888-7-XLIBRIS
www.Xlibris.com
Orders@Xlibris.com
13736

Dedicated to my dearest love, my son, Gerry Haynes, who was my number-one fan. 1964-1994.

B.L.

ACKNOWLEDGEMENTS

I'd like to thank Meredith Suki Coonley and Steve Swires for their hard work and thoughtful editing of the manuscript. My special thanks goes to Joe Esposito for his foreword to this book and his friendship over the years. Thanks to Andrew Smith, Jessica St. John, Tom Eden, Skye Aubrey, Judith Baldwin, Marilyn Grabowski, Gary Cole and Ilya Salkind for their love, friendship, inspiration and encouragement. I also want to thank my mother, Edith McIntosh, for her support and belief in me. Additionally, I'd like to thank Dick Clayton and Peter Schmidt for telling me through the years I could do it. Thanks also go to Russ Howe and Tom Salva for their contributions of their Elvis Presley photo collection, and to Tim Hacker for his cover concept and photo arrangement. And a big kiss for all my fans who never forgot about me. This book is especially for them.

FOREWORD BY JOE ESPOSITO

I met Elvis Presley when we served together in the army, and was with him from the time we were discharged in 1960 until his death in 1977. I was his road manager, right-hand man, and close personal friend.

In those 17 years, I handled almost every detail of his personal life which, for a man with Elvis' schedule, was a 24-hour-a-day job. I got to know all of Elvis' girlfriends. One of my extra duties was organizing their flight and hotel accomodations, so that they could be a part of his hectic life. It was easy to recognize that most of these relationships fell into one of two categories: they were either relationships of convenience or relationships of trust. His relationship with Barbara Leigh was certainly one of trust.

Elvis met Barbara in 1970, while he was performing at the Las Vegas International Hotel. (His shows during this period are still considered some of his best.) After each show, Elvis would hold court in his dressing room, where celebrity friends and fans would gather. As soon as Barbara stepped into his dressing room that night, he couldn't take his eyes off of her. I watched E as he walked right up and sat down next to her. I don't think either of them spoke to another person for the rest of the evening. Not only was she his "type"—a brunette with sensual good looks—they also shared a lot in common. Both grew up poor in the South, and both knew what it was like to be looked down on by others who had money. The two had come a long way to get where they were.

Their attraction was immediate and, during the affair that followed, Elvis and Barbara spent a lot of time alone together. It's no secret that E had his share of ladies, but Barbara stands out in my mind. She was caring and funny, and everyone in Elvis' circle immediately took to her. She brought out the southern boy in him. As the rest of his life began to spin out of control, she was someone with whom he could be himself, someone who could help him touch back on his roots.

But with lives like they were living then, nothing would last forever. Although he'd end up getting a divorce only two years later, Elvis still was married to Priscilla, and the future for E and Barbara did not look promising. Barbara's career made her less available for his calls, and they grew apart. They moved onto other relationships, but remained good friends. He always kept track of where she was and what she was doing.

She was one of the first people I called when Elvis died.

He would have wanted her to know.

Joe Esposito
October 2001

INTRODUCTION

As a child, I don't remember ever dreaming about being famous, or for that matter, being particularly interested in those who were. Growing up in a small town in Georgia, I was never formally introduced to the outside world until I was nineteen years old. At this stage in my life I moved to Los Angeles and began a modeling career that would eventually take me all over the world. But looking back now, I realize that I've ended up spending a great deal of my life involved with men who were "famous" by every definition of the word. Men whom the public know as stars. Men whom I've known as friends and lovers.

This year will mark the twenty-fifth anniversary of Elvis Presley's death. A lot has been written about the man and the icon. A good majority of it has been negative, highlighting his gluttony and opulent lifestyle. Yet none of this has come close to describing the Elvis Presley I knew.

I met Elvis on August 30, 1970, in Las Vegas when he was headlining at the Las Vegas International Hotel. I was a fashion model and aspiring actress, who just happened to be his "type." We met backstage, and for the next two years of my life, Elvis Presley was a friend and lover.

During those years, I got to know Elvis as a man who was kind, sincere, gentle, funny, and even humble. He lived for his fans and gave them 100 percent of himself. In almost every way, he belonged to them. Because of Elvis' enormous popularity, he constantly struggled to maintain his privacy, his perspective on life, and eventually even struggled to maintain his sanity. I was with Elvis in the down time—those quiet hours between the shows, and away from the public. It was in those times that I really got to know just how lovely and complex he was. Yes, Elvis had his faults, but I've never met another man quite like him.

As a result of my love and respect for Elvis, I never spoke about our relationship while he was alive, and I've tried to carry on that tradition after his death. I did, however, grant two interviews. One was for Peter Guralnick's critically acclaimed book, *Careless Love: The Unmaking of Elvis Presley*. The other was a *big* mistake. The author's name was Albert Goldman.

Goldman's book, the despicable *Elvis,* was nothing more than an over-blown tabloid article. He chose to focus on the prurient, and he distorted the truth. Maybe that's what "enquiring minds" want to read, but it was misleading and wrong. I'm writing this book in part to set the record straight regarding our relationship.

However, I really can't complain too much. I've been lucky. I've had the opportunity to know some fascinating men in my life, such as Elvis Presley, Steve McQueen and James Aubrey, three of Hollywood's heavy hitters in the sixties and seventies. Few people have experienced the exciting life I've lived. I've been able to share these men's worlds and their lives, while still maintaining my own anonymity. I've had a great seat to the "show," and I've loved every minute of it.

Barbara Leigh
October 2001

CHAPTER ONE

Mexico City was glorious. Although it suffered as one of the poorest countries I'd ever visited, it was a beautiful land filled with romance, created by the history of ancient people. A land of mystery and secrets. It was intriguing to view all of this through the eyes of an American.

At the time, I was 31, a top model and was filming a commercial for the new 1978 Ford automobile.

Throughout the week, I had been carrying on a torrid love affair with a dark, handsome, former-Olympic-athlete-turned-movie-star who was adored by all of Mexico. We met when he visited my stage-set, watching me until the appropriate time to introduce himself. He was filming on another stage, and had heard there was an American model next door.

He was tall, dark, gorgeous—the perfect host. He was romantic, exciting, and loved the thrill of pursuit. Between my lover and my modeling assignment, I didn't have much free time.

On the morning of August 18, 1977, I flipped on the television before another long day on the set. As I stepped out of the shower, I caught a glimpse of the news in Spanish. The image on television is still vivid in my memory.

The broadcast showed a white hearse driving slowly down a street in what appeared to be the United States. Thousands of mournful onlookers watched the hearse, which was followed by 16 white stretch limousines.

Who died who was so important? I hadn't heard anything on the set, but then again, no one could possibly have known of my relationship with the man whose body now lay in the casket.

I toweled off, got dressed and made my way downstairs to the lobby. The limo driver and a male model already were waiting for me.

On our way to the studio, the driver, trying to make polite conversation, casually asked, "Did you hear that Elvis Presley died?"

I felt as if a bolt of lightning had struck my body. I wanted to break down crying then and there, but surprisingly, I kept my composure in front of these strangers. Actually, I was in too much shock to cry. I remained numb and speechless throughout the day's shoot.

When I finished work, I rushed back to the hotel to call Teddy's, my answering service in Los Angeles.

The first message left on August 16 was from Joe Esposito. Joe was Elvis' right-hand man and my friend. His message said: "Barbara, come to Graceland. Joe."

There was an urgency to the tone of the call. I knew it had to be true.

The King was gone.

It has been more than 30 years since I first met Elvis Presley. At the time, I was an aspiring actress and a successful print and television commercial model. My look was in sync with the 1970s: a hippie/flower-child who wore mostly wore jeans, tie-dyed shirts, headbands, beads and leather sandals.

I had a charmed life once I reached the sunny shores of Los Angeles in 1967. A few weeks after I moved to California, I was sitting outside a restaurant on Sunset Boulevard when a man approached me. This started it all.

"You have beautiful hair. I would love to shoot a commercial with you," he said.

He turned out to be a famous hairdresser named Gene Shacove, who was later the inspiration for Warren Beatty's character in the 1975 film, *Shampoo*.

Gene practically invented the term "celebrity hairdresser"; made friends with world-famous personalities, often becoming their long-time stylist and confidant, an association that granted him a movie star's social life.

Gene also owned the Candy Store, the 1960s and '70s-era

nightclub he operated beneath his Rodeo Drive salon, a move that made him the center of social L.A.

"Gene Shacove & me in his famous night club The Candy Store in 1969." From the Barbara Leigh Collection.

I made a move myself—into Gene's home once I shot his commercial. We lived together for about a year in his beautiful Bel Air home on Stone Canyon Road. The two of us were two peas in a pod, and both played the field. Of course, when both partners do that, it's hard to remain monogamous. Gene and I decided to part ways but our friendship remained intact for more than three decades.

Sadly, on September 5, 2001, Gene Shacove died Wednesday

of a thoracic aneurysm and subsequent kidney failure at Cedars-Sinai Medical Center. He was 72, but lived a very full life.

I saw Gene a week before he died at an animal fundraiser hosted by Buddy and Sherry Hackett. Even though Gene was 72, he looked great for his age, and as always, was so sweet.

Buddy, one of Gene's best friends, spoke at his funeral service and broke everyone at the chapel during his eulogy.

"I want to come back here in a year's time and see how much grass around this site Gene will smoke," Buddy joked. It was funny at a sad time.

It was during one of the many nights I spent in the Candy Store when Allan Rapport approached me and asked, "Have you ever thought about acting?"

Rapport was an agent for IFA who was getting out of the business, but he introduced me to the legendary agent Dick Clayton, who had discovered James Dean. Clayton signed me on the spot.

I had been using my married name, Barbara Haynes, as a model, but the Screen Actors Guild already had an actress with that name, so I had to change it.

Actress Vivien Leigh of *Gone With The Wind* fame died on July 8, 1967, the very same day I had to come up with a new name. My agent decided Barbara Haynes would become Barbara Leigh.

Dick Clayton managed to get me many acting jobs. My first was a TV movie called *The Ballad of Andy Crocker* with Lee Majors. I had a few scenes—that of a hippie. But my big scene was of me rolling a few joints in an alleyway—not much of a stretch!

Other film roles followed quickly. I shot two other films in 1969: *The Christian Licorice Store* with Beau Bridges and Maud Adams and *Love Is A Funny Thing* with Farrah Fawcett.

My next picture broke me out of small parts and into a major role. I starred in Stephanie Rothman's *The Student Nurses*, (1970) the first film made by Roger Corman's New World Pictures.

"Poster for *Student Nurses* starrring Elaine Giftos, Brioni Farrell, Karen Carlson and me."

It was also the same year I met MGM president James Aubrey. Aubrey was a legendary figure in Hollywood. Known as the "Smiling Cobra," and "Jungle Jim," he was the epitome of the soulless studio mogul. James was the inspiration for the Robin Stone character in Jacqueline Susann's best-selling novel, *The Love Machine*. He was 30 years my senior, 54 to my 24.

James had sophistication, worldly experience, education and money—all of the things I dreamed of having. He was my father figure, someone I could look up to. His age didn't bother me a bit. In fact, it made him even more attractive to me.

Because of my high cheekbones, long hair and freewheeling

style of dress, James nicknamed me "Indian," and that's all he ever called me.

"Indian," he asked one day, "how would you like to go to Las Vegas and see Elvis Presley?"

"Are you kidding?" I squealed with delight.

"I'm totally serious," James said.

MGM was financing the 1970 documentary *Elvis: That's the Way It Is*.

I had always wanted to meet Elvis; he was kind of my first love. I was in third grade when he made his famous appearance on *The Ed Sullivan Show* in 1956. The cameras only filmed him from the waist up, because his movements, people said, gave youth "impure thoughts." I thought he was fantastic. I immediately got up off the floor and tried to imitate him, but I was quickly sent to bed by my foster dad, a religious zealot who automatically didn't like the young man who caught my attention, teaching me provocative moves. A little girl didn't move like that.

The rebel image Elvis conveyed, combined with his southern down-home charm, drew me to this mysterious singer on the television. I have never taken to anyone like I did to Elvis Presley on that day. I can still see him in my mind's eye; he was the greatest.

The day after James' phone call, I went shopping for a dress on Sunset Boulevard. At the time, Hollie's Harp was the place where many celebrities and starlets went to buy that special dress for that once-in-a-lifetime experience. I bought a black, Grecian-goddess-style, spaghetti-strapped evening gown that tied under the breasts and at the waist.

August 30, 1970, was a night I'll never forget. James and I flew to Las Vegas and checked into a luxury suite at the International Hotel. I must say, James did everything in grand style.

At 11 p.m., I sauntered out of the bathroom wearing my black evening gown, high heels and a perfect tan I had been working on for weeks.

"You look stunning, Indian," James smiled.

We went downstairs and joined the standing-room-only crowd

of fanatic Elvis followers. The head waiter escorted us to the best seats in the house: first row booth, dead center. Elvis' booth.

The energy in the room that night was mind-boggling. James and I were enjoying small talk and a drink with other couples at our table, when a man with a twinkle in his eye and a lot of charisma walked over to greet James. I didn't know who he was, but I knew he was important.

"And who's this lovely lady you're with tonight?" the man pleasantly asked.

"This is Barbara Leigh. Barbara, I'd like you to meet Joe Esposito, Elvis Presley's road manager," James said.

Joe took my hand, looked me straight in the eye and said, "It's so nice to meet you, Barbara." His smile radiated warmth and sincerity. I liked him immediately.

There are certain people you connect with right away, and Joe was one of those people. Eventually, we would become close friends. In fact, I introduced him to his future wife, my friend Martha Gallob, with whom I attended high school.

Joe was extremely protective of Elvis, because many people wanted to get close to him for all of the wrong reasons. Joe was the man who decided who met E and who didn't. As I would eventually discover, Elvis always got the best-looking girl, Joe got the second-best-looking, and so on down the line. Joe possessed an easy charm, and a friendliness that won the girls over.

Joe looked at me and asked with a smile, "How would you and Jim like to come backstage to the dressing room after the show and meet Elvis?"

Not wanting to show James I was too excited or make him jealous, I put on my best poker face and said, "That would be lovely." Inside, I was as excited as a teenager. I was going to meet my idol. For the time being, I passed the test—James didn't have a clue how excited I was.

At midnight, the lights dimmed and the opening music filled the room. The music pulsated in a frenzied beat that hit the audience square in the face. If you were dead, you'd surely come alive.

Goose bumps covered my body and butterflies filled my stomach. I'd never experienced anything like it.

Elvis slowly walked onstage wearing a high-collared jumpsuit, jewelry and a silk scarf. He strode across the stage with a cocky strut that said, "I'm in command now." The entire audience went berserk and came to its feet. Senior citizens looked as if they discovered the fountain of youth when Elvis hit the stage. I'll never forget the sight of seeing them jumping up and down, clapping to the beat, shaking like they were young again. He brought everyone in the audience to life.

Elvis exuded an energy on stage that was something to behold. His show was second to none, for he was and forever will be The King Of Rock 'n' Roll. He was nonstop singing, dancing, walking, talking and continual motion for 90 minutes. He was as powerful as dynamite. Every woman in the place was swooning.

During the concert, I felt as if Elvis was making eye contact with me, but then I asked myself, *Why would he be looking at me? He could have any girl in this place.* Then I'd be damned if he wouldn't be smiling at me again. Eventually I learned via Joe that Elvis was definitely aware of me, because Joe had told him about me earlier: "Check out Jim Aubrey's date tonight. She's beautiful." Joe instinctively knew Elvis would like me.

Elvis was experiencing a major comeback at this point in his career and he was riding the wave of popularity again. The Beatles had invaded America in February 1964, and remained at the top until they broke up in 1970. During that period, Elvis focused his attention on his movie career. As a result, his music took a different direction. Drugs, promiscuity, flower power, the hippie movement, Vietnam and all of the other phenomena the turbulent 1960s brought about seemed to make Elvis a relic of the past.

**"Elvis announcing to the world that he's planning a return to the stage in Las Vegas in 1969."
Photo courtesy of Joe Esposito.**

Elvis was morally against most of those things and was now looked upon by the youth as part of the establishment. In the beginning, he had been the black-leathered, greasy-haired, snarling-lipped rebel. Now the rebel had grown up, gotten married, became a father and had even been received by President Richard Nixon at the White House. He hadn't had a No. 1 hit in seven years. All of that changed in 1969 with the single "Suspicious Minds." Once again, Elvis was hot.

That same year, Elvis started performing again to sold-out shows across the country, including Las Vegas. He was packing them in every night. People of all ages, sizes and walks of life loved Elvis. They came from all over the world to see him perform. His crowds were a mix of young and old, married couples, and, much to my dismay, young, beautiful, single girls.

The show ended with Elvis' signature song, "Can't Help Falling In Love." He then blew a kiss good night, which made the audience even more frenzied. I felt excited and exhausted at the same time. I didn't realize until I sat down that the audience had been on their feet the whole time, me included.

"Well," James smiled, "let's go meet Elvis." My body tingled with anticipation. Red West, Elvis' chief bodyguard, escorted us backstage to E's dressing room. Surprisingly, it wasn't that big, and was sparsely decorated with a table in the middle and a couch at one end.

When I walked through the door, I could feel the excitement of being in the dressing room of The King. I felt special just walking through those doors.

The bar was to the left. Behind it was a mirror and rows of glasses sitting upright. Next to the couch was a small table and lamp. To the right was a double bathroom that opened into Elvis' dressing room. Security guards at the door kept their eyes glued to it, waiting for his entrance. My heart was pounding.

I remember that the room was light yellow, and it seemed to glow. I thought I was walking into a little bit of heaven. The feeling was electrifying.

I followed James' lead, sitting next to him at the table, shaking hands with Chris Nelson, the wife of singer Rick Nelson. I sat quietly while James talked with Chris. I was too shy to speak up, having little in common with these celebrities. I felt as if I was being watched. I couldn't quite explain it, but the feeling was there—a sixth sense, perhaps. Call it intuition, call it whatever. I call it luck.

Abruptly, James got up and went to talk to someone in the corner of the room. The next thing I knew, Elvis snuck in and sat down right next to me.

I turned my head, and stared directly into the eyes of Elvis Presley. He gazed at me for a few seconds before saying anything.

His attention was focused only on me. I must confess, there is nothing more attractive than a man who is giving you his full attention.

Elvis' fans refer to this time as his "Greek god" period, and it was true. At 35, he was thin and tan, his hair was jet-black, and he had the most gorgeous blue eyes. But it was his smile that I remember best; it was the most beautiful smile I'd ever seen. He had mastered his look to perfection.

"Hello," Elvis said, as he took my hand, "I'm Elvis." Of course he was Elvis! Everybody in the world knew who he was, but he had to break the ice somehow.

I melted at his touch. "Hi, it's nice to meet you Elvis. I'm Barbara," I said with a slight southern accent, which Elvis instantly detected.

"And where are you from?" he asked.

"I'm a Georgia girl," I answered shyly.

He smiled, "Well, I could pick up on that right away, darlin'!"

Oooh, that "darlin" made my head spin.

We made small talk. I told him I was an actress and model living in Los Angeles.

"I knew it," he smiled. Then he told me I looked beautiful in my dress.

When Elvis told me I was beautiful, I could have died right then a happy woman. It was the greatest compliment of my life. He never took his eyes off me for a second. I don't think he cared that James was in the room. He simply went after what he wanted, and, at that moment, he wanted me.

"Well, what'd ya think of the show?" I noticed he didn't ask about what I thought of him. He asked specifically about the show.

I looked him straight in the eyes and said with genuine enthusiasm, "I think you're the greatest! I loved your show!" Elvis smiled warmly and laughed. I think he liked my honest response. He knew he was the greatest.

I could feel James' eyes burning through the back of my head. He wasn't going to make a fuss because of his ego, but he certainly was going to watch this scene play out between Elvis and me.

While James was throwing daggers in my direction, Elvis said in a hushed tone, "I'd like to call you. Will you could give me your phone number?" As he asked this, he slipped a small pad of paper and a tiny pencil to me under the table. *Sly little devil,* I thought. *He had this whole thing planned out.*

For some reason, I wasn't shocked. When I had watched him on the stage, I knew that I was going to be with him. I knew it. I wished it!

When I thought no one was looking, I wrote my phone number on the pad without looking down. Then I slipped the number into his hands, looking away as I handed back the pad and pencil to Elvis. He pocketed the paper without anyone noticing.

We were still talking when James walked over and put his hand on my shoulder and said, "Indian, it's time to go." My heart sank.

Elvis looked at me, gave my hand a squeeze and said, "I'll see you again real soon." He could see by the longing in my eyes that I wanted to be with him. He winked in acknowledgement. I knew exactly what that wink meant; that he was going to call me.

Did I feel guilty about giving Elvis my phone number while I was with James? I can't say that I did. It didn't matter that I was in love with James. It didn't matter that Elvis was married to Priscilla. I had no illusions. Elvis didn't have the time to invest in lasting friendships. His life revolved around music, trendy hobbies and women. But he was The King and this was a once-in-a-lifetime opportunity.

As James and I walked to our room, he was a bit frosty toward me—and deservedly so. Whenever he got upset, he pouted. He would drink, get really quiet, then pout. At times like that, he would shut me out. Through a lot of good-natured teasing, loving, touching and playing, I could eventually change his mood. But not tonight. He could tell that Elvis had touched something deep inside of me, and he was livid with jealousy, although he didn't show it. James was incapable of showing much emotion.

As we turned out the lights to go to bed, he wanted to make love. Normally, if James said, "Let's make love here," we did. But tonight I told him no.

My head was still in that dressing room going over and over my conversation with Elvis. I just wanted to relive that moment. I was under Elvis' spell. Had James left the room that night, I would have been thrilled beyond belief. I know that sounds mean, but my heart was with Elvis.

Eventually, we ended up making love so that he could go to sleep and leave me to my thoughts, but for the first time my heart wasn't in it.

James and I flew back to Los Angeles the next day, driving straight from the airport to Malibu for a beach party, where we spent the entire day. At the end of the evening, James took me to my car and I drove home to my apartment in Hancock Park.

I heard the phone ringing as I pulled up. I knew it was Elvis.

I rushed to answer the phone, leaving my suitcase in the car, a Porsche 914 convertible.

I picked up the phone and sure enough, it was Elvis. "I've been callin' ya for days, darlin'. Where ya been?"

"Oh Elvis," I laughed, "I've only been gone for a day."

"Yeah, well, it feels like you've been gone for days!" he teased. Then his tone became serious, "I'd like to see you again. When can ya come back?"

At the time, I was shooting a movie called *Pretty Maids All in a Row,* and was booked solid for the next week.

"Can't cha come back any sooner?" he persisted. Elvis didn't like to take no for an answer; I'm positive he always got his way. If any man had all of the angles figured out, it was Elvis Presley.

"What about on the weekend?" he queried. "I know they don't shoot movies on weekends, darlin', so what do you say this weekend I fly you up to Vegas to see the show?"

James had planned on taking us on a boat cruise over the Labor Day weekend starting on Friday. So, I had to plan carefully.

But Elvis was most persuasive; and since this was what I really wanted, it made no sense to play hard to get. I told Elvis I could come on Thursday night, but would have to be back Friday morning.

I didn't tell Elvis that I had plans with James, but I suspected that he knew. He was too sharp and perceptive not to put two and two together.

After hanging up the phone, I remembered I had left my suitcase in the car. In a panic, I ran to the parking lot. Sure enough, it was gone.

All of my jewelry, my beautiful black dress from Hollie's Harp and my money were gone.

Although I was living an exciting life hobnobbing with celebrities, I didn't make much money. Models back in the early '70s didn't have the earning power that they have today.

Now I had to buy another dress for my next trip to Las Vegas, because naturally I had to impress Elvis all over again. After shopping and not finding anything, I was in a complete funk. I eventually settled for a gray and lavender dress that was dowdy and boring. Elvis absolutely hated the dress and told me so.

Somehow, I had to convince James that I was leaving town for one day. I made up a story that I was going camping with friends in the desert at Joshua Tree. It was the perfect alibi, because he couldn't call to check up on me. He may have questioned it in the back of his mind, but he didn't say a word. The plan was foolproof, or so I thought.

"Just don't forget, we have a cruise on Saturday, Indian," he reminded me sternly.

With that, I gave him a kiss and left for Vegas and Elvis.

Anytime Elvis made plans with a woman, he left the details for Joe Esposito to work out. Joe had carefully prepared my flight schedule and hotel accommodations.

He also gave me his phone number and told me that if I ever needed to get in touch with Elvis, I was to call him first and he would dispatch The King.

Elvis, I would discover, was a master planner of covering his tracks. As one girl exited, his bodyguards brought in another. He needed a woman around him constantly. Amazingly, I don't think Priscilla ever caught him with another woman. She may have had her suspicions, but she never actually caught him. Of course, he had the money, manpower and resources to pull it off, but all the same, he was quite gifted when it came to hiding his romances.

I arrived with great anticipation in Las Vegas at 7:45 p.m., and was greeted at the gate by Joe. On the drive to the hotel, Joe shocked me with the announcement that I wouldn't be attending Elvis' first show.

Alarmed, I asked him why.

"Jim Aubrey showed up with Joanne Pflug at the first show, and it doesn't let out until 10:30," Joe said.

Damn Jim Aubrey!

Now, I had no right to be mad at James, since I was doing the same thing he was. Nonetheless, I was fuming.

Looking back, I realize why James didn't get too upset about my trip to Joshua Tree—he had planned a little trip of his own.

When we arrived at the International Hilton, Joe escorted me to a suite that Elvis reserved specifically for his ladies-in-waiting. It was decorated with a woman in mind and boasted a round, pink bed with lush pink carpeting. It was really something special for the "girls." I watched television to pass the time, but didn't pay much attention to what was on. More accurately, I stared into space. I paced the suite, called my answering service in Los Angeles and downed a Coke. With nowhere to go, I sat on the edge of the bed, staring at the floor, trying to keep up my spirits.

While waiting, I was personally introduced to Charlie Hodge, Elvis' friend and member of his entourage. Charlie was kind and sweet-natured. He was humble, yet content to be in the background. I felt a little sorry for him, because he was very short and was often the butt of Elvis' teasing. But it was apparent that Elvis loved him, which made it easier for Charlie when Elvis was up to his jokes.

After waiting for what seemed an eternity, Elvis gave Charlie the go-ahead to escort me to his penthouse. This suite was decorated in a more masculine style—mainly blue and yellow, a stark contrast to the all-pink suite I had just left.

Elvis flashed his sexy smile at me as I walked in.

"It's good to see you again, Barbara. I'm glad you could spend this time with me." Elvis had a way about him that made you feel as if you were the only woman in the world. It was one of the many special qualities about him. He took my hands in his and gave me a quick, soft kiss on the lips. It was our first kiss. I melted.

Turning around, he introduced me to his large entourage, the infamous "Memphis Mafia," as the press had dubbed them.

Besides Joe and Charlie, the group that evening included Sonny West, a tall, good-looking man who at 6-foot-3 inches was as big as a football player. Sonny was Elvis' other bodyguard and a friend since 1960 when Elvis returned home from the Army.

Also hanging around was his step-brother Ricky Stanley, whose main job seemed to be fetching for Elvis and the guys. Most of the time, Elvis had a few members of his entourage with him wherever he was.

Although we got along, his Memphis pals were kind of quiet when I was around. When Elvis was in the room, he had to be the center of attention. Everything said and done in the room revolved around Elvis. The guys weren't particularly warm to me, but they weren't mean, either. It's just the way it was. As long as I made Elvis happy, I didn't care. I wasn't allowed to talk much to these guys other than Joe or Charlie, otherwise, Elvis would get annoyed at the attention I was giving, or getting. He was definitely the jealous type.

I learned quickly that when Elvis sat down, my place was right next to him, and that's where I stayed. Elvis loved women who waited on him hand and foot. If he wanted a drink, his woman got it for him. If you didn't instinctively know this, you were out the door. Luckily, I passed the first test. I attribute that to my Southern upbringing. Southern women are taught to be gracious and charming—a "Stand By Your Man" mentality. The guys also helped me by steering me in the right direction. If a woman made life easier for Elvis, it made life easier for them, too. If they taught her well and she learned fast, then she pleased The King, and the guys had less to do.

On this night the suite was filled with beautiful women vying for Elvis' attention. They all wanted him, but they invariably ended up with one of the guys. Elvis, of course, got first crack, and then the rest was a free-for-all. Even so, there was always the underlying feeling that every one of these women wanted Elvis and would do anything to get his attention. They all competed to be the most charming woman in the room. I hated it.

Since Elvis had invited me to Vegas, I didn't think I should have to compete for him. I'm sure other women in his life must have felt the same way. It was exhausting to have to constantly be "on." I learned I had to either accept it, change it, or leave. I tried to change it.

Later in a private moment, I told Elvis what was on my mind; that I didn't like having all of the girls around; it was just too tiring. He understood and liked my honesty. With Elvis, if you told him the truth, he could deal with it. Sometimes.

Still, that didn't win me any brownie points with the Memphis Mafia.

I'm positive the guys loved Elvis, but I don't think they had much respect for women. They only saw women coming on to Elvis to get something from him. They didn't see their human side. They didn't think that any of these women could possibly have loved Elvis. All they saw were young girls coming at him in droves. I'm sure they viewed me as just another "starfucker," nothing more than a notch on Elvis' belt buckle.

As 3 a.m. rolled around, Elvis led me to his bedroom and told me that I could freshen up in the guest bathroom while he was in his.

In a way, it was so old-fashioned and romantic. He wanted his woman to come out with fire in her eyes, ready to seduce her man and satisfy his every desire.

I didn't bring a nightgown with me, so Elvis offered me a pair of his red silk pajamas.

"Tomorrow," he yelled out loud enough so that I could hear him in the bathroom, "we'll get you all of the things you need."

The silk pajamas still carried his scent, a mixture of sweet oak with a dash of Old Spice. I've always thought it was the perfect scent for a man.

When I came out of the bathroom, Elvis was already in the bedroom. I quietly sat down next to him at the foot of the king-sized bed.

"I'd like you to have this," Elvis said, handing me a medallion of Jesus Christ. Elvis loved giving gifts. I don't think anything else in the world made him happier than to give people gifts. He wasn't looking for approval or to buy friendship. He was just one of those people who loved bringing happiness to people, and giving gifts was his way of expressing his love. He gave people jewelry, clothes, cars and even homes.

This particular gift had special meaning. How did Elvis know the importance of Jesus in my childhood? The answer was, he didn't. Simply, he was just sharing with me a part of his childhood. A tear came to my eye, because I had never met such a gentle and sensitive man. I thanked him and leaned over to give him a kiss.

If anything was foreplay to Elvis, it was kissing. He loved to kiss. His mouth was round, full and soft. Our heavy kissing led to our first night of lovemaking.

That first night left me in awe of him.

Elvis was very passionate and sensual. He had a little bit of his character in *Jailhouse Rock* in him, and kissed me over and over. He eventually worked his way to the back of my neck. From there, he slowly kissed downward, first touching, then kissing my breasts and then down my arm to the back of my hand where he stopped briefly.

For some reason, we began to laugh and then he grabbed me again. We kissed even more passionately, almost out of control. He was spontaneous, hungry and made love with the enthusiasm of a teenager. It was a dream to be with him, to kiss him, to smell him, to taste him, and finally, to feel him inside of me.

And through it all I kept thinking, *I'm with The King. I'm with The King.*

CHAPTER TWO

Elvis had a lot of energy and wasn't ready to call it quits, even at 4 a.m. After making love for a second time, he began questioning me on numerology, one of his hobbies. I didn't have a clue what numerology was, and I told him so. "Good," Elvis smiled. "When the pupil is ready, the teacher is willing."

That particular saying was one of his favorites, and he used it with me all the time. It defined our relationship: He was the willing teacher, and I was the eager student.

Elvis liked to spend his time with pretty, young women. They were in awe of him, and he thrived on their adulation. He was at his happiest when he was in his teacher mode. Part of it was ego, I'm sure, but part of it was his generous nature. Elvis wanted to share himself with the people he cared about. But it was about more than just his money and the material things he could give them. Elvis wanted to share his knowledge, his love and his spirituality; he wanted to share who he was.

Once he spent time with a person, he could see them as a real person, not just as a beautiful object. Of course, he was attracted to physical beauty, but he looked to the next level to see if the beauty went inward, if you were genuine or fake. Elvis gave everyone an opportunity to show him their inner beauty. He was very intuitive and insightful.

Elvis, smiling, pulled out his favorite book on numerology, *Cheiro's Book Of Numbers*, then asked me my birth date.

He told me I was the spiritual number seven, based on my birth date of November 16.

Knowing I was from the South, where religion was deeply ingrained, he asked if I had a personal relationship with God.

"Yes," I replied quietly.

Then he asked me about my parents, although he seemed to be more interested in my mother. I told him that my father had left us when I was young, and my mother wasn't physically or emotionally able to raise me or my two brothers and three sisters. So I grew up in a series of children's homes and some times with foster parents.

Elvis seemed surprised. He reached over and took my hand, kissing the back of it softly. My story had touched him. Maybe he saw the sad child inside of me, and that's why he instantly became my teacher and protector.

He wanted to know more about me, especially about my childhood.

The subject of my childhood usually was taboo. I didn't like bringing up my past, because it was too confusing, which led to questions I didn't want to answer. While growing up, whenever anyone asked me about my background, I usually lied. It was so much easier than telling the truth. But because I knew Elvis was sincere in asking, I revealed myself to him. We had both been raised in the South. It was easier for him to identify with my past, and with me.

So I told Elvis my story that night.

Most people know who their fathers is, but I can't say with certainty that I know who mine is. I've been told a couple of versions by various members of my family. My mother never got her story straight, so I've relied on my grandmother and aunt for their version of the truth. For whatever reasons, my mother blocked out the truth from her mind. I think it was painful for her to remember.

My mother, Edith Childers, married Clyde Kish, an upholsterer by trade. They had two children before Clyde was drafted into the Army in World War II. When he came back, he was a changed man, and he had become an alcoholic. His memories of the war brought to the surface many personal demons, and the alcohol managed to dull the horrifying things he must have seen.

Sober, he was sweet as could be and earned a decent living, but once that can of beer reached his lips, he became verbally and physically abusive; a bully who couldn't handle his liquor. His alcoholism caused an ugly transformation in him that my family came to fear.

When I turned 21, my Aunt Eileen, my mother and I were visiting my grandmother in Ringgold, Georgia, when the discussion turned toward me. Aunt Eileen asked my mother, point blank, "Are you ever going to tell Barbara the truth about who her real father is?"

I looked at my mother, questioning her with my eyes. She shrugged her shoulders sheepishly, as if to say, "Well, I guess she's going to find out now."

Mom remained quiet as Aunt Eileen spoke. Clyde was away fighting in the war, and my mother was left at home with her parents. One day on a bus ride across town with my sister, Jean, and my brother, Jimmy, my mother met a teacher from the local military academy. His name was William O'Nesta. He took an immediate interest in her, and they became friends. I am supposedly the result of their love affair. Clyde came back from the war, and I was born "prematurely" six months later.

"Why do you think you look so different from the rest of the kids, Barbara?" my aunt asked rhetorically. I asked my grandmother for confirmation, knowing that she'd never tell me a lie. She said it was true, or at least, that's what she thought was the truth. I guess the only people who know the real truth are my mother and William O'Nesta.

Imagine a secret like this being kept from me for 21 years! I was surprised and a little shocked. I looked at my mother, but she couldn't meet my eyes. Years later, after my grandmother and Aunt Eileen had died, my mother vehemently denied having an affair with William O'Nesta.

What I do know is that when Clyde came back from the war, he tore up any information regarding my birth he could get his hands on.

So who is my real father? Deep down in my heart I think he's William O'Nesta. The sad part in all of this is that my mother once confided to my grandmother that William O' Nesta was a good and decent man; a man with a heart of gold. He would have been the kind of father I always dreamed of having. I was later told that when I was 3, he came back to Georgia looking for my mother and for answers to some questions. Clyde wouldn't let him near me or my mom. Clyde would never know the pain his actions inflicted upon me. I grew up thinking Clyde was my real father.

I was Clyde's favorite child, or so he told me. I worshipped him for the short time I knew him. I didn't sense being different, and it was a surprise when I found out that I wasn't his.

I guess it doesn't matter who my real father was. One was an alcoholic who eventually abandoned his wife and children, while the other never knew for sure I even existed. Later, through therapy, I discovered that I was constantly looking for a father image. I've finally stopped looking.

Elvis was so taken by my story, he didn't respond right away. I paused to get his reaction. By the look in his eyes, I could tell he was fascinated. I was flattered. Trust me, it took a lot to hold this man's attention.

"Please don't stop," Elvis said. "Keep going. I want to hear it all tonight!" he said with boyish enthusiasm. He was a fantastic listener; making me feel as if I was the only person in the world. He was sympathetic and sexy at the same time. He sincerely wanted to hear about my past, so I continued. Also, he was playing the mating game.

Three more children were born after Clyde returned from the war: my sisters Sharon and Patty, and my brother, Lonnie.

By the time I was 5, Clyde had abandoned us. The responsibility of feeding six hungry mouths made my mother worn and frail. She also was diagnosed with ovarian cancer. I remember people from the local hospital taking her away on a stretcher in an ambulance with the lights flashing. The two older kids, Jean and Jimmy were taken in by relatives, while the four youngest (me included) were hauled away to a state-run children's home for juveniles, delinquents and orphans in Kindle, Florida.

"My mother, Edith, sisters Sharon and Patty; brothers Jimmy and Lonnie, and me in the bangs. My oldest sister Jean was in Tennessee. Circa 1952." From the Barbara Leigh Collection

My childhood was officially over.

The children's home had separate buildings for girls and boys. The babies and toddlers lived on the bottom floors, and the kids 5 and older were on the top floors. My baby sister, Patty, was only 18 months. My younger brother, Lonnie, was almost three. Sharon was 4. I was the oldest at 6. It was easier for us three girls, since we were together in the same building. Sweet little Lonnie spent most of his childhood alone. The "home" had bars on the windows. Even if we were good, we were locked in our rooms at bedtime. If we had to use the bathroom during the night, we were out of luck. I often stared out the window, wondering where my mother was. I dreamt about her constantly. It was such a lonely place. No one ever explained why we were there, or if we would ever go home. We were scared and lonely. We didn't have a sense of who we were; for most of our childhood, we simply existed.

I was in kindergarten at the time, and attended a public school with other children who had normal, happy lives. When the school bell rang at the end of the day, they had a mother, father and a family pet to go home to. I went back to the orphanage.

Kids can be ruthless at that age. They teased me constantly. I was labeled
"the kid from the home." It wasn't hard to tell which kids came from the orphanage. We had awful looking bowl haircuts. Our bangs were chopped off at the forehead and hung right above the ears. Our clothes were hand-me-downs. Usually, we had to wear the same clothes two days in a row. It was humiliating.

I think Patty and Lonnie were affected the most by our awful childhood. Patty was a drug addict by the time she was 14, and Lonnie was shipped off to Vietnam to keep him out of trouble. Like his father, he emerged from the war a different man. He didn't follow in Clyde's footsteps and became an alcoholic. But he wasn't able to forget Vietnam, and was an emotional wreck. He has never fully recovered from the psychological effects of the war.

Mom visited when she had the energy, but her visits were sporadic. There were times when she took us back to live with her, but she'd have a relapse. She eventually beat the cancer, but she couldn't take the pressure of having six kids to nurture, feed and raise. It was difficult for her to cope with us for very long; so back we'd go to the children's home.

When I turned 9, my luck changed. The Reverend Luther Key met my mother at church and struck up a friendship with her. Reverend Key was the pastor of Miami Baptist Church, the largest church in downtown Miami.

When Reverend Key visited us in the home, he fell in love with me instantly. He leaned over and whispered, "I want to adopt you, but I want you to meet my wife first." Mary Key loved me right away, too, and I went to live with them that day in their beautiful home. Reverend Key made sure that my brother and two sisters also were well taken care of. He arranged it so that they were transferred from that wretched home in Kindle to a much nicer children's home in Lakeland, run by the Baptist Church. Each child had an adult sponsor who would write them letters, and send them birthday and Christmas gifts. Things were definitely looking up.

Why did the Keys pick me? Maybe they sensed I had so much love to give. My mother always said that I was the most loving child. When I lived with her, I wanted to please her and I took every opportunity I could to spoil her. When she came home from a hard day's work, I greeted her with a bucket of warm water for her feet. I rubbed her back and brushed her hair at the end of the day. I was her caretaker.

It was a dream come true for a lonely little girl from the orphanage to be chosen to live in a lovely home. The Keys insisted I call them "Mom and Dad," and I was only too happy to oblige.

It was a safe and loving environment, and for once in my life, I had a new dress. Mary Key took me shopping, letting me choose it all by myself. I remember it to this day. It was red, my favorite color.

At night, Mary would brush my hair in gentle, loving strokes, and Reverend Key would read to me. Then they'd tell me they loved me and kiss me good night. Often I would awake after a nightmare and find Reverend Key sitting next to me on the bed, soothingly telling me, "Princess, you're OK now, go back to sleep and I'll see you in the morning." This was the life I'd dreamed of at night in the home.

I lived in this dream for two years. Then it, too, came to an abrupt end.

My mother was concerned that the Keys were becoming too important in my life, and she feared they would start adoption proceedings and take me away from her. Not wanting to let me go, she placed me back in the home, rather than risk losing me. The Keys had no choice but to give me up. I was hurt and angry with the Keys, because I couldn't understand how they could allow this to happen. I loved my mother, but I was so happy with the Keys. It broke my heart to leave them and their beautiful home, and, most importantly, my friends at school and church.

The Keys drove me to the children's home where my sisters and brother were living. I didn't hug or kiss them goodbye, or thank them for their love, care and concern for me. I couldn't. I wasn't equipped emotionally to deal with the hurt of losing them. I was alone again, and didn't understand what was going on.

I seethed inside; feeling that the Keys had abandoned me. How could they say they loved me, then turn around and leave me? Anger toward my mother never entered the equation; I never saw her part in it.

Unfortunately, the Keys caught the brunt of it. I experienced a pain in my heart that wouldn't let me talk during the entire drive to Lakeland. They bought me a can of sugar nuts on the trip, but I never opened it. I kept the unopened can by my bed for a year, then threw it away. The Keys had rejected and thrown me aside, just like that can of nuts. A child's thinking.

The Lakeland Baptist Children's Home was a big improvement over the home in Kindle. It was large and imposing, and resembled a college campus. The horseshoe-shaped buildings surrounded a grassy courtyard.

It was bittersweet family reunion: My two sisters and brother were there to greet me. Even though this was a nicer facility than the first home, it didn't necessarily mean it was an easier place to grow up. We spent a lot of time in church, which was our happiest time. I worked hard to memorize all the books of the old and new testament, and can still recite them today.

Living in a children's home is a lot like living in the Army. Life was regimented, and run according to the bells. The first bell rang at 6 a.m., waking me. I quickly made my bed, cleaned my room and did my assigned chores, so that when the second bell rang, I was ready for breakfast. There was a bell for school to begin, and a bell for school to end. There was a tardy bell, a dinner bell, other bells.

Bells, bells, bells!

There was no warmth or love at the home. There was no parental guidance other than our house mother, and she seemed to dislike kids. One day, I asked her to help me put my hair in a ponytail. She said she wouldn't.

"Oh blast it," I replied. I didn't curse or stomp my feet. I simply said, "Oh blast it." I reacted as any child would, but I didn't think it would garner such a violent reaction from her.

This woman, my house mother, this supposedly religious woman, slapped me across the face and yanked me by the hair. She screamed, "Never talk back to me young lady! Now, go to your room," which I immediately did. I was only 11, dying inside to be a little girl, but I was forced to grow up in a hurry. I learned never to deal directly with my house mother again. I kept my distance.

We weren't even allowed to have candy, except at Easter, unless friends or family brought it to us. Once when my mother visited, she gave me a nickel to buy some candy. I chose a bar of black licorice, which I hated, but I bought it because I knew it would last a long time. In time, I grew to love black licorice, and still love it.

I have one pleasant memory of that children's home. It's where I discovered boys. My first boyfriend was Larry Golden. I would see Larry on bus rides to school, or at church.

I was infatuated with Larry. He had a smile and a laugh that attracted me to him. It was an innocent love; a happy feeling, something pure, something completely good, and someone to look forward to seeing.

At about the same time, I discovered that I got along better with boys than I did with girls, a trait that has carried over into my adult life. For some reason, women have been jealous of me for most of my life. I can remember the first time someone became jealous of me. A group of girls ganged up on me, because one of them didn't like her boyfriend flirting with me. She turned it around to make it my fault. Often, my open and friendly personality is mistaken for flirting. Besides, the boys always took up for me and treated me better than girls, although I longed to have a close girlfriend.

For two years, the Keys worked on my mother to get her to allow me to return to their home and my friends. I was 12 when they finally managed it, but by then my feelings had changed. I had two years' worth of anger inside of me, and it only got worse as time went on.

Deep down, I felt the Keys had abandoned me, and I vowed that I would never love so completely again. I always held a part of myself back after that. I buried my deepest feelings of love for them; I buried them so deep that I never allowed myself to call them "Mom and Dad" again, which absolutely killed them. I even took that a step further: I spoke to them, but I didn't address them by name, which drove Mary wild. Our relationship quickly deteriorated after one day at the market, where I spotted two of my friends from school. Mary smiled and asked me who my friends were.

"This is Nancy and this is Bill," I said curtly, never bothering to tell my friends who Mary was, or introducing her in any way.

Mary was crushed because I didn't tell my friends she was my mother, and that was pretty much the beginning of the end. She drove home, trying to hold back the tears. When Reverend Key came home and found his wife crying in their bedroom, he knew something was wrong. After hearing her story, he was mad as hell, and demanded to know why I had deliberately hurt Mary.

He was even more infuriated by my glib answer, and by the fact that I could so casually go back to reading my romance comic book. Reverend Key yanked me out of my chair, hauled me into the garage and whipped me with his belt. That was the first and only time he ever spanked me. I was deeply hurt, and retreated from him more than ever. I really did love them both so much, but I was a child. I was terribly confused, completely tied up inside. I couldn't tell them how I really felt because I didn't know how to express myself. I was afraid of getting hurt.

I went to school the next day with welts on my legs and, of course, all of the kids spotted them right away, and asked me what happened. I never said a word. Instead, I wrote to my mother and begged her to bring me home.

In no time my mother called the Keys and demanded for my return. At first, they said no, telling her it was a simple matter of discipline.

My mother didn't take no for an answer. She appeared on their doorstep, and threatened to show up every Sunday at church in the loudest dress she could find. She vowed to sit in the front row, knowing full well this would cause a controversy, which would drive out the congregation in droves. It was a big church, and I'm sure the Keys didn't want to see any kind of dissension among the congregation over this. Also, it probably made them consider their job security with the church, so they gave me back. In my heart, I know they loved me and didn't want to give me up, but they had no other choice. They probably felt they had already lost me, which they had.

When it came time to leave, I hugged the Keys and told them I loved them, but I didn't trust them any longer. I would act differently today, but then I was so young and had no control over my emotions. I was just a kid with very little self-esteem, afraid of getting hurt because of all the disappointments I'd had in my life.

By this time, Jean was in Tennessee and Jimmy was old enough to live with my mother, and now me. But Sharon, Patty and Lonnie were still living in the Baptist home. I was thrilled at the chance to live with my mother again, but I soon found out it wasn't going to work. She was never home. She usually was out working or playing. Mother had a lot of boyfriends, and often would leave and not say where she was going or when she was coming back. Jimmy and I were forced to grow up fast. We were mostly alone a lot of the time but when my mother was home, she showered us with lots of love.

Thinking this was a good time to move on to other subjects, I asked Elvis about his mother, Gladys. It was obvious that she meant the world to him. He had a certain sparkle, yet sadness, whenever he spoke of her.

"I never loved anyone like I loved Momma," Elvis confided. "I lived to take care of her. I loved my daddy, too, but it was always Momma who tried to give me everything she could and more."

"What happened to her?" I asked gently, caressing his hand.

"She died right before I left for the Army in 1958, from acute hepatitis, or at least, that's what the doctors told me. Just about broke my heart. I don't think I've ever gotten over it, to tell ya the truth." There was an uneasy quiet in the room after he said that, and Elvis got this faraway look in his eye, like he missed her.

No man ever loved his mama more than Elvis did.

Born into poverty, Elvis and his mother shared a special bond when his father, Vernon, went to the Mississippi State Penitentiary for altering a $4 check when Elvis was 3.

Vernon had no real job prospects, and moved wherever he could find work. Gladys took refuge from their desperate poverty by showering Elvis with all of her attention. He was her pride and joy.

On Elvis' 11th birthday, his parents bought him his first guitar. Elvis originally wanted a bike, but Gladys revealed the cost was too much, and feared he might get hurt. So she and Vernon settled on the guitar.

The rest, as they say, is history.

After what seemed to be an eternity, Elvis recovered, smiled and said, "My momma always told me I'd marry a brown-eyed girl, and you just might be the one!"

He threw that killer smile at me, and I burst out laughing. Elvis said it in such a way that I never took his words seriously, but every now and again, he would repeat those sweet words to me.

Elvis sat with his knees pulled up to his chest and his back against the headboard, and stared at me thoughtfully.

"I'm sorry for interruptin' darlin'," he blurted out. "You finish your story. I wanna hear more about your momma."

"Well," I said, "I do know that none of my other relatives opened their homes on a permanent basis to any of my mother's children, except for Jean and Jimmy. Mother was kind of the black sheep of the family. They had their own families, and were unable to take all of us in." But as a child I couldn't see that. Once again, I had his undivided attention.

My mother's family was never able to understand her, especially her sisters. Mom was closer to her brothers, my Uncle James in particular. My mother was a tomboy, preferring to hunt, fish and be with the guys. She had a warm, vivacious, outgoing personality. She loved to flirt, something I definitely inherited from her.

Later I accepted the fact that my family couldn't take us in, and left it at that. I learned to live with many disappointments in my life. Knowing the whys didn't change the facts. I learned to live with my circumstances, hoping to change them when I became an adult.

When I turned 14, my mother married a wealthy man from Lexington, Kentucky. Soon after their marriage, my brothers and sisters and I went to live with them in his house, a place that rivaled Graceland in its magnificence and splendor. The estate boasted acres of green grass, horse stables and plenty of prized horses. Inside the entryway to the house was a large winding staircase, the kind you only see in the movies—the kind found in beautiful plantation homes. How exciting. We were going to be a family once more!

Did I dare believe this dream? Hadn't I learned never to trust anything that good?

Once my mother's new husband got a taste of domestic bliss, he decided he wanted nothing to do with her children. He told her we were a "crazed pack of wild Indians," always chasing his prized horses around. He also was diabetic, and unable to deal with the stress and strain of us "wild ones." He told my mother she could stay, but her kids had to go.

Again, my mother was forced to make a choice, a choice she had made many times before. She needed time to figure out what she wanted for herself and her life, and once again, the man in her life took priority.

The kids were sent packing.

Because it was summer and school was out, I asked mother to let me visit my Aunt Belle in Chattanooga, Tennessee. That way, I avoided going back to the orphanage for three months. Going to Tennessee bought me more time to ponder my options.

Not long after I arrived in Tennessee, I went on a date with a guy named Finley Haynes. Finley was a handsome 20-year-old Golden Gloves boxer, who came from a very good family and attended school with my cousins.

A few years before, Finley had dated my sister Jean. She kept a scrapbook with his pictures in it, but she married someone else and broke young Finley's heart. It was through Jean's scrapbooks that I developed a big crush on Finley. I thought he was gorgeous, and was dying to meet him. As fate would have it, he happened to be home on leave from the Marines. A couple of years later, Finley would survive the Bay of Pigs fiasco in Cuba.

I begged my cousin Nancy Miller to introduce us. I told Nancy to tell Finley that I was 16, not the immature 14-year-old that I really was. I was so attracted to the guy that I was willing to lie about my age to get a date with him.

Finley's upbringing was from a Southern "holy-roller," fanatically religious family, and like the good choir boy that he was, he wanted to have sex with me. He manipulated me by insinuating I was a "bad girl." By the end his leave he had done his number on me, and I relinquished my chastity in the backseat of his 1954 Ford.

A few weeks later he was back on active duty at Camp Pendleton in California. A month later he wrote to me, apologizing about how sorry he was for taking my virginity. He also confessed that he already had a girlfriend. Surprise, surprise.

Before I had a chance to read the letter, Aunt Belle opened it. She was deeply offended that this experienced, older man—all of 20—had taken advantage of her depraved 14-year-old niece. She felt he had taken what should only have been given away on my wedding night. Aunt Belle changed my life forever by invading my privacy and reading my letter. For years I resented her for it.

Aunt Belle picked up the phone and called Finley, informing him of my real age. I'm sure he thought, *Oh my God, what have I done?* Now he was in for a real shocker. My aunt told him that either he was going to get his Marine butt back to Tennessee and marry her teenaged niece, or she was going to call his superior officer and have him charged with statutory rape, which was and still is a felony offense in most states. I had no say in the matter; it always seemed as if my destiny was in the hands of others.

The summer was quickly coming to an end, and I would shortly return to Lakeland Baptist Home. I dreaded the thought of it. Aunt Belle had only agreed to take me for the summer, and hadn't offered to extend my stay. I had nowhere else to go. I had told all my friends in the home that I wouldn't be coming back, and now, that's exactly where I was going. I would rather get married than go back to the orphanage. On September 23, 1961, I became Mrs. Finley Haynes. My sister Jean and her husband, Dick Beene, were our witnesses. Finley and I were married in Ringgold, Georgia, the little town where I was born. I was 14. I bore a son a few years later. We named him Gerry.

"But Elvis, that's another whole story!"

Elvis was relieved that I didn't go on. He didn't like hearing about other men in his women's lives, and he especially didn't want to hear about any children. He was only interested in my background, maybe my childhood, but not about child bearing. He leaned over, hugging me for a very long time. I felt close to him. I had "spilled the beans" as they say. I was glad I didn't have to pretend now. We never discussed my marriage again, nor for that matter, his marriage to Priscilla. I made sure *not* to ask him any questions about his private life, knowing that my probing might end our relationship quicker than it started. On the other hand, he was always inquiring to what I was doing.

If Elvis wanted to know something, he came out and asked it. Whatever he felt was necessary to tell me, he told me. I didn't do much asking. That was okay with me.

"My first modeling job for Kodak film. Circa 1967." From the Barbara Leigh Collection.

I could tell Elvis was getting tired, and this was the perfect place to end my personal history lesson.

Elvis excused himself, and got up from the bed and went to his bathroom. He kept his bathroom habits as private as possible. One thing he didn't keep private was a black overnight bag containing all kinds of pills. When Elvis returned, he was wearing blue silk pajamas and had a little twinkle in his eye. He handed me a little red pill and a glass of water.

"Here, take this," Elvis offered. "It'll help you sleep."

Elvis had the same type of pill for himself, only his was bigger. He swallowed his "bedtime baby," then turned the air conditioning up full blast. It was so cold, you'd swear you were in Alaska.

I didn't have the nerve to ask him what I was taking. I trusted Elvis with blind faith, and I swallowed the pill without question. Hey, it was the '70s!

Elvis had another strange bedtime habit: He slept with cotton in his ears. He'd wet the ends of the cotton ball in his mouth, twist them neatly into straight lines, roll the cotton into a ball and then stick it in his ears. It was habit-forming. Eventually, I found myself performing this same ritual to drown out loud noises.

Elvis wanted his woman by his side at night to make sure he was tucked in safely. I quickly learned not to pass out on him, because he liked to fall asleep first. I had to wait for his pill to kick in before mine did. In those situations, it became mind over matter.

As he nestled comfortably into bed, Elvis kissed me softly and whispered, "Good night, darlin'. See you in the morning. Get a good night's sleep."

No sooner did he say those words than he passed out. I'll never forget laying in bed, looking at him and stroking his black hair thinking, *My God, I'm with Elvis Presley. Out of the millions of women he could be with, why did he choose me?*

It was all a matter of timing.

About 15 minutes later, my pill took effect and I was out like a light.

In the morning I got up the courage to ask Elvis what the pill was. He said it was a Placydill—one of the many drugs he would later become addicted to.

As for me, I was on a natural high. I had spent the night with the one and only Elvis Presley. He was The King and I was his princess.

If only for one evening.

CHAPTER THREE

The original plan had been for me to stay to see Elvis perform a second time, spend a couple of hours alone with him and then high tail it back to Los Angeles, where I would spend the Memorial Day weekend with Jim Aubrey. James' unexpected date with Joanne Pflug changed my brief visit with Elvis into a long weekend in the arms of another man. Events were beyond my control, so I rolled with the punches and came out the winner.

E's hours were the opposite of the average person. Time didn't exist for him as most of us know it. Elvis controlled everything, including time.

He was a sound sleeper; I don't think I ever heard him snore in all of our nights together. I studied his famous face as he slept. His features were so perfect; he was the most beautiful man I had ever seen.

It was a long way from Georgia to Las Vegas. So many things had happened in my life to put me here in bed with my idol.

We slowly began to stir in the early afternoon. I looked at Elvis, and he smiled back at me. Amazingly, his hair remained perfectly in place.

"Good morning, darlin'!" he said as he reached out to me.

I scooted up next to him. "Good morning, darlin!" I replied. We both laughed and kissed and hugged again.

"Are you hungry?" he asked.

"I'm starving!" I said.

"Good, we'll order up a big breakfast. Darlin', you get dressed and after we eat, I'll have Joe arrange for someone to take you shopping for clothes for tonight's show." I adored a man who took charge and made all the plans. It was exciting.

Elvis was beaming as he continued, "I'm so happy you've decided to stay. You don't mind seeing my show every night, do you?"

I thought he was joking. Mind seeing his show every night?

"Oh, Elvis," I almost panted, "I can't wait to hear you sing again!"

He smirked with self-assurance, "Good, that's what I wanted to hear. I like a little enthusiasm!"

We went to our separate bathrooms to get dressed. No two people at one time were allowed in his bathroom. It was a strange quirk of his, but not an outrageous one.

I've seen worse.

I put on the same clothes I had worn on the plane, and headed for the dining room to wait for Elvis.

Never for one moment did I believe that I was Elvis' only girlfriend. I definitely was a naive Southern girl, but I wasn't stupid. Even though I wasn't an educated woman, I possessed "street smarts," and I always knew there were others. Lots of them! It was an accepted fact. I had "others," too, but none were as exciting as The King.

Elvis walked into the dining room dressed to the hilt. He looked more handsome and radiant than I'd ever seen him. He sported tight black pants and a white shirt with a high collar, as was his fashion and his usual jewelry.

By this time, Joe Esposito had joined us.

"Hey Joe, let's get some room service up here," Elvis said, then teasing me. "My honey's hungry!"

Wherever Elvis Presley was, you could always find Joe nearby. In a flash, he had room service on the line, giving our orders of scrambled eggs, bacon, toast, milk and orange juice.

"Oh, please," I asked, "may I have some coffee?"

Elvis looked at me seriously through his smile, "Anything you want, you just say it."

I shyly smiled, softly whispering, "Thank you."

"Elvis with Joe Esposito preparing for the 1968 Comeback Special for NBC." Photo courtesy of Russ Howe.

"You're welcome, darlin', but you don't have to be so polite," he chuckled. "It's that 'Southern upbringing' of yours. You remember what I said, just ask, anything you want. You're my girl."

My head was spinning. *Anything I want.* I don't think I'd ever heard those words before. It was beyond my comprehension to ever question anything Elvis said or did. Only once did I go against his wishes, and that was toward the end of our relationship when Steve McQueen came into the picture.

We enjoyed our first breakfast together. Joe left the two of us alone to share a few intimate minutes together. It was an unusual moment because the Memphis Mafia was usually around most of the time.

Although I was very hungry, maybe even hungrier than Elvis, I was too excited to eat. I picked at my meal, and Elvis took notice. He watched me for a minute.

"I thought you were hungry," he said.

"Oh, I was, I mean, I am. Guess I'm just too excited."

Elvis wiped his face with his napkin, got up from the table and excused himself to go to the bathroom, where he emerged about 10 minutes later with a renewed vigor. I assumed he took an upper, because his legs and hands seemed to be moving in time with some godly rhythm in his head.

He went over the day's game plan. "OK, honey, Joe's taking you shopping for clothes. Make me proud!" I beamed. Nothing makes a woman feel happier or sexier than when she goes shopping for a new dress. I wanted to look especially good, as I would be watching the show from Elvis' special booth.

Joe took me to the women's dress boutique in the Hilton hotel. Elvis chose to put Joe with his girls, because that way Elvis could keep tabs on them at all times. I was fortunate that Joe and I got along so well. To me, Joe knew Elvis well. He read him like a book. He knew when to approach him, when to avoid him and how to detour the moods. He was the troop leader.

The shop was bright and elegant; a little flashy, which was typical Vegas glamour, but wonderfully exciting. I was over the moon with joy. We didn't have much time to shop. With Elvis, the clock was always ticking. Joe had a lot of prep work to do for E's show, and he was always on the go as well. He stopped when Elvis stopped, and more often, he worked long after. His was a demanding job.

The sales people in the store knew who Joe was, and were especially attentive and complimentary to me. I felt like Cinderella. Of course, my salesperson knew the clothes were for Elvis' new girl. I was enjoying every minute of it.

I picked out a white peignoir set, something I knew he would like. I also chose a a long, multicolored satin Geoffrey Beene dress, along with a pair of black satin evening shoes with a matching evening bag.

The clothes were a bit too sophisticated, not really to my taste, but then again, I was dressing for E. Actually, the dress was too sophisticated for Elvis, too.

Joe had my new clothes and accessories sent up to the suite, which I couldn't wait to model them for Elvis. When he came back from rehearsal, I was in the bedroom and the clothes were laid out on the bed waiting for him to inspect. He laughed as he always did, saying how much he liked my dress, and how beautiful it would look on me.

"Where are the others?" he asked with concern.

"What others?" I asked.

"The other clothes. Is that all you bought? You can't wear that dress again tomorrow!"

I hadn't wanted Elvis to feel as if I was taking advantage of his generosity, so I had picked out only one gown. Feeling a little embarrassed I said, "Elvis, I don't mind wearing this again."

"What's the matter?" he asked. "Didn't you find anything you liked?" He sounded as if he had let me down.

"Well, they were a little too sophisticated, but if you want me to look again, I will."

"No," he said with resolve in his voice. "Charlie will take you to Suzie Creamcheese. She'll have lots of things you'll like." The man had a solution for every problem, and he was quick to make decisions. With Elvis, there were never any moments of uncertainty.

Lightening up a bit, he commented, "You did good, honey, especially that nightgown!" He loved to flirt, and loved the art of seduction.

Changing subjects, Elvis went over the evening's agenda. "Tonight, after the show, Charlie will pick you up from the booth and bring you back up here to the suite. There's always a barrage of people hanging around after the show, and I need to say hello to them, but it won't be long. Most of the guys will be here with you." He then added, "I'll miss you, baby."

Elvis suggested I model the new dress for him. I couldn't wait to try it on for him, and feel beautiful all over again. I could tell by the way his eyes grew bigger and his smile got wider, that he really liked me in the dress.

"Hot damn!" were the words out of this Southern gentleman's mouth.

While I was putting on the final touches, Elvis went over the celebrity list with Joe, finding out who would be his special guests for the evening. The King always had celebrities coming to his shows, for his were the hottest tickets on the Vegas Strip. Elvis was gracious to his celebrity guests, and most were invited back to his dressing room. They absolutely adored him as much as his fans. Elvis wasn't a phony from Hollywood, who was nice to your face then stabbed you in the back when you left the room. He was a true Southern gentleman; famous for his good manners. It was a special trait that made Hollywood sit up and take notice. He possessed a boyish charm and charisma, combined with the presence of a masterful show business giant made Elvis the star he was. Elvis also had a certain innocence that stood out beyond all that power.

"Elvis during his sexy Greek God period. This is the Elvis I remember." Photo courtesy of Tom Salva.

Elvis asked for a few moments alone to make a phone call. I guessed he was probably calling Priscilla, but it didn't bother me. I was the one he was going to be with that night.

As I walked into the living room where the guys were gathered, the room fell silent. Joe broke the silence.

"You look beautiful, Barbara." As always, Joe was the most kind and gracious member of E's entourage. He really knew how to treat a lady.

"I helped her pick it out," Joe told the others, boasting of his impeccable taste in women's clothes.

I looked at Joe and smiled, "You sure did."

The doorbell chimed and one of the guys quickly ran to answer it. It was clear he was anticipating company. He came back leading several beautiful women. They were the guys' dates for the evening. The guys had their usual groupies as well.

Elvis finished his phone call and yelled out, "Joe?"

Immediately, Joe appeared at the door. "Yeah, boss?"

"Take care of Barbara, and put Sonny with her. Make sure she eats her dinner tonight."

"I will, E," Joe solemnly promised.

Joe left, and Elvis kissed me passionately.

"I'll see you soon, honey," he said sweetly. "I'll sing for you tonight." Just the thought of it gave me goose bumps. Cloud nine was beckoning.

He kissed me again, then left with Joe, Red West and Alan Strada. The three men escorted him to a private elevator that led directly to the stage.

I made a few phone calls, and wandered around his bedroom. My eyes were drawn to E's white silk shirt that he had just taken off and placed on the back of a chair. I picked up the shirt smelling it—it definitely had his distinct aroma. I carefully placed the shirt back on the chair. I looked at each of his books, which were mostly religious or spiritual. Elvis loved books, and they were piled high everywhere. His bottles of pills—in all varieties—also caught my eye. Was it the beginning of his addiction? I can't say for certain, but he could have opened his own pharmacy. Next to the pills were bottles of Mountain Valley Spring Water—his personal favorite. I wanted to touch everything that was his, as if they held some kind of magical power. I felt like I was in a shrine.

At the end of my solitary tour, I sat on the edge of the bed waiting to be led downstairs. Again, I felt like Cinderella before the ball.

I went into the bathroom for one last look. I wore my hair simple and long, parted in the middle. It was in stark contrast to the teased, big-hair look that Elvis liked. However, he liked me as I was. I didn't wear foundation, just eye makeup, and a lot of it. He never asked me to change my looks, as he reportedly did with other women. I guess I was made-up enough. Maybe he liked my look.

I had my own distinct look and was not a look-alike for Priscilla, although I think she is a very beautiful woman. The only trait we shared was long, dark hair, and, of course, Elvis.

I must admit that I didn't give much thought to Mrs. Presley that first weekend I spent with Elvis. Throughout our affair I tried to be respectful, never touching any of her things in the four different homes I visited.

"OK, you look good," I told myself as I looked into the mirror. "Now go out there and mingle." A part of me definitely wanted to mingle, but the other part didn't know if I could handle this fast-paced Vegas crowd. The little girl from Georgia wanted to stay in Elvis' room and dream.

Sonny knocked on the bedroom door and told me it was time to head downstairs to the show.

I opened the door and discovered not only Sonny, Red and Ricky Stanley but five new girls to boot, all very attractive. Another rough night of competition.

As we all crammed into the elevator I couldn't help but think about my past. Here I was wearing an elegant new dress and being escorted to Elvis Presley's table to watch his show as his No. 1 girl. I remember thinking that I would have gladly gone through my childhood again, just to be rewarded with this moment in time. It was a silly thought. But what were the odds?

The elevator doors opened, and our group was quickly led to two booths reserved for E's special guests. They were by far the best seats in the house. Joe was there to greet us, making sure he took special care of me, as requested by The King.

"Now Barbara," Joe said in a fatherly tone, "E wants me to make sure you eat something. You don't want me to get into trouble, do you?" he teased.

I smiled back at him. "No Joe, I promise I'll eat something tonight."

Throughout the whole weekend, I'd barely touched my food, because I was too excited. I figured I'd better eat that night, or I'd get sick. In addition, I didn't want to get Joe into trouble. If you were employed by Elvis Presley, you did what you were told.

Elvis, in a nice way, had told me to direct my questions and concerns only to Joe. I didn't have a problem with that, because I liked Joe. He was kind, loving, charitable and genuine. I felt as if he didn't judge me; he accepted me for who I was. He also was an invaluable help, giving me pointers regarding Elvis; his likes and dislikes. I felt we would be good friends, and time has proven me right. We're still the best of friends. Whenever I'm with Joe, I'm so reminded of Elvis that I can't help feeling Elvis' presence. When we reminisce, it's as if Elvis is still alive.

As I finished my dinner, I noticed people were staring at our table, whispering to each other, trying to figure out who we were. What a thrill for a shy girl from Georgia. I was living a fantasy.

The lights in the room dimmed, and the opening theme for the show filled the air. The music was loud and the normally more reserved Las Vegas crowd trembled with excitement, cheering wildly—it knew The King was about to enter. I felt like screaming with the rest of the crowd, but I had to be cool, so I behaved myself and quietly sipped my white wine. I sat there trying to be ladylike, feeling anything but.

As if out of nowhere, Elvis appeared, strutting across the stage.

He looked magnificent in his white satin jewel-studded jumpsuit, complete with cape. All of the women in the room fawned simultaneously.

He sang in that wonderful low, sexy voice. He shook and gyrated, and incorporated a few karate moves and kicks before closing.

For the encore, he looked directly at me and said in a low voice, "Barbara, this is for you." Then he sang, "The First Time Ever I Saw Your Face," made popular by vocalist Roberta Flack. I was absolutely entranced as he courted me with his music. I couldn't wait for the show to be over so I could be with him again, touching his face, smelling, kissing, caressing, laughing and sleeping with him. Being alone together, just the two of us, was worth any inconvenience.

Joe whisked us out before the crowd left, while Elvis headed to his dressing room to change and greet his guests. He was very fast with the backstage pleasantries that evening. Before I knew it, he was in the suite, walking toward me asking, "How did you like the show, honey?"

"Oh E, you were great! I loved it!"

He kissed the back of my hand and said, "Good!"

The guys surrounded Elvis, introducing him to the new girls. The realization finally hit me that this was standard operating procedure, and I didn't like it one bit! The girls flirted outrageously, trying to charm Elvis—and he ate it up. I knew my work was cut out for me. I had to be more beautiful, more charming, more desirable than any of them. It wasn't easy.

The girls were very pretty, handpicked by the guys. Let's put it this way: They had to be the cream of the crop to get into E's suite. I had to compete for his attention, so I played the game. I watched him carefully, studying his reactions to each girl. I thought, "How can I change this?" Elvis would glance over at me from time to time and wink, but he kept on talking to the girls, flirting in his own way. I made sure to smile at him every time he winked, to let him know that his actions didn't bother me. After all, I was the one who would be in his bed at the end of the night.

The evening dragged on for what seemed to be an eternity. Finally, the party began winding down around 5:30 a.m. This was my second night with E, and I wanted him to know I was getting tired. I stretched my arms and yawned. At one point, Joe came over to check on me and I asked him, "Joe, is this the way it is every night with all the girls coming up after the show?"

"Pretty much when the wives aren't here." Then he smiled, "Hang in there, kid."

I managed to crack a fake smile, "Thanks, Joe, but I'm getting pretty tired. Can I go to the bedroom?"

"No. Not yet," he said firmly. "Everyone waits for E to retire." Once was all I needed to hear that.

So this was the protocol. The King even dictated when you slept. I soon learned that you didn't do anything without asking Elvis. Even if you went to the bathroom, you had to let him know exactly where you were going. I suppose this was in case he needed you. Elvis didn't like waiting for anyone, unless it was cleared through "control headquarters." Later on, when I traveled with Elvis and felt tired, I would have almost killed to sneak away, lock myself in the bedroom and switch on the TV for some mindless relaxation.

Just as I was beginning to nod off, Elvis stood up. That meant, "It's time to retire." He called Joe over and they chatted for a few minutes. Finishing their business, Elvis held out his hand to me. I took it and stood up. I guess by that time the guys had sorted out which girl was going to be with what guy. Elvis and I headed for the bedroom, and once the door closed he belonged to me. He was a different person behind closed doors, he was a normal human being.

I changed into my beautiful new white nightgown, sprayed on a tiny bit of perfume and waited for The King. He came out wearing polyester and silk pajamas. We immediately embraced, but instead of making love right away, he started talking about religion and the Bible. My former in-laws belonged to the Church of Christ, an evangelical, fire-and-brimstone religion. I attended many tent revivals, where my mother-in-law went into a trance and spoke in tongues. I didn't understand the nature of the religion or the gifts of the spirit, but I did appreciate the virtue in which they received their inspiration.

Elvis quoted scriptures to anyone he thought would appreciate hearing his words of wisdom. He instinctively knew who would be receptive and who wouldn't. I was a Bible child, so was he. I clung to and cherished every word he said as if it were the Gospel truth.

In those first nights with Elvis, I learned a lot about him. He was a very spiritual man; his soul was on fire for music. He was a giving person who not only shared his talent but his spirit, and his insights into life, as well as his body and soul. He did what a lot of famous people don't do; he shared his time and he did it lovingly.

After we finished our religious talk, we cuddled for a long time. I'm very affectionate, and it's easy for me to show someone I love how I feel. Elvis was just as loving and affectionate. We got along perfectly.

"Did you enjoy the show, honey?" he asked for what seemed the hundredth time. He loved my excitement, I think that's why he asked time and time again. I always answered with the same enthusiasm as the first time.

"Yes, oh yes!" I answered the only way I knew how, and planted a kiss on his soft, wonderful lips. That led to necking and kissing. We were like two kids in love, and in lust.

During these moments in my arms he was mine, only mine. I didn't have to share him, and I realized then how very lucky I was. After more talk, more kissing, cuddling, loving each other, he reached his hand out to me.

"Here darlin'" he said, "take this."

I knew it was the little red pill. I washed it down—I now had my own bottle of Mountain Valley Spring Water—and we talked more about our lives and what it was like growing up in the South. As the pills took effect, he talked about the next day.

"Charlie will take you to Suzie Creamcheese. You pick out whatever you like. I want my girl to be happy," he said, then fell fast asleep. I felt my pill kick in, too, and I snuggled close to E in his loving arms. I fell into a deep sleep, knowing that I was his at least for another night.

CHAPTER FOUR

The next day, Saturday, would be my last full day and evening with Elvis; Priscilla and the wives of the Memphis Mafia were expected Sunday afternoon. I got used to the near-freezing room temperature but woke up once or twice, which happens to be an annoying habit of mine to this day. Quietly, I got up around noon, went to the bathroom, then slipped back into bed without waking up Elvis. I stared at him. He was so handsome. He wasn't big, I'd say he was medium-sized, but he was strong, lean and in perfect shape.

Only once during those three days with Elvis did I think of Jim Aubrey and our previous plans for the weekend. Only once did I have a brief flash of what he must have been thinking. My mind had thoughts of only one man—the man lying in bed next to me.

We awoke to Joe knocking on the door.

"Boss, you've got a phone call." That was Joe's subtle way of letting Elvis know that Priscilla was on the line.

Waking up, Elvis reached over and hugged me, then yelled back in Joe's direction, "I'll take it in the bathroom."

He grabbed a bottle of water at the side of his bed and headed for the bathroom.

"Wait for me here, honey," he said as he left.

I got out of bed and brushed my teeth. I took a glance in the mirror and noticed how tired I looked. All the excitement of that weekend kept my adrenalin pumping. I was revving at full throttle and didn't have time to rest.

Elvis came out of the bathroom smiling, wide awake, calling for Joe.

"Joe, I want Charlie to take Barbara to Suzie's after we eat breakfast. Make sure he takes good care of her." Elvis turned to me, asking, "Did you eat your dinner like a good girl?"

"Yes," I laughed, looking at Joe for validation, "Didn't I Joe?"

Joe smiled, "Yeah boss, I fed her." The three of us laughed, then Joe left the room.

"Get dressed and I'll see you in the dining room," Elvis said. "I'll order your breakfast. Scrambled eggs, bacon, toast and coffee, right?"

"You remembered," I smiled with a big look of surprise. "Yes, that's right. Thank you, Elvis."

"OK, see ya in a few. I need to talk with the boys," he said, closing the door behind him.

Once the door was shut, I rushed to the shower, quickly dressed and went to breakfast. I didn't want to miss a thing.

"Good morning, everyone," I said entering the dining room. Elvis was going over his schedule with Joe, Sonny, Red and Charlie.

All of them smiled at me and responded together, "Good morning, Barbara." Everyone seemed pleasant and content.

The two of us sat down to our last breakfast together. The plan was for me to leave early Sunday morning while Elvis would still be sleeping. We ate, chatting about mundane things, and every now and then, he'd reach over and squeeze my hand. I was in awe just to be there sitting next to him, watching his every move, and as he liked to say, "Taking care of business."

As soon as we finished breakfast, Elvis was off with his entourage. Charlie escorted me to the boutique, where Suzie was waiting for us. She was a tiny woman, a hippie in her early 30s. She had long, wavy hair, and wore blue jeans and a lot of Indian jewelry. Yes, this was certainly my kind of place. I felt right at home.

There were so many beautiful dresses, pant suits and pieces of jewelry that I didn't know where to start. Since I loved black (and so did Elvis) I looked for anything in that color. The shop didn't have any Grecian dresses like the one Elvis loved, so after trying on several evening dresses, I settled on a long, white crochet-knit dress with cut out lace on the bodice and no straps. To complement the dress, I selected a pair of high-heeled shoes and a pair of rhinestone earrings.

Charlie took care of the bill, then we headed back to the hotel with the day's purchases.

I laid out my new dress for Elvis to inspect, and waited for him to arrive.

Eventually, the door opened and the guys filtered in one by one.

"Hi, honey," E greeted me. "How did we do today?"

"Great," I answered. "I picked out a beautiful white dress."

"I like white. Bet you look like an angel," he said. Elvis always had a way of making me blush. He loved to tease. He sat down next to me. Quickly, we were joined by the ever-present entourage and watched television to pass the time. I remember it was always on, even when everyone was talking.

Elvis suddenly got up, leading me toward the bedroom.

"Let's see what you picked out," he said.

He opened the door, and there was my white dress, laying on the bed. I waited anxiously for the verdict.

"It's beautiful, darlin'," Elvis declared, "but not as beautiful as you!" He was forever complimenting me.

The dress accentuated my tan and my white teeth. I may not have had pretty clothes growing up, but I was blessed with healthy, straight, white teeth. I was eternally grateful for that.

"Why don't you model that for me?" he asked in a powerful tone.

I went into the bathroom to change.

Unlike his stage persona, Elvis was, in reality, a very shy person. So am I. Neither one of us liked to walk around naked. He liked a little intrigue, a little mystery in his women. He liked sheer, flowing nightgowns. I never actually saw him walking around totally naked, either. He preferred his pajamas when he wanted to be comfortable.

"WOW!" E remarked as I made my entrance from the bathroom. "You do look like an angel!"

I smiled bashfully, "Thank you, darlin'."

Elvis laughed at my feeble imitation of him.

"Now, let me see your earrings." He pulled my hair back, inspecting an earring in his hands.

"They're pretty, but I've got something for you," he said. He disappeared, and returned moments later with a jewelry box. Opening it, he took out a gold ring with a small crown hanging from the center on a simple gold chain.

"Here," he said, "wear this," as he put it around my neck.

It would be the most precious thing he would ever give to me next to the medallion.

"Now you're perfect," he said with a smile. Then he hugged me so close I could feel his breath on the back of my hair.

A knock on the door made us unlock our embrace. Joe was informing his boss that it was show time.

Elvis kissed me long and hard. "Darlin', see you after the show. You be good now."

Usually Elvis had Sonny or Red watch me, but I was never left alone with the other women who were hanging around. Some were friends, some were pickups the guys met in the audience or in the casino.

Elvis left with his entourage, and I waited for the show in anticipation, just as I had the two previous nights. By this time, the girls began to show up in the suite. There were even more than the night before. As I walked out of the room, I could see envy in their eyes. They saw the white dress and the gold crown I was wearing. They knew I was the No.1 girl.

Like the night before, a group of us headed down to the show. The show seemed to get better each night, and the highlight of each evening was watching Elvis throw his scarves into the screaming sea of fans.

Once again, Elvis dedicated "The First Time Ever I Saw Your Face" to me. (I guess that was his favorite song to dedicate to all his girls.) This time, it brought tears to my eyes. I knew it would be my last show for awhile.

When Elvis sang, his voice was somewhere between a lover and a gospel singer. It was pure, sexy and righteous.

I didn't want the evening to end. I didn't want to leave Elvis or Las Vegas. It was a perfect weekend. I wished we could be together forever.

After the show, but before the house lights came back on, we were led to the elevators. More girls had joined our group to get in line for a chance encounter with The King. Elvis did his usual entertaining in his dressing room, then came back for the nightly party. The routine was pretty much the same, and by this time, I was really tired, but getting the picture loud and clear. Once Elvis made his gesture of acknowledging me, he made his way around to everyone in the room. Like always, the girls flirted outrageously while Elvis ate it all up, winking at me every so often to show me I was still his No. 1 girl. In return, I would dutifully smile.

The evening came to a close around 6 a.m., and Elvis and I escaped to his bedroom. We closed the door, started kissing, fell onto the bed, and made love. We made love every night we were together, but this particular night was the most memorable of all.

After showering, we slipped into our respective night gown and silk pajamas. I finished first, waiting for E in bed. When he came out of his bathroom he had a beautiful black jewelry box, which he placed between us on the bed. He methodically went through every piece, pointing out which ones were his favorites and why.

He loved jewelry, and the bigger, the better. He especially liked Indian jewelry, which was a big craze in the early 1970s. He also loved diamonds in his rings.

I don't know why, but I suddenly got emotional. Like the first night, I reiterated to Elvis about all of the girls that I had to contend with. I told him I hated competing for his attention, and how draining it was on me.

He pulled me to him, hugging me. "You're No. 1, and don't you forget it," he said with all of the sincerity he could muster. In reality, I was his 10th No. 1 girl.

During the next few hours, he talked about upcoming shows, a new song he was considering, another tour he was planning. He never discussed personal dreams or family plans. And once again, it was time to go to sleep. We took our pills and fell asleep in each other's arms.

I had to leave the next morning, before the wives arrived. I awoke to Joe's quiet knocking, and I hurriedly dressed and gathered up my things. Elvis woke long enough to say goodbye. He kissed me gently, then fell back into a deep sleep.

I crept out of the bedroom and met Joe on the other side of the door. As I walked past the living room, I noticed something strange—a stuffed animal on the coffee table, which had a mongoose in strike position moving in for the kill on a cobra. Now that Elvis thought he stole me away from Jim, he nicknamed himself "The Mongoose," because it was the only animal that could kill the Cobra. He was so proud of himself for stealing me away from Jim and loved to brag to the guys how the "the mongoose killed the cobra." That was his distinct sense of humor.

Once Joe and I got over a quick fit of the giggles, we made our way downstairs to the waiting black Cadillac.

In the car, Joe tried to make me feel better. "E will call you, so check in with your answering service."

As he handed me my ticket at the airport, he smiled and said, "See you soon, kid." Then he drove off back to the show.

I checked in at the ticket counter, and then purchased a much-needed cup of coffee.

The plane ride back to Los Angeles passed quickly. I spent most of that hour staring out the window, gazing at the mountains and the desert, and dreaming about Elvis. I wondered if and when I would see him again.

I had a busy schedule ahead of me with the filming of *Pretty Maids All in a Row*. It wouldn't be easy to just pick up and go whenever Elvis wanted me. But, as I was to discover shortly, that's the way it would be. He juggled his women according to the mood he was in. Some of us "girls" were experiencing parallel relationships, doing primarily the same things with Elvis, but on different days of the week.

"Rock Hudson and me in Marina del Rey shooting *Pretty Maids All In A Row*." From the Barbara Leigh Collection.

For the most part, Elvis was a creature of habit with the exception of "new things" he periodically brought into his life. It could be guns, jewelry, cars, philosophy, police badges, huge flashlights, wrist guards or whatever else might catch his fancy. Anything new intrigued him. Having a new girl in his life was another new thing. It kept his attention.

The plane ride was smooth, and before I knew it, we were at the gate. As I deplaned, my thoughts shifted to James. While I waited for my overnight bag, I called my answering service. Four calls from James, a couple from my friends, one from my agent and one from my mother.

I couldn't wait to call my mom with the news about my weekend with Elvis. She was proud of me when I became a professional model and actress, and she got a huge kick telling her friends. I knew she'd be tickled hearing about Elvis.

As I headed for my car, I wondered if I had enough money to pay for four days of short-term parking. I had only planned on being gone one day. I rarely had much cash on me, always surviving on credit cards. Luckily, I had the money and breathed a sigh of relief.

My relief was short-lived, because as I pulled away from the airport, my thoughts went back to James. I knew I had to face him. Cinderella was home from the ball.

Several possible stories swirled around inside my head. Being an actress, I wasn't at a loss for good material or a possible scenario. I could tell James my mother was sick and I had to take care of her, but there would be the question of why I didn't phone him. Then again, I could just face the music and tell him the truth. After all, he was with another woman. What could he say to that? Still, I dreaded having to come clean with him.

I drove in the direction of Hancock Park, knowing that a serious confrontation awaited me. I unpacked my things, then reached for the phone, slowly dialing James' number. His phone rang three times before he finally answered.

"Hello?" His voice sounded abnormally low and depressed. Guess his ploy was shot.

"Hello," I said back with an airy spin.

"Where have you been, Indian? I've been worried sick!" he shouted. That was a switch, he rarely showed any emotion.

"I'll tell you when I see you," I said quietly, but firmly.

"I'm waiting for you. Can you come now?" he asked impatiently, again, not his usual, cool self.

"I'm on my way."

I changed into some jeans and a T-shirt and grabbed my tote bag, adding a few personal effects—just in case.

He sounded as if he missed me. I loved him. In fact, I was plain crazy about him, but I still was going to level with him about Elvis. And I definitely was going to bring up Joanne Pflug. I wanted him to know that two could play this game. Why should men have all the fun?

Driving up Benedict Canyon, I was anxious, gripping the steering wheel tightly. Would this break us up? I was prepared for the worst.

James lived in a small but very elegant house at the top of Tower and Seabright drives. The location commanded a breathtaking view of both the city lights and mountain tops. He was forced to sell his beloved house 20 years later because of a lawsuit. Ironically, he called me on his last night in the house, totally lost. He loved his casa; it was his castle.

I let myself in the front door. James was sitting in the living room, drinking a glass of Almaden wine, which he bought by the half-gallon. I could tell he was mad and slightly tipsy.

"Well, Indian, glad to see you're OK," he said with a slight hint of sarcasm. "Where have you been? You know we had this boat cruise to the Catalina Islands planned for some time."

He must have hated the fact that he had to pay for the cruise anyway, even though we didn't go. James was not an overly generous man. Although quite wealthy, he was very thrifty and was consumed with the thought that people (mainly women) were after his money and his powerful connections. He wasn't only tight with his money but also with his time, affection and emotions. The thought of helping someone get ahead never crossed his mind, and that included his ex-wife and children.

"James, I'm sorry, but I was in Las Vegas with Elvis," I blurted out.

There it was. The cat was out of the bag, and I expected all hell to break loose.

His face turned red, but before he could answer, I continued, my confidence having risen a notch or two.

"James, you lied to me about going to San Francisco," I pointed out. "You took Joanne Pflug to see Elvis in Las Vegas." Now I had his attention. He was busted!

Before I let him get a word in, I continued my lament. "I was going to Las Vegas for one night to see his show and you turned up, so I got mad and stayed the weekend."

After a brief pause, James fumed, "Well, you and I are both liars, I guess. What happened to Joshua Tree?"

He had me there. I placed my hands on my hips, standing over him, not giving an inch.

"Does this make us even?" I asked, ready to give him a fight if he wanted one.

His demeanor changed suddenly, and he said with a defeated tone, "Come here, Indian." He reached up to grab me, and I let him. I could tell he had missed me. I sat on his lap and he started kissing me on the neck, then worked his way up to my lips.

James was a very sensual, sexual man—a great lover. He was mechanical, but to give him his due, a great lover nonetheless. He also was neurotic and meticulous. For instance, his house had to be in impeccable order. If an ashtray were turned the wrong way, he would straighten it. James was the living, breathing embodiment of Felix Unger from *The Odd Couple*. I was neat, too, but nowhere near as compulsive as James.

The fact that I had been with Elvis probably gave him unwelcome pangs of jealousy. He was a champion competitor, ruthless in his business dealings and not particularly well-liked by the Hollywood community. The word "cold" fit him to a T. After a few minutes of kissing, he offered me a glass of wine, which I gladly accepted. We officially made up, and he chose to forgive me for these last few "miserable days" as he put it.

"James Aubrey and me during happier times."
From the Barbara Leigh Collection.

We spent the rest of the evening together, later dining at Nicky Blair's, a posh Beverly Hills restaurant that was our favorite hangout. James and Nicky were friends, and it was in Nicky's old restaurant, Stephanino's, where we first met and had our first date. Nicky was as popular back then as Wolfgang Puck is today.

Back at the house, James lit a fire and we drank more wine. Believe it or not, being with James made me forget Elvis. I was head over heels in love with this tyrant. Why, I don't know. Maybe it was because of his good looks; he was tall, had a gray mane of hair (which I loved), piercing blue eyes and a great body, which he kept in shape by daily jogging and intense calisthenics. Maybe it was his intelligence. Mostly, it was his power. He would be one of the two boyfriends that I later questioned becoming involved with, but for the time being, he was the dominant force in my life. Whatever the reason, I loved him.

We spent several hours in front of the fireplace sipping on glasses of wine. We talked about what we wanted in life, our careers, and our futures. Our stomachs were full, and we were content from a great meal of pasta and salad, our favorite dinner. It was time to kick back and relax.

We lay there looking at each other, knowing what was going to happen next. Our shoes hit the floor in front of the roaring fire. Next, it was our pants, then our shirts. We walked toward the bedroom while undressing each other. We arrived there stark naked, laughing and falling into a passionate embrace. We made love all night and into the next morning. Was this night of lovemaking specifically for me, or was it a man reclaiming his woman? I couldn't tell. What I could tell was that I liked it.

The next morning James was up early.

"Indian," he whispered, "I'm off to work. Lock the door behind you. I'll call you later."

I instantly I fell back to sleep. I awoke to his maid, Anna, coming in for the day. *Did he kiss me goodbye?* I hated it when he left, and couldn't remember if he had properly said goodbye. *Of course he did,* I thought, and got dressed in a hurry. I waved goodbye to Anna, closing the door behind me.

I drove home, thinking of the week that lay ahead of me. I fed my cat, Ashley, the minute I got in the door. I could tell she was mad at me for leaving her to be cared for by my neighbors.

I showered, threw on clean clothes and made a pot of coffee.

My head was spinning from too much wine.

With coffee in hand, I called my commercial agent, Randy Fred.

"Barbara, I was just about to call you," he said. "You have a call back for Aqua Net Hair Spray." He filled me in on the particulars. I ended up getting the commercial, which turned out to be one of my best moneymakers, grossing in the neighborhood of $13,000, good money in those days. The commercial, nostalgia buffs might recall, had two girls, one blonde, one brunette (me) going through a torture test to see whose hair would hold up the best. The blonde's hair held up because she used Aqua Net. I, alas, used an inferior brand, and my hair looked like a rat's nest.

Just as I was about to leave the apartment, the phone rang. It was James.

"Indian," he asked, "do you want to go to a dinner party tonight?"

"Yes!" I said without hesitation. I was in the mood to do something fun.

"Fine, meet me at the house at seven."

That was another little quirk of James'—he always wanted me to drive up the hill to his house. He liked his castle where he was King, and that's where he wanted to be. Only a couple of times did he ever pick me up at my apartment. One time it was a proud moment in my life when James did show up.

My son Gerry, who was visiting me from Tennessee, was being looked after by a babysitter when the door bell rang. I opened the door and Gerry ran out in front of us to shake James's hand. They both had big smiles on their faces—mine included. It was the cutest moment, and totally unexpected.

My beautiful blonde-haired, blue-eyed son looked more like his father than he did me. Gerry was raised by his father, Finley, and his stepmother, Alice. He also had a younger half-brother named John. They were very close.

Gerry lived with them in a quiet, family-oriented suburb of Chattanooga, Tennessee, where he was born. There, he had a stable childhood I couldn't give him. He had his own bedroom, a big yard to play in, a pet dog and lived the normal life of a young boy. He took the bus to school, played the trumpet and marched in the school band.

"Me and my precious six-year-old son Gerry."
Photo taken by Charles Bush. From the Barbara
Leigh Collection.

Though he yearned constantly for my love and affection, my life at that time was too unstable; not the type of environment to bring up a young boy who needed guidance from his father.

I loved Gerry too much, and did not want him to grow up with the nagging insecurities that plagued me growing up, not knowing where I'd live next or with whom. It simply wasn't the type of life for a child. We both learned to accept it and tried to make the best of his living with his father, whom he also loved very much. I knew it was the best thing to do at the time.

In Tennessee, Gerry had his grandparents, numerous cousins, aunts and uncles all living normal lives with regular schedules. There was direction in his life with academic and social goals. The influence of his family gave him a sense of who he was, and it was there that he truly belonged. He was a part of a large extended family— something I knew very little about.

It was hard for me to let go of Gerry, but in my heart, I knew it was the best thing for him. I tried to see him as often as our schedules would allow, and we always were just a phone call away. But no matter how often we saw each other or how much we talked, we missed each other terribly.

Not being around for Gerry's upbringing was the biggest regret of my life. At 17, I was much too young to be a mother. I wasn't financially able, or emotionally mature enough, to raise him on my own. I wasn't the mother he deserved even though I truly loved him with all of my heart.

Once back at home, my shoes came off, and my body demanded a rest. I took a well deserved nap. I hadn't slept much the last four days. When I awoke, I got ready for the dinner party, putting on my best mini dress and pumps.

As I was pulling into James' driveway, so was he. Our timing was perfect.

"Indian, you look great," he commented.

I returned a smile, then asked him, "Where are we going?"

"To Sue Mengers'," James answered.

Sue Mengers was the single most powerful and influential agent in the '70s, bar none. She represented a who's who of movie and television stars and directors, including Barbara Streisand, Cher, Faye Dunaway, Ali MacGraw, Candice Bergen, Tuesday Weld, Cybill Shepherd, Sidney Lumet, Ryan O' Neal, Gene Hackman, Bob Fosse, Peter Bogdanovich, Arthur Penn, Herbert Ross and a host of others. Sue also later represented former President Jimmy Carter, bragging to everyone that she could get him a movie deal with the snap of a finger. She lived in a palatial home in one of the canyons in Beverly Hills on a winding, narrow street.

We were greeted at the door by her butler, who escorted us into the living room, where everyone was drinking and talking. Sue cut off in mid sentence the person she was talking to, and sauntered over to greet us.

"Jim," she said, all smiles.

Sue was a very large woman, very charming and very successful. If she was your agent, you were sure to be submitted for the juiciest parts. She handled only the cream of the crop, and her being your agent was a sign that you had arrived.

Sue smiled and shook my hand. The three of us walked over to the bar and got a glass of wine.

After dinner, we went into the living room, where I drifted over to the couch and plopped down. James was schmoozing away with various people in the movie industry. I quietly watched him work the room.

A few minutes later, Sue sat down beside me. She was blunt and straight to the point.

"If you're thinking of marrying Jim Aubrey, you can forget it," she coldly told me. Our conversation stopped dead in its tracks. Who the hell was she to make such a bold proclamation?

Her remark annoyed me so much that I looked to James for comfort, but he was deep in conversation across the room.

I looked right at Sue Mengers and told her, "I love James enough to marry him, but the thought never occurred to us."

I remained angry with her for a long time, but now I realize she was only trying to warn me. She did it in a very rude way, but, as it turned out, she was right on the money.

I was uncomfortable for the rest of the evening—my mood took a drastic turn for the worse. My stomach churned, and Sue Mengers' words ate away at me.

After a couple of looks from me and another hour of schmoozing,

James was ready to go home. We dutifully said our goodbyes and left—thank God.

I was in a deep trance on the ride home, thinking hard, looking straight ahead at the road. James' soothing voice broke my concentration.

"Indian, are you tired? You're so quiet tonight."

"I'm OK," I said in a voice just barely above a whisper. "I guess I am tired."

Actually, I was depressed. It seemed as if I was always loving the wrong man.

I decided I wasn't going to let my depression spoil the rest of the night, so I put aside my thoughts for the time being. I wanted so badly to tell James what Sue had said, but what could he do? He'd probably agree with her, anyway. And that would only make me feel worse.

Once we were inside the cozy comfort of his bedroom, we undressed and made love, falling asleep in each other's arms. I felt such warmth in those arms. James was a lot like Elvis when we were together behind closed doors. He was just a man who needed to be loved. No deals, no studio problems, no hassles, no huge ego. Nothing but the two of us. If only this feeling could last. But that's the big problem: Nothing lasts forever. Only in the movies is there a happily ever after.

CHAPTER FIVE

Mystery was a dominating part of James Aubrey's character. Like an excellent poker player, he never placed all of his cards on the table. He preferred to watch and wait for his chance to pounce, never letting you know what he was thinking or feeling. The air of mystery that surrounded James was a big part of my attraction to him. Most women I know are inherently attracted to mysterious men, but mystery doesn't necessarily translate well in a relationship. Communication is the key to a lasting, loving union. During the beginning of my relationship with James I was attracted to his mystique. That mystique and lack of communication eventually became a big turnoff.

This much I do know: James Thomas Aubrey Jr. was born December 14, 1918, in Lasalle, Illinois, to James Thomas Aubrey Sr. and Mildred (Steven) Aubrey. James Sr. was a hard-driving advertising man. His career, rather than his wife and four children, remained the top priority in his life. The Aubrey family was uprooted several times in pursuit of James Sr.'s ambitions. The family lived in a series of cities, including Chicago and New York, finally settling in the affluent Chicago suburb of Lake Forest.

James rarely spoke of his father, and when he did it was never with love or admiration. As is often the case, the first born has it harder than the children who follow, and James was no exception. He had stricter rules to follow than his brothers, added responsibilities and higher expectations. Pressure was put on him to succeed at a very early age. His father displayed no sympathy and very little affection.

James adored his mother Mildred. They were extremely close. When James became a success, he always made sure he kept his mother's cupboard fully stocked in See's candy, her favorite chocolates. She lived to be 97, passing away in 1992. I heard through Skye she was a strong, beautiful woman.

What James Sr. couldn't give to his four children emotionally, he gave them financially, working hard to provide them the best that money could buy. His family had luxurious homes in the city, summer homes on the beach, vacations to Europe, new cars and beautiful clothes. He even provided a first-class education for James at Phillips Exeter Academy, an elite prep school in Exeter, New York. James lived at school for most of his childhood, and only spent semester breaks and summers at home. He was raised by a set of rules and regulations, rather than by a set of parents who would nurture him whenever he fell down or got a cut or bruise. Love wasn't a word that was loosely tossed around at Phillips Exeter Academy, nor was it a word that was used in the Aubrey household.

James entered Princeton University in 1938, where he majored in English, played end on the football team and belonged to the Tiger Inn Club. After receiving his bachelor's degree *cum laude,* in 1941, he enlisted in the Army Air Force, where he became a test pilot, facing death every day on the job. He reached the rank of major before his discharge, in 1945.

After World War II, James put as much distance as he could between his father and himself by settling in Los Angeles. He sold advertising space for Street and Smith and Conde Nast Publications for two years, then worked as an account executive at CBS affiliates KNX and KNXT from 1948 to 1955. By 1956 he had moved to the CBS television network's West Coast programming department. Accounting was second nature to James, but it wasn't exciting. He had mastered everything there was to know about accounting, and he yearned to work in the creative part of television.

In 1956, James and a co-worker, Hunt Stromberg Jr., worked on a story idea that originated with two Hollywood writers, Herb Meadow and Sam (*The Man From U.N.C.L.E.*) Rolfe. They turned the idea into an outline for *Have Gun, Will Travel*, an offbeat Western series starring Richard Boone, that became enormously popular and was a network hit for five years. James was on his way.

Stromberg introduced James to officials at ABC, which was the infant among the major networks and ranked dead last in the ratings. ABC desperately needed someone who had an understanding of numbers and budgets, yet was creative enough to understand the crucial elements in producing and packaging a television series. The president of ABC, Oliver Treyz, felt James was the man to take ABC to the top, so he hired him as vice president in charge of programs and talent. With Treyz, James initiated several popular television series, such as *The Real McCoys*, *Maverick*, *The Donna Reed Show*, *77 Sunset Strip* and *The Rifleman*. By 1958, ABC took a quantum leap in the ratings and was now within the competitive range of CBS and NBC. ABC was no longer looked upon as the new kid on the block. James Aubrey Jr. was now a force to be reckoned with.

In April of 1958, CBS realized it had made a huge mistake by letting James get away, and hired him back as vice president in charge of creative services. A year later, James was appointed president when network president, Louis G. Cowan, the inventor of the audience-participation format, resigned in the wake of the scandal over rigged quiz shows. During James' reign, he personally was responsible for bringing *The Beverly Hillbillies*, *Mr. Ed*, *Gomer Pyle*, *Petticoat Junction*, *Gilligan's Island*, *The Munsters*, *My Favorite Martian* and *Route 66* to television.

His climb to the top wasn't all rosy; James made enemies, because of his curt ways and ruthless personality. He was responsible for giving the ax to such old-time stars as Jack Benny, Gary Moore and Arthur Godfrey. He bruised a lot egos while he was riding the crest of success, and his critics and enemies patiently waited, sharpening their knives and biding their time for the right opportunity to thrust. They would have to wait many years to get their revenge.

Perhaps the biggest enemy he made was television mogul William S. Paley, who also happened to be CBS's owner and chief executive officer. You see, James had an affair with Bill's better half, well-known socialite Babe Paley. At first, the affair helped boost James' career as he zoomed to the top of the corporate ladder. Babe, I'm sure, more than put in a positive word with her husband concerning James' "abilities."

While Babe Paley was known to have had several affairs on the side, close friends of James' didn't think it was smart for him to keep it going. They knew that Bill Paley was a powerful man with an enormous ego who could damage his career, but James was stubborn and wouldn't heed their advice. Eventually, Bill found out about the affair and waited for the proper moment. When the opportunity presented itself, Bill fired James. All it took was for three of CBS's new television shows to fail. At the time of James' dismissal in 1965, CBS had 12 of the top 15 nighttime series on the air and all 12 of the top daytime soap operas.

The official reason Jim was dismissed was because of the three failed television series, but I have to believe his affair with Babe Paley was ultimately the reason his tenure with CBS was terminated. The simple reason he was fired was that he bit the hand that fed him.

At the time of his dismissal, the *Washington Post* reported, "No man in TV history made bigger profits—or more enemies." Author David Halberstam in his best-selling book, *The Powers That Be*, wrote: "Aubrey's success was very simple: He had a killer instinct for the lowest common denominator, and unlike others who had that instinct, he had no shame, no interest in respectability, or at least the traditional forms of respectability." His tenure at CBS was fictionalized in two novels: *The Cannibals*, written by ex-actor and former network programming associate Keefe (*The Eddie Cantor Story*) Brasselle, and Jacqueline Susann's *The Love Machine,* a best-selling book and later a successful motion picture directed by Jack Haley, Jr., in which the character based on James, named "Robin Stone," was played by John Phillip Law.

James' life was a mess after he had been dumped by CBS. A few years earlier, his marriage had fallen apart.

I think in his heart James truly regretted leaving his wife, the beautiful and gracious actress Phyllis Thaxter. Phyllis was the mother of his two children, Susan Schyler (Skye) and James Watson. The two met and married in 1944 when Phyllis was under contract to MGM and filming *Thirty Seconds Over Tokyo* starring Spencer Tracy, Van Johnson and Robert Mitchum. The two met on a blind date and fell in love. They divorced in 1963, when Phyllis finally tired of his infidelity.

"James Aubrey at his domain—MGM Studios in Culver City, California." Photo courtesy of Skye Aubrey.

In October 1969, MGM was in a state of total disarray. The studio had not had a hit in four years, since *Doctor Zhivago* in 1965. MGM was still spending lavish amounts of money on big pictures that tanked at the box office. The dividends dried up and majority stockholder Kirk Kerkorian, a Las Vegas real estate tycoon who owned 33 percent of the MGM stock, enlisted James' help, installing him as the acting president.

James immediately put a ceiling of $2 million on all MGM productions, and put out the word to all big-name producers and directors that the gravy train had run its course. They could either accept more realistic salaries or find employment elsewhere. With Kerkorian's approval, James sold off land owned by MGM and historical props and wardrobe, including Judy Garland's ruby slippers from *The Wizard of Oz*. Staffs were reduced to half (James personally fired some 3,500 people), salaries were drastically cut and all excessive spending habits were curbed, including turning off the heat in a few office buildings. By 1971, the studio saw its first operating profit in four years. With those cutbacks, and the success of the MGM Grand Hotel in Las Vegas, the studio was well in the black when James left in 1973. He was the first man ever to head a TV network and film studio.

The first time I ever laid eyes on James was in February 1970 at Jilly's Restaurant in Palm Springs, California. Jilly's was named after Jilly Rizzo, Frank Sinatra's best friend. The food was of course Italian, but it played second fiddle in comparison to the stars who frequented the eatery. Jilly's was the in-place to be seen in Palm Springs, and was patronized by the likes of Sinatra, Sammy Davis Jr., Cary Grant, Peter Lawford, Dean Martin and a lot of Hollywood's old guard. I was with my boyfriend, Ed Garner, whom I describe affectionately as a "Beverly Hills brat." His grandfather was the famous actor, H.B. (*The King of Kings*) Warner.

Eddie worked mainly as an extra in the Frankie Avalon and Annette Funicello beach movies under the American International Pictures banner. He also managed the band Dino, Desi and Billy, all kids of famous parents. Eddy ran with a fun, glamorous group of Beverly Hills elite. It was always a party when I was around him.

Five of us were sitting in Jilly's at a corner booth, not behaving too well, I might add, when someone passed a joint of marijuana around the table in Frank Sinatra's best friend's place of business. Not too smart. At first, the thought of smoking pot scared me. I hadn't grown up with the privileges and freedom of these spoiled kids, and I was petrified of being arrested. The rest of the group only laughed, so I got with the program and took a puff.

Before the main course arrived, I noticed four people walk in and sit down in the next booth. One of the men was Cary Grant, a childhood hero of mine. But it was the other man, James Aubrey, who captured my attention. Both men were with dates. Because of the configuration of the booths, I was sitting in direct line with James, and I couldn't help but stare at him. He was the epitome of what I thought my dream man would be. James wasn't nearly as handsome as Eddie, but he had an air about him that stood out, attracting me to him even more than to the legendary Mr. Grant. I don't know why, but he reminded me of a Texas oil tycoon. He caught me staring at him, so he smiled back. I shyly looked away, embarrassed at being caught.

Once dinner was over, I glanced one last time at James, I thought, *It's a shame I'll never see that man again.* Little did I know that I would see him the next day.

He was lounging pool side at the famous Racquet Club Hotel. He watched me as my friends and I arrived to have lunch by the pool. James watched in a detached manner, trying to appear that he wasn't staring at me, but in reality he was fantasizing about me (he told me this later when we were dating). I spent the rest of my time in Palm Springs with my friends having a wild, wet weekend, drinking and having fun.

A week later while visiting my girlfriend, Judy Baldwin, I picked up a copy of Time magazine, casually flipping through it. There was an article with a stamp-sized picture of James Aubrey.

"That's the guy I saw in Palm Springs, Judy," I declared, pointing at the picture.

Judy was a blonde-haired, blue-eyed former Ms. New Mexico turned actress. At the time, she was dating Mort Viner, a successful agent with Creative Management Agency (now International Creative Management). We thought maybe Mort might know who the guy in the picture was. Mort knew everyone in the businesss. Unbelievable as it seems, in my haste, I didn't bother to read the article, but I knew that I definitely wanted to meet this handsome and intriguing man. He reminded me of my mom's hero—Howard Roarke—from Ayn Rand's "The Fountainhead," who was beautifully portrayed by Garry Cooper in the movie. That was always my kind of man.

Judy and I were under contract to Twentieth Century-Fox for a pilot called *Bracken's World*, ironically, a series portraying contract players. The show was the fictional account of people in the movie industry. The pilot was successful; the series was not. NBC aired the show for a year and three months before canceling it. It was a great idea that was a little ahead of its time.

"TV promo for *Bracken's World*. Judy Baldwin is the beauty in the white cut out bathing suit."
Photo courtesy of Judith Baldwin.

As a result of the pilot, I developed a friendship with Judy. We had a ball on the pilot, filming in our bikinis on the Santa Monica beach and causing quite a stir. We both have great pictures from the show, Judy wearing her cut out bathing suit and me with my hair in a French fall ponytail. Definitely the '70s. So cute.

Judy offered to take the article to her boyfriend and ask him to try to arrange a date for me. I thanked her, but I wasn't the kind of girl to sit around waiting for the phone to ring, so I didn't give James another thought until a couple of days later, when Judy called me.

"Mort knows James Aubrey!" Judy said, with a touch of excitement. "It turns out he's the president of MGM Studios."

"Wow, I guess I should have read the article!" We both had a good laugh over that one.

"Mort's fixed you up on a blind date with James on Friday at 8 p.m. at Stephanino's," Judy added.

Judy told me that Nicky Blair would take care of the introductions.

"Thanks Judy, I owe you one," I said as I hung up the phone, pumped full of life at the thought of meeting this man. From that phone call until I actually saw him face to face, I thought of nothing else but James.

Ed Garner and I weren't getting along too well at the time: He had a severe drinking problem, and James quickly became my No. 1 fantasy. I was nervous at the thought of meeting him, wondering if he would like me.

Friday rolled around and I got dressed in my best clothes, a miniskirt, a silk blouse and high-heeled pumps. As I approached the restaurant, I had to wait for three cars in front of me to get valet parking, making me late. I was hoping James wouldn't be mad at me. I was sure no one had ever made him wait before.

Once inside, I was greeted by Nicky Blair himself. Gracious as always, Nicky escorted me to the table where James was already seated. A big smile came over his face as we were introduced. I knew right away that he liked me. I sat down and he poured me a glass of white wine, the first of many I had that night.

"You're the girl at the pool," he said in amazement.

"What pool?"

"The pool at The Racquet Club in Palm Springs. I saw you there," he told me.

I was flattered he remembered me. That sealed the deal—we were both hooked on each other.

From that moment on, my relationship with Ed was history. Up to then, most of my boyfriends had been near my age, but secretly I had always wanted a relationship with an older man. I was looking for a surrogate father to teach me about life, about things I didn't know—someone who could teach me about love and kindness as well. I was hoping that James could fill that void in my life. Ha!

I'd like to be able to say that I was a good girl and didn't go home with James that night, but I can't. The fact that he wanted me as much as I wanted him was too much to fight.

We drove up the hill to his house on Seabright Drive, and made love. James was a fantastic lover, everything he was said to be and more, if he wanted to be. That night, he wanted to be.

Just like my first night with Elvis, James wanted to know everything. I cautiously told him about my upbringing, saying as little as possible, sparing him the details when I could.

Where was I from? What did my father do for a living? What nationality was I?

The first two questions were given cursory treatment, but I answered in full what my nationality was.

"I'm part Cherokee Indian, part English and part Italian," I replied.

"Well, you look like an Indian princess, so I shall call you 'Indian' from now on."

I must admit, I liked it. It was the 1970s, and America was going through its "Hail to the Indians" period. I thought the nickname was special.

"A shot of me in the Grand Canyon from my May 1973 *Playboy* pictorial." Photo by Charles Bush and courtesy of P.E.I.

James had a way about him that glamorized everything he said or did. His proper schooling and privileged upbringing lent him an air of royalty, at least to me. I hadn't dated anyone quite like him. More specifically, he was my knight in shining armor, riding high in the saddle on that white horse, just what every little girl dreams of. He was the man on the cover of a romance novel, holding me in a daring and provocative embrace.

James was used to being with sophisticated women who were educated, well-dressed and glamorous. He mainly dated models, but had many highly publicized affairs with Babe Paley, model Dee Hawks and *Women's Wear Daily* fashion writer Carol Bjorkman. Carol was one of the great loves of his life. The two met through author Jacqueline Susann, and their relationship lasted for years, until Carol's early death from cancer. In an uncharacteristic display of love, James was at her bedside when she died, clutching her hand in his. James' daughter, Skye, was Carol's best friend.

I was the little girl from the wrong side of the tracks, but he liked that. He could educate me in the ways of the world, and often would.

Whenever I mispronounced a word or got my facts wrong, James was there to correct me in private, never in front of other people. He was gracious that way, making sure never to embarrass me in the presence of others or exploit the fact that I was uneducated.

At first, my relationship with Skye was a bit touch and go. Growing up with James Aubrey as a father was a trial for any young girl, and Skye suffered through years as her father's "beard" on numerous dates. She accompanied him to many restaurants while he was courting young, beautiful models, even while he was still married to her mother.

Skye never betrayed her father's trust, but all those years of playing second fiddle to his women ate away at her heart. In retaliation, she would get even with James by having affairs with her father's best friends, including actor and dancer Gene Kelly, who asked Skye to marry him. She also had an affair with Anthony Quinn, a man three times her age. George Peppard was another older actor with whom she embarked on an affair. He also wanted to marry her. Skye eventually married someone her own age, movie producer Ilya Salkind. Ilya and his father Alexander produced the *Superman* movies, along with other well-known films.

At 17, Skye left home for England to study at the London Royal Academy of Arts. She didn't take a penny from her father her first year away, working instead in a clothing store on Kings Road, which she found to be a blast. She broke down her second year away, allowing James to help her with room and tuition. Skye was and is a very proud woman.

Skye became friends with a lot of James' girlfriends, but she did the choosing, picking the ones she particularly liked. She would watch and wait to see who really loved her father, knowing that many of them only wanted to take advantage of his position in Hollywood to further their careers. She was an old soul for a young girl; very hip to the Hollywood scene at an early age. Although Skye and I weren't good friends while I dated James; we ironically became friends the day her dad and I ended our relationship.

James' son, James III, or Jay as I liked to refer to him, wasn't around often but I distinctly remember him as a very quiet and shy little boy. He seemed afraid of his father, or at least, afraid of disappointing him. Years later he became a movie producer, working on several projects with his dad.

By April 1970, James and I were an item. By then, he had broken off his relationship with his longtime girlfriend, Del. I met her by accident one evening at James' house, and it wasn't a festive occasion.

James had asked me to come to his house, which I happily complied. When I arrived, I noticed a car in the driveway but went inside anyway. Del was there. James casually introduced us and poured me a glass of wine. I didn't have a clue as to what was going on, but I played it cool. Del lost her composure, storming off into the bedroom with James a step behind her. Once in the bedroom, they quarreled loudly and then she bolted for the front door, slamming it behind her. I felt badly for her. As for me, I felt as if I had gotten in the middle of something, but I was so naive that I didn't see the big picture.

Looking back, I'm sure that James' intentions weren't good. Later in our relationship, James tried to put me together with himself and several women, but never succeeded. I'm almost positive that's what he tried to do with Del and me that night; it was probably the reason she made such a scene, and left. I don't blame her one bit. The very idea was way too bizarre for me. I found out later from Skye that James and Del had dated for a couple of years, until I arrived on the scene. James had chosen me over her.

That night we casually went about our routine, choosing to ignore what had just happened. He didn't seem to care that Del left, so I didn't either. It wouldn't have been wise to rock the boat; after all, I was the one who had pursued James and I didn't want to spoil the evening. We drank our wine, talked and eventually made love well into the night.

It wasn't long into our relationship when James took me to the bright lights of New York City, where MGM had an apartment in the famous Carlisle Hotel on Madison Avenue and 77th Street in Manhattan. I landed a big, national commercial for Ponds cold cream, which was being filmed not too far away on Long Island. After I finished the commercial, James flew to New York on business and we spent a couple of interesting days together.

Walking into restaurants with him was like entering a room with a king. The restaurants we frequented were the ones he regularly ate in when he was president of CBS. Our entrances were dramatic: The staff and patrons turned to stare at us, whispering who knows what. We always got the best table and the royal treatment. It was intoxicating.

My first time at the internationally known 21 Club was especially memorable, because James had arranged for the captain to show me the famous room and doors in the basement that are legendary from Prohibition days, when it was illegal to drink liquor in this country. The captain showed me shelves of expensive bottles of wine labeled with family names like the Rockefellers, Duponts and the Vanderbilts. Some of the bottles ran into the thousands of dollars. The tour was was very impressive and can still be taken today—a must if you ever eat at the 21 Club.

Coming back from my last day of filming the Ponds commercial, I walked into the hotel room dead tired. I wanted to rest, but instead, found James in the living room with a tall, beautiful black actress drinking wine. James got up from the couch and gave me a hug. I was a little bit surprised and alarmed to see him with this woman, but I decided to remain calm, cool and collected. In reality, I was extremely upset.

"Indian," he started the conversation, "would you like a glass of wine?"

He went over to the bar and, like a perfect gentleman, poured me a glass of wine. I was only 24 and very naive, so I remained polite while conversing with the two of them. I refused to reveal my feelings, but inside I was very anxious, knowing something was not right, but unable to put my finger on exactly what was wrong.

The three of us were waiting for a limo to take us to dinner, while we polished off another bottle of wine. The wine hit James, and he started making overtures as to what he wanted—a threesome—but that item wasn't on the evening's menu.

I began fuming. He had never given any inclination that he was interested in such a thing. The night with Del didn't hit home until long after, so I wasn't prepared for this. How do you prepare for a proposition like that? They don't teach you those kinds of things in Ringgold, Georgia!

The limo driver phoned from downstairs to let us know he was there. When James went to the bathroom, I grabbed my purse and left the room. I took the elevator downstairs, taking the limo that was meant for the three of us. I asked the driver to take me to the Village, with a side trip through Central Park.

I was hurting inside, and at the same time furious with James. So I exacted my revenge by taking his car and driver, and not going back to the hotel for a few hours. I thought it was a good plan; I didn't care about the consequences.

To keep my mind off James, I talked with the driver, rambling more than talking. He drove me to the Village where he parked, and we both downed Nate n' Al hot dogs. After our elegant dinner, I walked around window shopping until an ivory chess board caught my eye. To drown out my depression, I bought the chess board, which I kept for many years. I learned to play chess on that board. To this day, I love the game.

I kept the car and driver out until 11 p.m., when I decided I'd better head back to the hotel. Of course, I was dreading every minute of it.

I thought I was going to teach James another lesson, but he proved me wrong. I was an amateur compared to him. When I walked back into the suite, the black actress I saw earlier was putting on her jacket, looking very happy. I walked into the bedroom, slamming the door behind me. Shortly after, James started pounding on the door with his fist. He was livid. I wouldn't open the door or answer him, which made him even more enraged. He continued knocking, but I wouldn't answer. Finally, he stopped knocking, electing to sleep in the other room for the rest of the night. I cried a little, got mad all over again, and finally fell asleep.

The next morning he knocked gently on the door, cooing softly, "Indian, I'd like to talk to you. Please open the door." After a good night's sleep I relented, giving in to him, and opened the door. We looked at each other without saying a word and kissed. I was so crazy about him, I foolishly let him talk me out of being mad.

"Why did you leave me when we had dinner plans?" he asked in all sincerity.

"Because I didn't want to have sex with that woman and you," I answered sternly.

"I was only kidding," he blurted out with a laugh.

I knew he was a lying dog, but I wanted him so much that I talked myself into believing him. I ultimately forgave him, and pushed this dreadful incident into the back of my mind for the time being. He knew how I felt now; I'd made my point. Deeper into the 1970's, other men also tried to repeat this scenario, but by then I wasn't so shocked. I had lived in Hollywood long enough to understand that some lived by a different standard. Three-way was something a lot of men wanted with me, but I always thought a one-on-one relationship was more romantic. I couldn't imagine sharing my lover with another person. Nothing is better than passion between two people.

"Picture of Jessica St. John and me. Jessica is one of my dearest friends throughout the years."
From the Barbara Leigh Collection.

In retrospect, I should have listened to my friend Jessica St. John, who dated James a few months before me. Jessica was a tall and beautiful model who lived in New York, and was introduced to James by a friend. They went out about 10 times and her opinion of him wasn't high. She said she stopped seeing him because of his improper behavior. When I asked James about her later on, he chose not to remember. That way, he had less to explain.

I believed Jessica. We were friends from way back. We met in Las Vegas, and were roommates in the late '60s. She was my best friend.

One day while chatting away on the phone, I said, "I'm dating a guy named James Aubrey." There was a silent pause. "He's the president of MGM Studios."

"That's funny," said Jessica, "so am I."

Of course, I was upset because I loved him, but I wasn't giving him up. I chose to believe him when he said it wasn't much of a romance, and as far as he was concerned he barely remembered her. Looking back, he was using both of us. James Aubrey wasn't capable of loving or being faithful to one woman. It wasn't part of his makeup. He loved women, but wasn't able to love just one woman. Sound familiar?

Why did I stay with this man who was incapable of love and monogamy? Like I said before: I was in love with him, plain and simple. Another reason was the power he wielded, and maybe the glamour that came with it. James and I attended a lot of black-tie events, and there were always lots of parties. This gave me the chance to wear beautiful evening gowns, which afforded me a lot of attention and the opportunity to meet glamorous people. When we walked hand-in-hand to these events, the paparazzi would swarm around us, flashbulbs would go off; people would stare, wishing they were in our shoes. To a young woman in her early 20s, attention is a powerful aphrodisiac.

One of the other benefits of being with James was the people I'd get to meet.

Many were powerful, interesting, eccentric, exciting and never dull. One of my favorite people that I met through James was Ed Hookstratten. Not only was he James' attorney, he also represented Elvis Presley (he handled Elvis' divorce from Priscilla), the Los Angeles Rams football team, and many movie stars, news and sportscasters. He was his own man.

Ed was married to the charming Patricia Crowley, star of the television series *Please Don't Eat the Daisies*. The two of them hosted many dinner parties, where Ed would cook delicious gourmet meals while Patricia played the ultimate hostess. They were a wonderful couple.

Ed and James owned real estate together, and were as close as friends could be. I adored Ed from the moment I met him. He has remained a good friend through the years and would later represent me on my movie contract regarding Vampirella.

Ed was a man's man, but at the same time, he was a true gentleman who respected women. He was handsome, charming, and always had a twinkle in his eye. He was a loyal ally, and definitely someone you'd want on your side.

Once Ed had to bail James out of jail, after he and I had a fight. I can't recall how or why the fight began, but it was related to the time I spent with Elvis, when I broke a date with James to go off with Elvis for the weekend. When I did finally show up at James' house, we got into a big shouting match, which led to my getting back in my car and driving off.

Whenever James was upset, he would drink Smirnoff Vodka, and this was definitely one of those times. He let his guard down, and had one too many. He wasn't the cool president of MGM Studios that night, but rather an enraged and jealous boyfriend. He decided that he was going to get even by making me pay. James marched into his master bedroom closet, where I had a lot of clothes. He grabbed every article of clothing that was mine and threw it into the trunk of his car, with the idea that he would personally deliver them to my apartment.

The vodka had definitely affected his driving. He was swerving and weaving on Sunset Boulevard, when he was pulled over by the police. After checking the inside of his car, they ordered him to open his trunk, where they discovered a wardrobe full of women's clothes. Who knows what they thought, but they hauled him off to jail. James called Ed to come and bail him out. I thought the whole thing was endearing, because it revealed the human side of James. He was acting like a spoiled child, not the hard-nosed movie executive he was.

But the moments when James wore his heart on his sleeve were few and far between. One of his favorite sayings was that he hated "shitters and weepers," meaning animals and children. In his later years, he had a Doberman named Max, whom he absolutely adored. Max was completely loyal to James, but was extremely possessive, biting anyone who got close to James, including his daughter. Max bit Skye in the face, almost causing her to lose her eye and permanently scarring her. Seeing the blood pour down his daughter's face made James think that he had no other choice but to shoot Max. I know it hurt James to kill his loyal pet, but he'd rather shoot him than have someone else put him down. I felt horrible for James; he showed no emotion whatsoever when he came back from the mountains. It was scary, and I couldn't quite put my finger on it, but there was a dark side to him that no one could heal. Still, I chose to forget all the bad things about James, because I loved him so much.

James screened a lot of the MGM films, as well as other studios' films. He used a little room at the Beverly Hills Hotel, which I enjoyed immensely. I rarely, if ever, paid to see a movie in those days. Usually, a small group of producers and executives, along with Skye and myself, previewed a movie in that room. Skye and I were very sensitive, sometimes we showed our emotions or got upset by a certain part, and James was embarrassed by our display of emotion. He hated vulnerability, but we couldn't help it. We were honest.

Skye and I cried a little during one particular movie. Other tears were flowing as well. James was brewing inside over our emotional display, but didn't say anything until we got home. He thought we looked silly.

"You're not allowed to go to anymore screenings with me," he said matter of factly.

Stunned, I asked in shock, "Why?"

"Because you and Skye were a complete embarrassment tonight."

"Why? Because we cried at a sad movie?"

James remained silent for a moment, then relented. "OK, I'll give you another chance. But if you cry one more time, that's it. You will not be invited back. Do you understand?" He hated tears.

Surprisingly, I chose not to fight James on the issue. I promised him never to cry at another one of his private screenings and I kept my promise, although there were times when I fought back the tears. James was like a robot who was afraid to show any emotion, while I always cried during sad movies. With Elvis I could laugh, cry and be myself. Even though I loved James, I sometimes felt stifled and controlled.

By Christmas 1970, James and I were closer, after having survived the episode with Elvis. Although I adored Elvis, he was still married to Priscilla. That kept me from giving up James completely. Not that he was ever mine.

I knew that one day James and I would break up. It would be for a multitude of reasons: the age gap, his indifference toward marriage, his inability to be faithful. Even with all of those sound reasons, I kept hoping he would change. Maybe, just maybe, I could help him to change and that we could remain together.

Why do women always think they can change a man?

Through an extraordinary amount of heartache, I would learn that a tiger never changes his stripes, or in my particular case, that a cobra is never short on venom.

CHAPTER SIX

Elvis and I finally managed another rendezvous at the end of November 1970. The Christmas season was in full swing, and Priscilla and Lisa Marie were visiting family in New Jersey, or so was the story. Elvis was coming to Los Angeles and wanted me to see him at his house in the exclusive Trousdale Estates. I was ecstatic, to say the least.

I had seen him once since Vegas, and it was just a brief visit at RCA Studios on Sunset Boulevard. Elvis had cut two songs in Nashville in late September called, "Rags to Riches" and "Where Do They Go, Lord." He was going to review the final tracks before "Rags to Riches" was released as a single.

Joe Esposito called me and told me I had to be at the studio around 9 p.m. if I wanted to see Elvis. It was the first time I had ever been to a recording studio, so I didn't hesitate to say yes!

I got dressed in a sexy mini-dress and headed for RCA Studios. I parked my car on Sunset and practically ran to the front door, where I was greeted by the doorman. He asked me to sign in, gave me a badge, and pointed me in the direction of the elevator. As the elevator door opened, there stood Joe E., waiting for me with a big smile on his face. I'm sure he knew this was a treat for me. I bounced over to him, giving him a big hug and a kiss. It was always good to see Joe.

Joe took my hand and led me down the hallway where I heard the faint sound of music pumping. As we opened the control room door, there was Elvis along with all the other guys.

"Hi Barbara, glad you could make it," Elvis said with that southern drawl with an accompanying smile and a gentle kiss.

"Thank you for having me," I beamed.

"Wanna hear my new record?" Elvis asked with the enthusiasm of a little kid. What could I say? Of course!

"Okay, let it roll," Elvis told a sound engineer. I looked down and noticed for the first time the music console all lit up with all sorts of buttons and knobs.

As the music engulfed the room, Elvis smiled the entire time. It was obvious to me he enjoyed listening to his own music and couldn't get enough of it. But once or twice wasn't enough for the King of Rock and Roll, we must have listened to "Rags to Riches" at least 50 times. Elvis played the song over and over again until I could recite the song lyrics.

It was fun for a while, but as the hours rolled by, I could see the other guys were getting tired as well. Not Elvis. He had the constitution of an iron horse when he came into a recording studio.

"Elvis in front of the RCA Studios in Los Angeles, circa 1970." Photo courtesty of Russ Howe.

"It's a hit, Elvis," one of the guys said to him, as it crept into the wee hours of the morning, subtly hinting that perhaps he should call it a night. But Elvis was wired and had outlasted everybody in the room, and nobody could tell him when to call it quits. That's how it was with Elvis—he'd completely exhaust any and everything until he wore it out. About 5 a.m., Elvis decided to wrap it up.

Elvis said his goodbyes and we kissed goodnight, and then he handed me off to Joe who would plan our next rendezvous. As it turned out, the next time I saw Elvis, he would come to see me at my place of work at MGM Studios, where I was busy filming *Pretty Maids All in a Row*. The film was directed by Roger Vadim, and starred Rock Hudson and Angie Dickinson.

I landed the part when I was walking on the beach in Malibu, and Roger Vadim came running up to me from his beach cottage. He told me frantically that he was casting his next movie, starring Rock Hudson, and asked if I wanted to be in it.

Rock Hudson was a gentle and kind man. He was the most giving and considerate actor I ever had the pleasure to work with. A true pro. I knew from the beginning that he was gay, but it didn't matter to me. I just thought it was a terrible waste of a gorgeous man. I think I somehow bonded with Rock in a strange way because I played his wife on screen. Rock always made it a point to visit me on movie sets whenever he found out I was filming. In real life, he was the epitome of his character in *Giant*, for he was truly adored.

I especially got a huge kick out of watching the other actresses, who didn't know Rock was gay, hitting on him. Joanna Cameron had a crush on him, and thought they would have an affair. Rock found it all very amusing.

Elvis, Charlie Hodges and Sonny West had arrived together on the MGM lot, but Elvis stayed back in one of the executive suites. He sent Charlie to get me. I was flattered that Elvis would make the trip to the studio from Trousdale, and even more flattered that he fit me into his busy schedule.

When I arrived at the suite with Charlie, Elvis was waiting like a big kid, with two presents all wrapped up.

"Hi, darlin', thought you'd never get here," he said with that wonderful sense of humor, as we embraced.

I noticed Sonny in the corner, and we exchanged greetings. I didn't know Sonny that well because Elvis didn't like me talking to the boys although Sonny seemed to be nice, and genuinely loved Elvis.

I also noticed Elvis didn't like to give passionate kisses in front of the guys; he was a private person. I always wanted to be alone with him at times like this, but he had a routine and we had to abide by it. He was rarely alone.

Elvis then handed me two presents—ring boxes.

"Here's a little present for you," Elvis said proudly. "Hope you like them. I picked them out personally."

I gushed a thank you. He smiled that wonderful, crooked smile of his. I hesitated, wondering if I should open them. I didn't know the protocol.

"Go ahead, darlin, open them now," he prodded.

The first box held a darling gold love knot ring that was popular in the 1970s. The second was a gorgeous gold owl ring with sapphire eyes. Oddly, James later gave me the same love knot ring, which I in turn gave to his daughter, Skye.

"Oh Elvis, they're beautiful. Thank you so much," I said, leaning over to kiss him on the cheek.

"Try them on. See if they fit."

They were both too big, but I put the love knot on my right index finger.

"Looks great," Elvis said, trying to cover up his embarrassment because they were too big. Oh well, it was the thought that counted.

"The owl is to see where you are at all times," he joked and laughed, as only he could do.

Elvis took me in his arms and kissed me. Joe and Sonny left, giving us a few moments together. It was a brief reunion; I had to get back to the set.

He held me tenderly and kissed my face. Again, I was overwhelmed by what was happening—I was being kissed by The King. We held hands on the way to his car, and kissed goodbye. Then I thought of James, who was on the lot at the time, and wondered if he had witnessed or heard of our encounter. I quickly headed back to stage 10.

Now I was driving up the hill in Trousdale Estates, to 1174 Hillcrest Drive. The French-Regency style house had been purchased by Priscilla in 1967 for the then astronomical sum of $400,000. Priscilla wanted the house so that she and Elvis would have a place away from the constant presence of E's entourage at Graceland, where they could have some privacy. Little did she know that he entertained other women in there when she was gone.

As I rang the doorbell, I got weak in the knees—Elvis was the only man who ever brought out that reaction in me.

Joe Esposito answered the door. I stood there for a moment, then Elvis came over to greet me. I was wearing a white blouse and vest, and a black miniskirt. No jeans were ever allowed in the Presley household. Elvis always preferred pretty and feminine clothes to casual. So did I.

"Hi, darlin', you look beautiful," he said as he grabbed my hand. We walked toward the living room and he gave me a kiss. The television was on and Charlie was in front of it, clicking away with the remote control.

"Tell me what you've been doing with yourself. Have you missed me? Are you wearing those two rings?" He rattled the questions off in one breath.

"Yes, I'm wearing my love knot," and I held up my hand to prove it. "I haven't taken it off, except to wear my owl ring," and then I smiled at him.

"I'm glad you like them," he said. We hugged and kissed again. I was so excited to be in his home.

Grabbing my hand, Elvis took me on a tour of the house. It was cozy and quaint. It sported three bedrooms, an Olympic-sized swimming pool and a guest cottage. It was very modern and nice, but certainly not my favorite out of all the houses that he owned. That was Graceland.

When he finished giving me a tour, I asked to use the bathroom. Elvis told me to use the one in his bedroom, but I felt uncomfortable. Priscilla's things were everywhere, unlike the Las Vegas suite, which was mainly for Elvis' use and held little of her. I couldn't help but notice her perfume and jewelry box in this bathroom. It was definitely the first time I was aware of her presence.

Placing my guilt behind me, I headed for the living room where Elvis sat with the ever-present entourage. As usual, they weren't doing much; watching TV, chatting, laughing. At times, I thought it was ridiculous that Elvis paid them for doing so little. At other times, I knew they got paid less than they were worth. I think the bottom line was that they were paid to keep Elvis company and to protect him. They were good ol' hometown Southern boys in which Elvis could be himself—and that was priceless to him.

Elvis was in a really good mood that day. As I stated before, one of E's hobbies was buying gifts. Depending on his mood, it could be a dress, it could be a car. That day it was a car—a Mercedes Benz—and Charlie was the lucky recipient.

Elvis was monkeying around, and in midstream of this fun he announced, "I'm buying Charlie a car today." Everyone broke out in applause, because Charlie was genuinely liked by everyone. I secretly thought that I'd like one, too, especially since Elvis had made fun of my 914 Porsche, calling it ugly. E read my mind and asked me, "Darlin', would you like a new Mercedes? We'll call it a late birthday present and an early Christmas present."

I was floored. Most people would have faked an obligatory, "No, Elvis. I'm fine with what I have," but I wasn't too proud to say yes. I eagerly responded, "Oh Elvis, would I!" I know my response bugged some of the guys; they thought I was a gold digger. But I thought, why not me? They all received presents, including cars, and they didn't think anything of accepting his generous gifts.

It wasn't like I had asked him for a car. He asked me if I wanted one, and I accepted it. I didn't try to impress Elvis by pretending not to want a Mercedes, nor did I fake humility by offering to take something less expensive. It was all timing. He was on a Mercedes Benz buying spree, and I just happened to be there. It easily could have been a Cadillac buying spree, and I would have been driving that instead. Lucky for me, it turned out to be a Mercedes buying spree.

It has always hurt that one of the guys—Lamar Fike—put me down in his book for taking a car. Even though I didn't know him all that well, Lamar wasn't really a bodyguard—he was E's court jester who got teased a lot about being fat. He provided a lot of comic relief for Elvis and the Memphis Mafia.

Elvis later soothed my feelings. "He's just jealous, honey. I wanted you to have it. Can't have my girl driving no ugly car!" and then he laughed that crazy laugh of his, which immediately made me feel better. Elvis knew who loved him and who tried to use him. He wasn't a dummy.

We arrived at the Hollywood Mercedes dealership at Sunset and Wilcox. Before we arrived, Joe had called the owner and had him open up the dealership specifically for us that night. Elvis wanted to buy the cars right then and there. Joseph Gold, our salesman, was only too happy to oblige, and let us look at new Mercedes to our hearts' content. He probably was going to make his whole year's quota in one day.

One car instantly caught my eye: A brand new brown 250 C Mercedes with tan interior.

"You don't want that, honey," Elvis said, knowingly.

"Why not?" I asked, daring to question him.

"Because it's a 250, not a 280."

"Well Elvis, I kind of like this one because it goes with my coloring," I said sheepishly.

"But it's not as good as a 280," Elvis argued. He wanted me to have the best; that was his only dispute.

"Elvis, I really like this one," I said like a child. "Plus, don't you want me to get what I really want?"

I didn't know the difference between a 250 and a 280, and I didn't care. The 280 was bigger, but I fell in love with the two-door coupe—and that was all I needed.

Elvis chomped on my words for a few seconds and relented. "I want you to be happy, darlin', so if this is what you really want, then this is your new car."

"Oh, thank you, thank you," I squealed with delight.

Elvis and the guys started to walk into the showroom, but I couldn't tear myself away from that little brown Mercedes. I was transfixed.

"Elvis was as generous as he was beautiful."
Photo courtesy of Russ Howe.

"Barbara, are you coming, darlin'?" That got my attention. Elvis rarely said my name; he usually used terms of endearment like "darlin'," which I preferred anyway. Growing up, I never wanted my mother to call me by my name. I liked "Baby doll" or "Sweetheart"—terms of endearment.

"Elvis, could I stay here and look at my car, please?" I begged.

He was firm, "No, you stay with me. You'll have plenty of time to see your new car."

I relented, and fell into step with the rest of the guys.

Once inside, Elvis showed me a 280. It was breathtaking, white with a blue top, but no matter how gorgeous it was, I had my heart set on the 250 C. Elvis and Joe made arrangements with Mr. Gold to have my and Charlie's cars delivered the next day. I snuck out the door to get another look at my beautiful new car.

Mr. Gold called out, "Barbara, would you like to pick out your new license?"

"Yes, thank you," I blurted out as I bounced back inside toward his desk. Elvis was laughing at me.

"Honey, you're just like a little kid!" he said.

"I know," I smiled at him, then went over to give him a great big hug. I was presented with two different numbers to choose from; 111CPT or 777CRS.

I looked at Elvis and asked, "Well, Elvis, what do you think?"

"Honey, I like the 111, uno, uno, uno," he said, then winked. That did it.

"OK, it's 111," I said. I was leaning toward the 777, but they both added up to a three, numerology-wise. The number three represented creativity, and that sealed it for Elvis. They were good numbers.

Before we left the dealership, Elvis asked me one last time, "You sure you don't want that new 280, darlin'?"

"I'm very sure, E," I said in my most positive tone. I looked over at the brown Mercedes one last time as we pulled away.

"You'll have it tomorrow, darlin', so hold your britches," Elvis laughed. I was a bit embarrassed, so I thought I'd better settle down.

I told him one last time, "Thank you E, I love it so much," and then pulled him closer to me, snuggling up against his arm. It gave Elvis pure joy to watch someone's face light up when he gave them a present. I didn't disappoint him.

We were all starving when we got back to Trousdale, so we headed for the kitchen. I was too excited to eat, but settled on a peanut butter sandwich and Mexican wedding cookies, which Elvis loved.

After making love that night, Elvis wanted a few more cookies and milk, which he followed with the usual evening cocktail of pills. While we were sitting in bed, watching television and eating cookies, Elvis started to nod off. His mouth was still full of cookies, and he began choking. I jumped up, grabbed my glass of milk, ran around to his side of the bed and started yelling, "Elvis, wake up! Drink this, Elvis!"

I gently held the back of his head, giving him milk a little at a time, all the while talking to him as if he were a child, "Elvis, drink up, swallow your food!" He coughed up some of the milk, and after a few minutes his throat cleared of the cookies. He finally got all of the milk down before passing out again. I never called Joe or anyone else for help, because it all happened so fast. If I hadn't acted so quickly, he might have choked to death that night in his bed at Trousdale. I later learned that almost everyone in Elvis' immediate circle had saved his life at one time or another.

I told Joe about the incident the next morning, and he warned me to watch E when he ate that late, knowing that the speed of his medications sometimes varied. This was new to me, but not to Joe.

From that time on, I watched Elvis like a hawk when we ate late at night. After ingesting his evening cocktail, I made sure that all of his food was gone before I went to sleep.

When Elvis woke the next morning, he didn't recall the previous night and how he scared me. He even woke up hungry!

We hung around the house the next day waiting for the cars to be delivered. Elvis played with his guns, showing us his latest addition. E's attorney, Ed Hookstratten dropped by to see Elvis about some business.

Also visiting that day were two young groupies Elvis liked, because they were especially sweet. I didn't feel threatened by these girls because they didn't blatantly go after Elvis in front of me like some of the other girls did. These two just liked to hang around Elvis and the guys. Elvis later bought them a car to share—a Camaro.

One of the girls took a liking to Ed and made a play for him, which Elvis loved. He got a kick out of seeing his normally calm, cool, collected and sophisticated attorney squirm and blush when this girl let it be known that she was his for the taking. Ed didn't take her up on it.

My new car arrived later that afternoon. I felt like jumping up and down, but tried to contain myself. Mr. Gold dangled the keys in front of me, "It's officially yours."

Elvis grabbed my hand and asked, "Well darlin', are you ready to drive your new car?"

"Yes, yes, yes!" I said playfully.

We walked outside and there it was; all new and shiny.

"I get to drive it first, honey," E said.

"Please do," I replied. It was just the two of us, no entourage, no Joe. Rarely did Elvis do anything without some of the guys tagging along, but today it was just the two of us taking turns at the wheel, driving around Trousdale. We even dropped by General Omar Bradley's house, which was nearby.

At the time, Bradley was the only living five-star general. He was brilliantly portrayed by Karl Malden in *Patton*, one of Elvis' favorite movies. As it happened, the general was in that day and we were greeted at the front door by his wife, who led us into the his office. The walls of the office were covered with photographs of the general with former presidents and celebrities. I didn't know who he was at the time.

"I really admire this man," was the only thing Elvis told me.

When General Bradley greeted Elvis, you could tell that the

legendary warrior had a genuine liking for him. Our unannounced visit was a surprise. Elvis liked to do things on the spur of the moment; it's a Southern tradition to show up without making prior arrangements. It's not necessarily a good tradition, but it perfectly illustrated how spontaneous E was.

We visited with the Bradleys for a while, then Elvis phoned Joe.

"Gosh boss, I was starting to get worried," Joe said. He had to know where Elvis was at all times.

Elvis let me drive the car back home. I wondered how I was going to get my old car back home. Before I even asked the question, Elvis spoke, "The boys will follow you home with your old car."

As I gathered my things and got ready to leave a few days later, I told E in all sincerity, "Elvis, I had a great time, and thank you so much for my new car. I love it!"

He took my hands in his, looked me straight in the eyes and said, "Darlin', you just drive it in good health. I'll be in touch, so stay near the phone. Joe will call you."

"I promise I'll be by the phone. I can't wait to see you again," I said with a smile and a kiss. Alan Strada and Sonny were waiting to follow me home in the Porsche and one of their cars to get back to Trousdale.

A quick story about my old, ugly car. Once while driving through Beverly Hills on Sunset Boulevard with my girlfriend, Judy Baldwin, Elvis drove up next to us in a black stretch limo. We pulled over, and he ran to my window to give me a kiss on the lips. I introduced him to Judy and then he was gone. The chances of that were rare. She was impressed by how natural he acted. He thought she was beautiful but luckily for me, she was blonde! Elvis joked that my Porsche looked like a vaccum cleaner.

Once behind the wheel of the 250 C Mercedes, I couldn't help but feel I was in a dream. I felt rich. Then reality hit. How was I going to explain the new car to James? After much deliberation, I decided to tell him the truth. He was too cheap to ever buy me a car; he wouldn't even buy himself a car! He was driving a black 1971 Lincoln Town car the studio paid for.

When James saw the Mercedes, he was surprised. "Did Elvis buy that for you?"

I gulped, "Yes, James, it was a birthday and Christmas present." Solemnly, he replied, "It suits you Indian. I'm happy for you."

Wow! That was easier than I thought!

James always tried to play it cool when it came to Elvis. To show jealousy would be admitting defeat. James only displayed his emotions when something interfered with his own agenda. I think my being with Elvis only made James want me more. Some men are like that. (Some women, too.)

By Christmas, James and I were closer than ever, especially after having survived the episode with Elvis and the Mercedes. James took me to Acapulco, Mexico, for the holidays—the trendy place to go for the Hollywood crowd. I also think James wanted to take me there because it was a million miles away from Elvis.

I had never been to Acapulco, and was delighted when James asked me to go with him for Christmas and New Year's. We stayed at the popular Viva Vera.

It was wonderfully romantic. Our room looked out onto the most beautiful view. Every night we sat out on the balcony eating sardines with crackers, drinking banana daiquiris, and watching the sun go down over the water. I had never eaten sardines before; the thought of swallowing a fish whole, head, eyes and guts was not appealing to me. Plus, they smelled something fierce. In spite of all the negatives, however, I grew to love sardines on that trip. It's all in the introduction.

The first day in Acapulco, James told me to buy a new swimsuit, which he picked out, but I paid for. Unlike Elvis, who was very generous, James expected me to dress well but at my own expense. The suit was a lot smaller than what I would have chosen for myself, but it was what he wanted. On our trip, we enjoyed lots of parties during the day, but kept pretty much to ourselves at night. I loved being in Acapulco alone with James when he could relax and be himself.

Despite the romantic setting, I often thought of Elvis, wondering what he was doing and when I would see him again.

The new year started off great. After a brief trip to Miami to see my mother, I went to visit my son Gerry in Tennessee. It was good to see family again, but when I came back to Los Angeles, it was to a hectic schedule. It was in 1971 that my career really took off. I signed with the Ford Agency, the most prestigious modeling agency in the world. I had commercial filming, plus photo sessions for "Vogue", "Mademoiselle", "LOOK", "Ladies Home Journal" and the cover of "Elle" in France.

Eileen Ford, head of the agency, was an interesting woman. On signing, she invited me to her townhouse in upper Manhattan. The main topic of conversation, interestingly enough, was James Aubrey. Specifically, she warned me about his womanizing. We sat on the edge of her king-sized bed talking like school girls while she quizzed me about him. At the same time, she gave me some friendly advice and motherly warnings. She probably had had a few run-ins with James when he lived in New York. He was notorious for chasing models, and he must have raided her stable of beauties more than a few times.

To give Eileen her due, she didn't lecture me and she didn't tell tales. She was very elegant and proper in protecting her girls. Because I was living in Los Angeles and flying to New York for shoots, I didn't have the luxury of being in her personal fold, so I got limited advice and didn't take any of it. I wasn't going to stop seeing James no matter what anyone told me—and that included Eileen Ford.

While James was busy chasing models, Elvis was busy chasing me. At the end of February, Elvis and I made plans to see each other in Las Vegas. I asked him if I could bring along my sister, Sharon.

"Sure darlin'," came the reply, "I'd love to meet your little sister."

As always, Elvis put Joe back on the line to work out the details. Elvis thought that Charlie might like my sister, and promised that he would take good care of her. Elvis' matchmaking efforts would have to be put on hold that trip, since Charlie's old girlfriend showed up unannounced.

"What should I wear?" Sharon asked me. Like most women, she was excited to meet The King.

"Whatever you want," I said, "but no pants and especially no jeans!" Elvis hated jeans. He thought that the only proper time for a person to wear jeans was when they were milking a cow. It was hard for me, because I loved wearing jeans.

When we arrived in Elvis' suite at the International, the living room was packed with groupies—their numbers were growing. They were being entertained by Red, Sonny and Ricky Stanley. In addition to the usual crowd that day, Elvis was being presented with an award by members of some civic group, who were accompanied by a few people from the media.

When it was over, he winked at me and smiled, which meant he would see me later. He dared not make a public display of affection toward me, especially in front of the press. I definitely understood that my presence could place him in a compromising position while he was still married, which is why I never insisted on taking a picture with Elvis, and how I kept a good secret for so long.

My sister and I waited in the suite with most of the guys, groupies and the rest of the entourage, while Elvis performed his second show. I took Sharon on a tour of Elvis' suite and then his bedroom, showing her his favorite books.

Finally, the door opened and in walked The King.

"Elvis," I squealed in delight, getting up to give him a hug.

"Hi, darlin'. Sorry I couldn't give you a hug before," he said sweetly into my ear.

I looked into his eyes and beamed, and in an instant, he knew I understood. "I want you to meet my sister, Sharon," I said proudly.

Elvis offered his hand to Sharon, and said with a smile, "Hi, Sharon, it's nice to meet you. Hope she's taking good care of you."

Sharon grabbed his hand and replied, "Thank you for having me. It's great to meet you."

Ever-efficient Joe asked Sharon if she needed anything. He made sure that she had a room of her own and spending money. Joe, as usual, was on top of things.

That night seemed long, and I couldn't wait to get Elvis alone behind closed doors. Things started winding down around 6 a.m.

"Are you ready to see the shows tonight?" Elvis asked Sharon.

"I wouldn't miss them for the world, Elvis," she said, absolutely melting.

"I've arranged for you and Barbara to come to both shows. I hope you enjoy them."

Sharon and I hugged and said good night, while Joe grabbed her bag and escorted her to her room. Elvis grabbed my hand and led me to his bedroom. The instant we shut the door, we were in each others' arms. We sat on the bed a few minutes, giggling like school kids. Then we readied ourselves for bed. The same routine; our routine, his routine.

When I came out of the bathroom, the placydills were neatly laid out, his on his side of the bed and mine on my side. After I swallowed the little red pill, I jumped into his waiting arms and we made love, the kind of passionate love I had been fantasizing about only hours before.

Whenever I was with Elvis, I didn't think of another man, even James.

When I was with James, I rarely thought of E. Later on, when I became involved with Steve McQueen, I didn't think of James or Elvis. I enjoyed the moment, and whoever I was with at the time was my main man. Why should men have all the fun of having more than one affair at a time? I definitely didn't believe in the double standard, and I didn't feel guilty about dating three men at once.

After we made love, I washed up and met Elvis in bed for the second time, kissing him for an eternity until we settled into comfortable positions, eventually falling asleep.

I never questioned taking the pills, because they helped me sleep soundly. The only problem was, I would wake up groggy. Toward the end of our relationship, Elvis started giving me a morning pill. That was how our routine went: there was one to knock you out so you could get sleep, and one to wake you up so you could function. It was a vicious cycle that eventually led to Elvis' death.

When we woke up, Elvis excused himself to make his daily call home. It was another routine that I accepted without question or resistance. I was, after all, the *other* woman. Sharon joined us for breakfast—the sight of Elvis eating pancakes and applesauce brought a smile to her face. Having breakfast with Elvis was an exciting experience for her. A once in a lifetime memory and definitely something to cherish.

As we ate, I thought back to our years in the children's home when I took care of my sisters. Now, here we were, those two little girls having breakfast with The King!

The night, February 19, a female fan rushed the stage, causing the microphone to hit Elvis in the mouth, chipping one of his front teeth. Being the ultimate professional, Elvis shrugged it off and continued with the show. The hysterical woman was grabbed by several members of the Memphis Mafia, and escorted back to her table.

After the show was over and Sharon and I were escorted back to the suite. Elvis burst through the door, mad as hell. His front tooth, I'm sure, caused him great pain, but it was more than that. Elvis was extremely vain, and the chipped tooth didn't go with his image—a feeling most people would share.

Joe already was on the phone before Elvis burst into the room. Elvis displayed a side to him I had never seen before, and I instinctively knew to stay in the background until his fury subsided. I could practically see the steam rising, he was that mad. Elvis was the sweetest man I ever knew, but there obviously was a flip side to him. He didn't get mad often, but when he did, he blew his top. That night in the suite, he was a full-blown volcano.

A dentist arrived, the chipped tooth was fixed and things got back to normal. After the second show, Elvis apologized for getting so upset .

"E, I never took it personally. I don't blame you for being upset," I said soothingly. Then Elvis kissed me sweetly on the lips.

In the ensuing months, I would once again encounter his rage, but this time it would be aimed directly at me. And it involved another man—Steve McQueen, the world's biggest movie star at the time. Steve would begin courting me, competing directly with Elvis for my time and affection. A rugged, handsome prince would enter the picture, and The King would not be amused.

CHAPTER SEVEN

On our last night together that weekend in Las Vegas, Elvis and I tried to schedule when we could see each other again as soon as possible. It was going to be difficult because my career was kicking into high gear, and I was busier than usual. And, of course, his schedule was even more chaotic. I was booked solid by MGM for the next few months. A publicity tour for *Pretty Maids All in a Row* would keep me busy with press junkets and movie premiere's in Atlanta; New York; Portland; Miami; Indianapolis; Charlotte; Denver; Jacksonville; Minneapolis; and, of all places, Memphis, the home of Elvis Presley. Elvis said he would try to be in town for the Memphis trip.

Usually when I visited Elvis in Las Vegas, I would leave on Sunday morning. That worked out well, because I had to work on Monday. It worked out especially well for Elvis, because Priscilla and Lisa Marie often arrived on Sunday afternoon. Elvis would then become a devoted husband and doting father once again, picking up where he left off.

I think it was easy for Elvis to live two separate lives. He lived the life of a swinging bachelor on the one hand, and he had the picture-perfect marriage and family on the other. He had the financial means and the manpower to carry out his liaisons. Elvis' entourage scheduled how to escort women in and out of his suite without them ever bumping into each other. The guys were equipped with walkie talkies, and were savvy enough never to get caught in an awkward situation. Elvis trained them well; they catered to his every desire, and those desires often came in the form of women.

The Memphis Mafia was once complimented by a Memphis reporter, stating that the Secret Service could take a few tips from those guys. It's true, they were so effective in running Elvis' professional and personal life like a fine-oiled piece of machinery. It was the highest honor anyone could have bestowed on those guys—and I don't say that with any disrespect. They were good at what they did—the best—and Elvis in turn took care of them by showering them with presents.

Not only did Elvis have the financial ability, he had the psychological make up to live his double life. I don't think it bothered him in the least, or that he felt guilty even one day about the fact that he constantly cheated on his wife. So many women went after him, and he had so much love to give, that he couldn't bottle it up or he would have burst. E loved women, and they couldn't help but love him in return. It was that simple. He was one of a kind.

In his heart, he was always faithful to his wife. She was his No. 1 love, and I understood that. I was his No. 1 "girl" for awhile. Elvis could easily block out his feelings and emotions when it came to fidelity. He was The King. He was wanted by millions of women all over the world, and he'd seen and experienced too much in his life to be monogamous; the temptations were just too great.

How does a man who can have any woman he wants cure himself of this affliction? He doesn't. That's why Elvis never remarried after his divorce. I believe that Elvis would never have divorced, because in his mind he never thought there was a problem in his marriage. Personally, I don't think Elvis had another marriage in him. There were stories of him proposing to his last girlfriend, Ginger Alden, but who knows if it really happened? I did dream about Elvis close to his death, and in the dream he said he was going to marry Ginger. I later told Joe Esposito about my dream, but he dismissed it.

He wanted to be taken care of, but he also wanted a variety of women. Elvis could do whatever he wanted, whenever he wanted, and generally did. I'm not saying Elvis didn't have a conscience—he did—but he had a separate set of rules for himself.

When the shoe was on the other foot and Priscilla had an affair with her karate instructor, Mike Stone, Elvis wanted Mike's head on a platter. It was a matter of pride as much as anything. The King detested being made to look like a fool. Even though Elvis had hundreds of affairs over the years while he was married, her one infidelity broke his heart. I believe that was the beginning of the end for Elvis and started a mental meltdown. His drug use escalated, his weight went up and an ever-present joylessness replaced his once-vibrant spirit.

I can't say I was never jealous of Elvis and the fact that he wanted to sleep with other women. I wasn't fooling myself. Elvis belonged to the world and I knew that from the get-go. I just enjoyed my time with him, and made every moment count. This is the prime reason Elvis and I remained friends long after our affair was over.

On the return trip to Los Angeles, Sharon and I giggled the whole time, rehashing the weekend. I was thrilled at the thought of visiting Elvis in Memphis, now that I was officially invited to his home, Graceland. I was forced to wait another month before I would see him again, but luckily, I had the movie premiere of *Pretty Maids All in a Row* in Atlanta to look forward to and keep me occupied.

My birthplace, Ringgold, Georgia, is about 100 miles north of Atlanta near the Tennessee border, and 15 miles south of Chattanooga. I was a hometown girl who had made good, and Atlanta rolled out the red carpet for me, even more than it did the other celebrities at the premiere: Rock Hudson and Angie Dickinson. MGM hadn't premiered a movie in the city since 1939, when Clark Gable and Vivien Leigh descended upon Atlanta for the world premiere of *Gone With The Wind.*

A limousine awaited me at the airport to take me to the Regency Hotel in downtown Atlanta. The Regency put up all of the guests in addition to hosting the big after-premier party. A 100-foot banner stretched from one side of the street to the other: "Atlanta Welcomes Barbara Leigh."

"Rock Hudson and I share a moment on the set of *Pretty Maids All In A Row*. Rock was one of the dearest men I've ever known." From the Barbara Leigh Collection.

I was overwhelmed. I didn't know how to react to such a grand gesture, and I was moved to tears. I had fourth-billing in the picture, but the town treated me as if I were the lead.

Barbara Leigh had arrived, or so I dreamed.

After the premiere, James promised to take me to Europe for all of my hard work on behalf of MGM. As a child I had always dreamed of traveling to Europe. But I never could have dreamed in a million years that James would take me. I think after my little excursion with Elvis, James wanted me all to himself.

The two of us left Los Angeles May 15 for Paris, where we had a connecting flight to Nice, the playground of the rich and famous. We stayed just one night at the Hotel Carlton, before we boarded Kirk Kerkorian's yacht.

Kirk was the majority stock owner at MGM. His yacht was imposing and obviously worth millions of dollars. Kirk docked to pick us up right across the street from our hotel. Once we stepped aboard, it was nonstop partying for days, from morning to night. The wine flowed, and beautiful women wore the tiniest of bikinis.

Kirk was a gracious host and assigned James and me a large, lovely state room for our stay aboard ship. He was rugged and manly, yet very polite and cultured—a very interesting man. Kirk and James seemed to be very close, like two old school buddies.

Kirk's girlfriend of many years was the actress Yvette (*The Time Machine*) Mimieux. The yacht was full of beautiful and exciting people, including Cary Grant and German car entrepreneur Johnny Von Newman, plus many more from the jet-set crowd.

Our first stop was St. Tropez, the village where Roger Vadim discovered Brigitte Bardot. It was a very small town in those days, built around its harbor, where many luxury yachts and small fishing boats docked.

The cruise to St. Tropez was an event in itself. James and I soaked in the sun, drank wine and people-watched. Along the way, we anchored at a small island to eat lobsters at a famous restaurant. It was the first lobster I had ever eaten. Before then, I had been strictly a shrimp eater, but I quickly switched my allegiance to lobster.

James was especially attentive to me, insisting I stay close to him at all times. He wasn't going to give me the opportunity to become infatuated with another man while he was with me. Back in Los Angeles, I did what I wanted, often making myself unavailable to him. I think it was frustrating for him, because most of the women he dated gave in to him, whereas I usually kept him at arm's length. Most of the time he never showed his frustration, but when I later met Steve McQueen we quarreled openly. I think he admired Elvis and had some small amount of affection for him—they had worked on a documentary, *Elvis: That's the Way It Is*—but not so for Steve McQueen. I think Steve's ruggedness presented an ever bigger threat to James' ego than Elvis did. Steve was his own man, a rebel, a solo act.

When we docked at St. Tropez, I was surprised; it wasn't exactly how I had envisioned it. It was much smaller, and not at all the glamourous setting I had hoped it would be. To me, Cannes was much more glamorous, grand and exciting. I must give St. Tropez its due, however; it is like a little jewel, and precious to the French, who appreciate its subtle beauty.

"Taken in Paris while visiting Vadim by the French press." From the Barbara Leigh Collection.

One afternoon in St. Tropez, I was talking with Cary Grant on the deck of Kirk's yacht, who was chatting me up. He very quietly and out of the blue asked if I would be interested in having his baby. Cary was a wonderfully sweet man; very classy, gracious and diplomatic, so much more so than James, who was always standoffish. I laughed, not taking him seriously. Mind you, he wasn't proposing marriage, he just wanted a child. It was an interesting conversation.

The most glamorous man in the world appeared very lonely. Years later, I learned that Grant had asked several other young women in Hollywood for the same favor. He eventually married a very young, beautiful Dyan Cannon and had a daughter with her. Dyan was 30 years his junior. I didn't mention my conversation to James. He probably would have laughed.

Several French jet setters were with our group. Once I caught four of them in our cabin, smoking cigarettes and flicking their ashes on the new carpet. I let them know what I thought of their manners. My scolding didn't have the effect I desired. "Stupid American," one of the men had the nerve to say to me under his breath.

I could see that they weren't going to leave the cabin, so I went back on deck where James was. I never told James what happened because I didn't want to make trouble, yet for the rest of the trip, I stayed away from the French. They weren't friendly from the beginning, and tended to keep to themselves.

Because I wasn't very secure back then, it hurt me that they shunned me, acting as if I didn't exist, but I dealt with the situation like a lady. After all, I'd grown up with kids in school who put me down for being from the "home." Surely I could handle these spoiled brats. I later had a better experience with the French jet-set crowd when I visited with Roger Vadim in Paris. I'm sure that being with a world-famous director boosted my self-confidence. If you were with French aristocracy, you were automatically accepted. Vadim was wildly famous in France, and was adored by everyone. After all, he had introduced Brigitte Bardot to the world.

James and I left the yacht on May 28 and flew to London, where we stayed for several days. It was fantastic! I can only compare it to New York City. I could not get over the black cabs, and the way that cars drove on the left side of the road. I was also happy to be in a country where English was the native language. For the most part, I found England to be a much more friendly place than France.

I wanted to learn everything I could about this enchanting country, so James bought me a book on English history. I pored over its contents, listing places we must see. James was a great sport and tagged along with me, squeezing a month's worth of sightseeing into a few days.

We returned to Los Angeles on May 30, and, after a couple of days rest, I checked in with my agent to find that work was not letting up.

I was asked to interview on June 2 with Dodge, for a large automobile campaign featuring young actresses as spokeswomen. I got the job and left for Idyllwild, California, the next day to begin shooting the commercial. Often a model or actress would be cast because of a preference by the client, director or agent. For example, a client might want you if your look was right, or you might remind them of someone. There were a lot of actors and actresses fitting the profile for every job, but fate, luck and personal choice often would be the real reason you either got the part or didn't. In this particular case, the client, Mr. Johnson (not his real name) a high-ranking businessman from Cascade Productions, became smitten with me. That was the sole reason I was hired. But it soon became a nightmare, because of his personal hangups and petty jealousy.

Idyllwild is situated in the hills directly behind Palm Springs. The town is surrounded by tall trees and charming weekend cottages; a California version of being in the Swiss Alps.

Joe Esposito called me that day, and I gave him my work schedule. I told him I would be working in Idyllwild shooting a commercial.

"That's right over the hill from E's house," Joe said enthusiastically. Besides his house in Trousdale Estates in Los Angeles, E also had a house in Palm Springs.

Elvis grabbed the phone and my spirits rose. "Hi darlin', glad you're home." He knew I had been in Europe with James, but didn't broach the subject further. "So, you'll be in Idyllwild? Do you want to come for dinner?"

"I'd love to Elvis, but how can I? I don't think anyone can bring me there, and I won't have my car. Besides, I have a call at 7 a.m. and I have to be ready to go with makeup."

"Don't you worry your pretty little head," Elvis said. "Let me work out all the details. I'll call you later tonight. See ya later, darlin.'"

Great, I thought. I get to work, possibly be the new spokesperson for Dodge, and get to see Elvis on the side. How lucky could I be? In the ensuing days, I'd find out just how lucky.

I started packing my clothes, wondering what Elvis had in mind. Knowing him, it was certain to be unusual. That would prove to be an understatement.

The next day I met with the client, director and crew. We flew into Palm Springs and then drove to Idyllwild. My prospects as the new spokesperson for Dodge looked great. When we arrived at the Idyllwild Inn, there was a message waiting for me from Joe. But before I called him back, I had a drink in the lobby with Mr. Johnson. I could tell he liked me, but I didn't give it a lot of thought—my head and heart were with Elvis for the moment. Mr. Johnson asked me to have dinner with him and I told him I'd have to let him know, because I was expecting a phone call. He told me to call him in his room.

I bolted to my room to make the call to Joe. He put Elvis on the line.

"Hi darlin', got a surprise for you. You're going to have dinner with me here in Palm Springs, and I'm sending Joe with a helicopter to pick you up. That way you can stay the night with me."

Uh oh, I thought, this could get me in trouble.

"But Elvis, I have an early call and I can't be late. I'm the only actress in the commercial," I tried to plead my case.

"You won't be late, darlin.' That I can promise you. The pilot will come back in the morning and have you back in plenty of time," Elvis promised.

How could I argue with The King? He had it all planned out; he had an answer for every question, and he wanted his way no matter what. Who was I to say no?

I finally gave in, but made him promise to have me back in time. I knew instinctively that I was making the wrong choice.

I also knew it wasn't smart to leave Mr. Johnson waiting by his phone wondering if I was going to call. Why didn't I level with the gentleman? I just couldn't bring myself to tell him that I was involved with Elvis Presley, a married man. Besides, it wasn't smart to mix business with pleasure.

I decided to call Mr. Johnson's room, but he wasn't in. I left a message saying I wouldn't be able to have dinner with him, and that I would see him in the morning. The hotel operator said that Mr. Johnson was out scouting locations for tomorrow's shoot, so I felt somewhat off the hook. Little did I know that I had just gotten *on* the hook.

I gathered my things for the overnight trip to E's and went to meet the helicopter, which was landing in the back of the Idyllwild Inn. I arrived in Palm Springs a short time later. E greeted me at his door with open arms.

Elvis had this huge Cheshire cat grin on his face, like he'd accomplished the impossible. "See darlin', I told you not to worry. I'd get you here safely."

I ran into his arms and we hugged and kissed, walking immediately into his living room. I was scared, wondering what consequences I'd suffer because of my foolish actions. I couldn't afford to dwell on them for too long, as Elvis picked up on everything, so I decided just to have a good time. He promised I would be back in time to fulfill my obligations, and that would be that.

E's house in Palm Springs was my least favorite of his homes that I visited and was uninviting. It had a small front yard and didn't have any grass—Southerners like lots of big trees and green grass. This yard was called "desert landscaping", which essentially was just dirt and rocks. And the house was surrounded by gates, which made me feel claustrophobic because it was too accessible and very close to the road.

A table and mirror were immediately to the right of the door as you entered, and Elvis never passed the mirror without stopping to check himself. Beautiful man? Yes. Vain man? Definitely. Allowed? Certainly!

The house was decorated in contemporary style, and divided into two parts;

Elvis' bedroom and the guest bedrooms where Joe and the guys slept were on the right side of the house, while the living room, dining room, kitchen and the maid's quarters were on the left. The living room looked out onto the pool, and had a panoramic view of Palm Springs. A private Jacuzzi was next to the pool.

E's bedroom was decorated like his Las Vegas suite, in navy blue. The centerpiece was a king-sized bed. The master bath was to the right, and windows on the left side of the bed looked out onto the swimming pool, but Elvis rarely opened the drapes to take advantage of the view. And, as usual, the bedroom was freezing cold. On each side of the bed were night tables that held his assortment of pills and books.

We spent the evening watching television with Joe, Sonny West, Charlie Hodges and a friend of Elvis' I had never met before, Jerry Schilling. Jerry was a very handsome man, and we got along famously.

Our dinner was catered. Most of the time it was either burgers and fries or fried chicken. The food was never from fancy restaurants, but mostly from greasy spoons or diners. Elvis was no gourmet, and probably would have gagged at the thought of eating sushi—my favorite food.

As midnight approached, I reminded Elvis that I needed to get some rest for the next day. The helicopter was picking me up at 6:15 a.m.

Early the next morning I quietly kissed Elvis on the forehead and crept out of the room, to meet the helicopter. He was dead to the world, dreaming in a world of prescribed euphoric drugs. He looked too peaceful to stir.

I was back at the Idyllwild Inn in plenty of time to have makeup, wardrobe and hair done in time for the 7 a.m. call. When I arrived on the set, the crew was silent. I knew something was amiss. Mr.

Johnson wasn't verbally abusive, but he was seething. I didn't tell him that I had been with Elvis. Maybe if I had, he might have understood. But in those days I kept my relationship with Elvis private, rarely discussing him even with my close friends, except my mother. I already had a name in commercials and modeling, but I wanted to be famous, not infamous. I respected Elvis' wishes that our relationship be discreet and kept out of the gossip columns. I didn't want to lose him.

Anytime I was fortunate enough to spend with Elvis was a good time with lots of laughter. Elvis had such a silly side to him and it was contagious.

I conducted myself on the set in a professional manner and did the best job that I knew how, but it wasn't enough. Later, someone in the crew told me that Mr. Johnson had kept calling my room all the night before. I had no obligations to this man other than to do a good job on the commercial, but he didn't see it that way. I had no idea that he liked me as much as he did. This was a job, not a romantic liaison. Mr. Johnson was way out of line to expect any more from me.

Needless to say, I lost the chance to be Dodge's next spokeswoman, an opportunity that potentially could have earned me a lot of money. The commercial ran only a couple of times, and I never heard from Dodge again. C'est la vie!

Was it worth it? I've asked myself that question a few hundred times over the years. It certainly wasn't worth it money wise. I could have used that money then, and I could have used the exposure from the commercial. But I had wanted to see Elvis so badly, that losing the commercial was the price I was willing to pay for one night with him. I made my choice to see Elvis, and I stuck by it. I may not have the money, but I do have a wonderful memory of Elvis making a romantic gesture to see me by sending a helicopter to bring me to him. No amount of money in the world can buy that.

Back home after shooting the commercial, I went on a blind date with a hot new writer who was represented by the same agency as me, the International Famous Agency. My agent, Dick Clayton, set me up with him. His name was Michael Crichton.

Michael is a remarkably intelligent person, and I just knew he was going to make it in Hollywood. But who could have foreseen that he would write the novel that would become one of the most successful movies in history—*Jurassic Park*. Michael would go on to write and direct movies, as well. Michael was very handsome, extremely charming and, at 6 foot 9 inches, the tallest man with whom I ever went out. We set another date for June 17.

That was the same day I would pick up a scene for an upcoming Sam Peckinpah movie, *Junior Bonner*, starring Steve McQueen.

Growing up, I loved science fiction movies that featured monsters. I especially liked *The Blob*, the 1958 thriller about a small town that was invaded by a gelatinous mass of goo. The movie was one of the first real monster movies and a fun romp, even though it scared me half to death. I loved Steve's performance, but to Steve this movie was always a source of embarrassment, considering his great list of performances in first-rate movies. Mostly, I remembered Steve as Captain Virgil Hilts, the Cooler King, from *The Great Escape*. That particular character, more than any other film character he played, I felt, was the epitome of Steve McQueen.

Junior Bonner is about the metamorphosis of a small western town that experiences a real estate boom that changes it forever. Steve plays Junior, an over-the-hill rodeo star who has the chance to shine one last time in his hometown. Steve was enthused about playing the part of a cowboy, and a stubborn one at that. The character was a lot like Steve, and I'm sure that appealed to him. After getting to know him, I would say that Steve, like Junior, would not give up on something he wanted. Junior wanted to win the rodeo the same way that Steve wanted to win anything. Junior's goal was to ride the bull, Sunshine—a bull no one had been able to ride and stay on for eight seconds.

I was submitted for the part of Charmagne, McQueen's girlfriend in the movie. I picked up the script, then met Michael for dinner. During dinner Michael talked about his former career, medicine. He was a doctor-turned-writer; an amazing man. Michael and I never had another date after that dinner and our paths have never crossed again—living in Los Angeles is like that. But I'm happy for his phenomenal success. He deserves it!

My fate was sealed when I picked up that script.

My agent called the next day with my appointment time with Sam Peckinpah. I was to read for Peckinpah at producer Joe Wizan's office in Studio City. I'll never forget that day. Knowing it was a rodeo film, I dressed in boots and an orange blouse, and wore my hair straight and parted in the middle.

I arrived a half hour before the scheduled appointment. There were several actresses ahead of me, and I sat down to wait for my turn, going over again and again the scene I was to read . Finally, 12:45 p.m. rolled around and I was ushered into a private room. As I walked in, Tiffany Bolling walked out. Tiffany was a very pretty blonde who had a lot more experience than me, and was a much better actress. She had recently appeared opposite Richard Benjamin in *The Marriage of a Young Stockbroker*, and posed nude for a *Playboy* pictorial. We smiled, acknowledged each other, and kept walking.

As I entered Mr. Wizan's office, I was a little stunned to find not only Sam Peckinpah present, but Steve McQueen as well. I had no idea that he would be there; I thought I was only there to read for the director. I was nervous to begin with, but now my palms started to sweat.

I'd love to say that I studied my craft and knew what I was doing, but that would be lying. I was an ingenue, totally inexperienced; and boy, did I start to feel the pressure of not being prepared.

Joe Wizan introduced me to Sam and Steve. They were both polite but short and to the point.

Settle down and do your best, I thought. One was the biggest box-office star in the world, and the other was the most original American director since John Ford. No big deal!

The first thing I noticed about the two men was that they were short, with Sam being the shorter of the two. Steve stood about 5 foot 10 inches, but he slouched and had a very wiry frame, which made him seem much smaller than he really was. When you grow up watching an actor you admire on the big screen, he becomes larger than life. His diminutive stature made him seem more human to me.

Steve asked me to sit next to him, and said that he would read with me. Even though I was nervous, he immediately put me at ease, which was nice. He wasn't dressed; sporting blue jeans, a white T-shirt and brown leather sandals. Steve started reading the scene with me and when I responded with my lines, Sam interrupted and gave me a little direction, and then we started from the top again.

The interview and reading took approximately 20 minutes and after we'd read the scene a few times, Sam abruptly stood up and said, "That's good. We'll let you know. Thanks for coming in." Instantly, I got the sinking feeling that he didn't want me, and that his mind was made up.

I was right.

Joe Wizan was sitting behind his desk, and smiled as he waved goodbye. Steve stood up and shook my hand, thanking me as well, and smiled directly into my eyes as he held my hand. I didn't give the gesture much thought—then. I found him charming and sexy, but I knew he was married—and I had my hands full with James and Elvis.

I walked out of Joe Wizan's office thinking that, while I hadn't gotten the part of Charmagne, at least I had done my best. I was almost to my car, keys in my hand, when I heard someone calling my name.

I turned and there was Steve McQueen, running to catch up with me. I was bewildered. He was a little shy as he said, "I don't think the part's going to work out, but I'd like to take you to dinner." Not a way to a girl's heart, especially an actress, but he was honest.

I was at a loss for words. He smiled that boyish, crooked grin of his. How could I say no? He was honest and forthright, so what did I have to lose?

I didn't think about James or Elvis, or for that matter, Steve's wife, Neile. Instinctively, I did what most women would do if a famous, charming movie star asked them to dinner: I said yes, and gave him my phone number. He smiled like a bad little boy who had just gotten away with something. We said our goodbyes once again.

As I got into my car, my head swirled with all kinds of thoughts: Did he find me attractive? Why did he invite me to dinner? Did he have romantic intentions? Did he just want to talk? I was excited, and a new adventure awaited.

By the time I got home, there was a message at my service from Steve.

I dialed the number right away. After all, it isn't every day that Steve McQueen calls. He answered the phone himself, and asked me to meet him that night at a Malibu restaurant on Sunset Boulevard near the Pacific Coast Highway, next to the Self-Realization Center. The building, long since gone, was out of the way, quiet and discreet.

Steve McQueen was a man who was very aware of his stardom, maybe more so than any other celebrity I knew, except for Elvis. He didn't like people approaching him for autographs, and avoided publicity if possible. His elusiveness made the public clamor for him all the more, and had the opposite effect of what he wanted it to have: his privacy.

After we hung up, I began to get that tingling sensation that meant I was getting myself into another situation that I shouldn't have. I didn't get the part, but I got Steve McQueen!

CHAPTER EIGHT

The rest of the day flew by and before I knew it, it was time to get dressed and head to the beach for my date with Steve. I put on tight blue jeans, white cotton shirt and boots. A little cowgirl in me, maybe.

All the way to the beach, I was anticipating a great dinner, remembering how gracious Steve had been during our reading together. When I arrived, he was already there, sipping a beer. The hostess escorted me to the bar, where I spotted his piercing blue eyes and craggy face waiting for me. This was one rugged, handsome man.

"Barbara, glad you could make it," the movie star said as he stood up, pushing his bar stool away, a big smile on his face.

I smiled back and we shook hands—held hands was a more apt description. He pushed out a bar stool for me, and then he sat back down.

"I'm having a beer. May I get you something?" he asked politely. He was quite the gentleman. I opted for something different than my usual wine.

He ordered a screwdriver for me and another beer for himself. We casually sipped our drinks, making small talk. Steve was by far the most casual of the magic three. Elvis had a similar upbringing, but years of being on stage had made him flashy and in need of constant attention. James was elegant, debonair and arrogant.

As we talked, we discovered that we had a lot in common. In fact, our backgrounds were almost identical. Both of us had lived in foster homes and children's homes. We had been deserted by our fathers at an early age. Both of us had mothers who were not equipped to raise us, mothers who were free spirits and had too many relationships with men throughout their lives.

After the second drink, I was feeling a little buzzed and asked Steve if we could eat. He laughed heartily.

"Man doesn't live by bread alone," he said, and we both laughed. A profound Biblical saying I'd heard quite a bit growing up. Steve paid the tab at the bar, asked for a table in the corner so we could have some privacy.

While we were eating, we talked more about our childhood, flirting all the while, even getting turned on. I'm sure the alcohol had something to do with that. I was having the time of my life, feeling pursued and excited at the same time. Steve began getting touchy, lightly stroking my hair, then reaching for my hand. I felt completely comfortable with him, as if I'd known him forever or maybe in a past life, if one believes in reincarnation.

After dinner, Steve asked me if I would come back to his place. I knew in the back of my mind that we were going to become lovers, but I didn't want to rush it, even though I wanted him as badly as he wanted me. I didn't want to be a one-night stand, so I made him wait like a good little boy. Surprisingly, Steve understood and was very gracious.

"We'll have plenty of time to get to know each other," I promised him. I was thinking *let's not rush into anything right now.* I smiled and planted a warm, sensual kiss on his lips—a promise of a future night to come.

"Sounds like a plan, Barbara," Steve laughed. "I'll call you tomorrow, and we'll set a time to get together again."

"Sounds like a plan," I responded with a smile, slightly teasing him.

It must have been around 11 p.m., which late for me. I was getting tired. Steve walked me to my car and kissed me again. I got in, rolled down my window and before I knew it, his head was inside my car window, kissing me again and again. It was obvious that he didn't want me to leave. I had to go, only I didn't really want to go, either. The magic was there, no doubt about it.

As I drove away from Steve, I could see him in my rearview mirror standing there with a bright smile on his face. I stuck my hand out of the window and waved as I sped away in my brown Mercedes—the one Elvis had given me. All the way home I couldn't help but think of Steve. He was intriguing; a rebel, a boy-man, and his charm was very much that of a bad boy. He had a wild aura about him. I just knew he would be good in bed.

I arrived home safely, a little tipsy from the alcohol, and certainly a little tipsy from the romance. I undressed and fell into bed for a not-so-good night's sleep. Drinking didn't allow me to get the proper eight hours of rest my body needed. At that age, you don't think of those things—especially when you're having the time of your life.

I awoke the next morning to the sound of the phone ringing. It was Steve.

"Good morning, Barbara," Steve said in that inimitable voice of his. "How would you like to have dinner with me again tonight?"

This guy didn't waste much time!

I said I'd love to, and gave him directions to my place. I had recently moved to a cozy little apartment in Westwood, on Kelton Avenue. It was a lot closer to everyone I was involved with, and so much more convenient than Hancock Park. Steve lived in Pacific Palisades, right off the Pacific Coast Highway. It was only a short jaunt away.

"See you later," Steve said with a touch of anticipation as we both hung up. I slowly got out of bed. I put on a pot of coffee, poured myself a cup and planned my day. I was to spend the day in Hollywood at the studio of photographer Charles Bush. Charles was a dear friend, and a talented photographer. He took hundreds of photos of me through the years, and eventually he convinced me to test-shoot for *Playboy,* which led to my first layout in the May 1973 issue titled "Indian, a pictorial" as a featured actress. He shot my entire portfolio of pictures, and we remained friends for many years. The advice given by modeling agencies to models is true: test, test, test, shoot, shoot, shoot—and make the most talented photographers your best friends!

I arrived home with a bag of groceries, and a six-pack of Budweiser for Steve. I took a quick shower and threw on a pair of blue jeans, something Steve liked as much as I did. He arrived sharply at 7 p.m., and buzzed me from downstairs.

Moments later, Steve appeared at my door. He held something behind his back. "This is for you," he said shyly, producing a single red rose—my favorite flower.

Steve was not particularly generous as far as gifts went. He wasn't like Elvis, who loved to give gifts and who expected nothing in return. But I understood why. He was a kid who had nothing, got everything, and spent the rest of his life worrying that somebody would take it away. The best description I ever heard regarding Steve was from his second wife Ali McGraw: "Steve always looked as if everyone was going to steal his second helping of mashed potatoes."

"Steve McQueen and me during the filming of Junior Bonner, just before the famous fight scene in the Palace Bar." From the Barbara Leigh Collection.

"Thank you, it's beautiful," I said, taking the rose from him, closing my eyes and sniffing its fragrance. It smelled so good. I was feeling a tad shy, but before I could even put the rose in water, Steve grabbed me and kissed me. That's the way it was with Steve—everything happened so fast.

Starry-eyed and weak in the knees, I broke our embrace to offer Steve a beer. As I opened the refrigerator to fetch his beloved suds, he looked around my apartment, eying my portfolio. He sat down at the dining room table and started flipping through its pages.

"Do you mind?" he asked me. What could I say? He already had his head buried in the book. Besides, I was delighted he wanted to see my pictures.

"No," I said politely, "please look."

He loved my pictures, and asked if he could keep one for himself.

"It's the only one I have, but if you really like it, I'll have a copy made for you."

"Yes!" he said, practically yelling. We broke out laughing over his enthusiasm, them he moved closer to me, grabbing me, pulling me to him, kissing me gently, yet passionately. This guy must have had some Italian in his background, as he was one of the hottest-blooded men I had ever encountered.

After Steve downed his beer, we made our way to Mario's, a small Italian restaurant owned by the Angeli family in Westwood. It was a quaint neighborhood hangout with checkered tablecloths, jugs of wine and candles on the table. The food was also out of this world.

During dinner Steve was twice asked for autographs. The fans were nice enough and sweet, but Steve wouldn't give them his autograph. He really hated giving autographs, especially when he was eating, and he wasn't particularly nice about it either. It embarrassed me that he wouldn't just quickly sign a piece of paper for people who appreciated and acknowledged him as a movie star. He was a little mean-spirited about it. He explained to me that it wasn't he who was being rude, but the fans. He pointed out that it was they who interrupted his dinner, with no regard for his privacy. It wasn't how I would have handled the matter, but then again, he was a superstar. It wasn't in my nature to say no to a fan, nor was it in Elvis' nature—he always said yes to anyone.

Despite the autograph seekers, we had a lovely dinner. Steve had his beer, I nursed my white wine. We delved into our complicated personal lives, though we were careful not to pry too closely. I talked about my son, Gerry, and Steve in turn talked about his two children, Terry and Chad, whom he dearly loved. He also spoke of his 15-year marriage to Neile and how it was nearing the end. He spoke of her with respect, which I found admirable. I think he needed to spread his wings and wanted to be free to take the next step in his life. The romantic part of his marriage was over and he wanted excitement. Sadly, Steve and Neile still loved each other deeply, but Steve, from what I knew and read, couldn't be faithful to her. He seemed a little lost and confused as to what he wanted in life.

When that subject became awkward, he switched the conversation to his upcoming movie, *Junior Bonner*. Shooting was going to take place in Prescott, Arizona, 90 miles northwest of Phoenix. He was very honest and forthright when he brought up the subject of the part I had read for, the role of Charmagne.

"Sam wants Tiffany Bolling for the part, but I wanted you," Steve said. "Sam's the director, so I have to go along with what he says."

I could tell the situation embarrassed him.

"And you already have me," I said to Steve, looking right into his eyes, trying to put him at ease by some gentle teasing. He smiled that boyish grin of his, and squeezed my hand hard with passion.

At least he didn't bullshit me by saying the part was mine, or lead me on to get a part in his movie by sleeping with him. He let me know right up front, before our relationship went any further, that the part of Charmagne was not mine. I respected him immensely for that. Besides, Tiffany Bolling was a more accomplished actress than I was and would have done a terrific job.

He asked if I would visit him on location, and I said yes without a moment's hesitation. Who wouldn't have wanted to visit Steve McQueen on a big movie set with real cowboys in a charming town located in the mountains of Arizona?

By the end of our dinner, we both knew that our destinies had brought us together. We would become lovers and friends in a very short period of time. The chemistry was undeniable, and neither of us was going to fight it. I didn't allow myself to think about the two of us on an intellectual basis, like where our relationship might go or if we would have a future together. I was living in the "Be Here Now" stage of my life.

Like my credo, I let things take their natural course. However, lurking in the back of my mind were James and Elvis. There seemed to be just enough time in my life for all three.

Steve had only five days before he left for filming in Arizona. We would certainly become lovers before he left. I wanted to, but as silly as it seems, I wanted to have one more date first.

Before I could say a word, Steve solved that little problem for me. "Can you go to dinner with me on Saturday?" he asked, smiling.

"Yes," I practically screamed, without a moment's hesitation. An electric shock went through me, and we both knew that Saturday night would be *our* night.

On the drive back to my apartment, Steve held my hand and lovingly pushed my hair off my shoulders. He loved running his fingers through my hair. I was relieved that I didn't have to say or do anything because he made me feel so comfortable. I had to be up early the next day. It was a perfect second date. Steve wanted to walk me up to my apartment to give me a proper "good night kiss." When we got inside, he gently pulled me to him and we kissed. After 10 minutes of pure bliss, he headed for the door and said,

"See ya, Barbara." He smiled that trademark half-crooked smile of his, and promised to call me. I knew he would.

I was floating. If all he was after was just sex, he wouldn't have been so sweet to wait. Yes, he really liked me! I liked him, too.

Steve called me the next day, to tell me where to meet him on Saturday. It turned out to be the same restaurant we went to on our first date. How romantic.

I arrived at the restaurant five minutes early, and sat at the bar. I ordered a glass of white wine. Promptly at 7 p.m., Steve walked into the place wearing a great big smile. He was dressed casually, sporting his normal attire—blue jeans, T-shirt, light jacket and sandals. In all the time that I knew Steve, I never saw him dressed up. I thought he looked so handsome in *The Thomas Crown Affair* in his tailor-made suits, but he preferred casual clothes for almost all occasions when he was with me.

Steve ordered a draft beer, and another white wine for me. There were sparks in the air. We ordered dinner and picked at our plates—we were too excited to eat. We flirted, laughed, talked, held hands and stroked each other's fingers, slowly building up to what we both knew the end of the evening would bring. There was so much sexual tension between the two of us, that we were practically going out of our minds.

"You want to see my little house?" he asked. That was the pass I had been expecting.

"Yes," I answered unabashedly.

He paid the bill, squeezed my hand tightly and we headed for our cars.

"Follow my car. My house is just a few blocks away," he smiled.

I followed his sporty looking Porsche up the hill to his rented tiny guest house on a side of Pacific Palisades near Gladstone's restaurant, overlooking the Pacific Coast Highway.

I pulled in behind him, and by the time I stopped my car, he was at my door opening it for me. Always the gentleman.

My heart was pounding. I stepped out of my car and we immediately started kissing each other wildly. Steve picked me up and carried me through the front door, straight to the bed. As I remember it, the guest house was just one big room with separate areas with his bed nestled in a cozy corner. We laid down and immediately went into a passionate embrace, a lover's dance.

We began to undress each other in between fits of laughter and French kisses. Steve buried his head in my hair, smelling it, stroking it and kissing my neck. I was kissing him back when I could, thoroughly enjoying the experience.

Steve McQueen was all I had hoped he would be: wild, provocative and passionate. He took pride in his body; he was stocky and strong. There was longing in his ice-blue gaze, a slight sadness. We fit perfectly as lovers.

After we made love, we showered, washing each other's backs and fronts. It was fun, like two kids exploring something together for the first time. We toweled off and I put on Steve's white terry cloth bathrobe, while he wrapped a towel around his waist. At that moment, I felt as if we were a couple. It all felt so right.

As I dried my hair, Steve made tea. While the water was boiling, he rolled a joint and we sat on the bed, talking, smoking and drinking Chamomile tea.

We made plans for me to visit him in Prescott, once he sorted things out with Neile. I didn't broach the subject of his family, and he didn't offer any information. With Steve, nothing was volunteered and everything was on a need-to-know basis. I couldn't complain. At least I knew where I stood, and I thought I could handle it.

I stayed overnight, cuddling close to him until morning. He was sweet and tender during those intimate moments. It would be our only night together before he left for Arizona, but we made the most of it. We made love three times, and hardly slept a wink.

I didn't think about whether our being together was right or wrong. Some would say I wasn't acting responsibly, and they'd be right. He was still married, but I believed what he had told me regarding his eroding marriage and trial separation. He was still spending a good deal of time at home in Brentwood but he said he was "working out the family details." I didn't push him in any way.

In the end, it was true. His marriage to Neile was over. They were married for 15 years and bore two wonderful children; a noble achievement in Hollywood.

Neile McQueen was his friend, lover, confidant, mother of his children, partner and everything else you could want in a wife. It wasn't easy for him to break his ties to this wonderful and beautiful woman who supported him financially when he wasn't a household name, remained faithful to him when he did make it, and was behind his career 100 percent. Steve was searching for love, and had it in abundance with his wife. But even though he had love, he wasn't satisfied. The excitement and newness of marriage had waned for him. Steve would marry two more times, but I believe his best years were with Neile. The sparkle was gone after his divorce from Neile. He became a hermit in the last years of his life, ducking the Hollywood limelight to live like a recluse in Malibu and Santa Paula, California.

We were both up early the next morning. We had a cup of tea (Steve preferred it over coffee) and he promised to call me from Arizona when he got settled.

"I'll miss you," he said as I left. For such a macho guy, he could be really sweet.

The memories of that first night with Steve more than 30 years ago are still as vivid today as they were then. Being with Steve was nothing short of fantastic.

All three men I was dating were great in bed, in their own unique way. Technically, James was the best lover. He knew what to do to a woman's body and how to get the best out of it. He pleased his woman first, through a strategic course of moves and maneuvers. Elvis, on the other hand, made love tenderly, but naturally straight. He didn't have certain moves down, but his moves were like his dance performance in *Jailhouse Rock*, and he was the greatest kisser of anyone I ever knew. Steve was the wildest, and a little on the rough side like the Heathcliff character from *Wuthering Heights*.

I freely admit, I love men. I feel safe and wanted in their company. The only drawback is that in the early years I was extremely naive, and believed everything a man told me, so I wound up being used more often than not. By nature I am a very trusting person. Possibly even too trusting.

Steve called me on July 1 from Arizona.

"Hi," he said in a perky manner, and Steve wasn't a perky guy. "I have a surprise."

"Really? Isn't that something," I said playfully. "I have a surprise for you, too."

"You first," he insisted.

"Well, I have that 8 x 10 picture you wanted of me when you came to my apartment."

"That is good news," Steve said, trying to stifle his laughter. "I have a bigger surprise for you."

This was intriguing. A bigger surprise for me. I loved surprises. "You know that picture you wanted when you first met me in Joe Wizan's office?" he asked.

Picture? What picture? I couldn't remember what picture he was talking about. "What picture would that be, Steve?"

"That would be *Junior Bonner*, Barbara."

"Can you be a little bit more specific, honey?"

"You've got the picture, Barbara! You've got the part of Charmagne in *Junior Bonner*! "

Finally, it sunk in. I screamed into the phone, beaming with joy. "I've got the part of Charmagne? I've got the part! I can't believe it!"

"Well believe it, honey," he assured me. "Of course, you'll have to high tail it here to Prescott by tomorrow if you want the part. Can you manage?" he asked in a teasing manner, knowing I'd say yes no matter what my schedule looked like.

I was at a loss for words—I mean, I was absolutely dumbfounded. Just like that, out of the clear blue. That was the single greatest thing to happen in my acting career, starring in a Steve McQueen movie directed by the great Sam Peckinpah. But that's Hollywood for you; overnight, anything can happen.

I hung up the phone, and called Joe Wizan at the production

office in Prescott in a frenzy. Joe answered the phone and said he'd been waiting for my call.

"Hi, Barbara. Surprise, surprise," he teased sweetly into the receiver.

"I can't believe what Steve told me. Is it true?"

"It's absolutely 100 percent true."

"What happened to Tiffany Bolling?" I just had to know.

"Tiffany got sick, and so now you've got the part. It's as simple as that." Then Joe switched gears. "Call your agent and give him my number, so I can work out the financial details. Your reservations are already made and your ticket will be at the airline counter; you'll have to be here by tomorrow."

Much like Joe Esposito was to Elvis, Joe Wizan was the "details" guy on this picture.

And there it was. In the snap of a finger I was to be Steve McQueen's leading lady. Then it occurred to me: *Not only did I get the leading man, but I got the part, too!* Who says you can't have it all?

CHAPTER NINE

By the time *Junior Bonner* came Steve's way, he had it all, too. He was the biggest star of the Beatles generation with hits such as *The Great Escape, Love With The Proper Stranger, The Cincinnati Kid, Nevada Smith, The Sand Pebbles, The Thomas Crown Affair,* and *Bullitt* to his credit. However, his fame rested uneasily on the shy, quiet farm boy.

Steve McQueen was born on March 24, 1930 in Beech Grove, Indiana. Like me, he had a hard upbringing. His father took a hike when Steve was just six months old, leaving his mother, Jullian, the unpleasant task of raising a son by herself.

Steve never knew his father, and was deeply haunted by that. Even more upsetting to him was the fact that his mother was an alcoholic, who had taken up with many men to pay the bills. Often, she abandoned Steve and left him with her brother, Claude Thomson, on his Slater, Missouri, hog farm.

As a result, Steve grew up on the streets, got involved with the wrong crowd and was sent to reform school by one of his many stepfathers. He grew up distrusting women and blamed his mother for a lot of his problems.

"How could that bitch leave me?" he often said of his mother.

When Steve discovered acting in the mid-1950s, he was a sensation. He electrified audiences and offered a unique gift to the world through his performing. In 1963, he became a bona-fide superstar when he stole the movie from a high-powered cast including James Garner, Richard Attenborough, Charles Bronson and James Coburn in *The Great Escape*. From 1963 to 1975, Steve McQueen was the biggest box-office star in the world.

I quickly made arrangements with both my commercial and

print agents to cancel the rest of my commitments for the next six weeks. I was in a state of euphoria, thinking only of Steve and the picture. I tied up loose ends and prepared to leave for Prescott the next morning, hardly sleeping at all.

I arrived under a blazing hot Phoenix sun. A driver from the set was there to greet me at the gate, pick up my bags and get me up to the rodeo grounds in Prescott, where the set was located.

"Me, an extra, and the world's biggest box-office attraction at the time—Steve McQueen, sharing a few moments behind-the-scenes." From the Barbara Leigh Collection

When I arrived on location just 90 minutes later, Steve dropped what he was doing to plant a big kiss on me. It was evident to everyone that we were together. Steve made sure of that. I guess that meant no sneaking around on this picture. Actually, I've always preferred the honest approach to things; so did Steve.

He introduced me to the crew, and Sam Peckinpah came up to me to say hello. He seemed nice enough. However, I think that Steve pulled some major strings to get me the part, because of the vibes I was getting from Sam. I later found out that I wasn't even Sam's second choice.

After exchanging pleasantries, I was escorted to wardrobe, where they tried several shirts on me. I wore the same outfit throughout most of the film. Steve was there to check out the clothes, helping make the final decision—a navy blue shirt with a beige design embroidered down the front. He was a perfectionist, even though he didn't appear that way. I wore my own blue jeans and boots, and no jewelry whatsoever. This definitely was not a high-fashion role. I was handed a script and a schedule for my scenes.

I had a room at the Prescottonian, but it was a farce because Steve had rented a small house at the foot of Prescott's Landscape Mountain, where I stayed with him almost constantly for the six weeks I was on location. Everyone else involved in the picture stayed at the Prescottonian. On many weekends Steve's children, Terry and Chad, would visit and I would go back to the hotel and make myself scarce. He and Neile weren't divorced and to Steve's credit, he didn't want the kids to be shocked by the new lady in his life. Eventually, I did meet his children, and was especially taken by his daughter, Terry. I gave her a special carnelian heart as a memento of her visit. She melted my heart, and was the little girl I had always wanted.

The other actors in the film included the great Robert (*The Music Man*) Preston, the legendary Ida (*High Sierra*) Lupino, Academy award winner Ben (*The Last Picture Show*) Johnson, a true gentleman cowboy, and the forceful Joe Don (*Walking Tall*) Baker. It was an incredible cast, which made it all the more intimidating for me. Luckily, they were a fun bunch to be around, and whenever I did stay at the Prescottonian, it was a riot. Ida and Robert were old friends and often left their doors open to welcome cast and crew to have a drink with them. When you finished partying with Robert, you floated over to Ida's for more of the same. There was a lot of partying going on throughout the filming of *Junior Bonner*. As a matter of fact, the Prescottonian was a behind-the-scenes movie in itself. Never a dull moment.

"Steve McQueen and Robert Preston share a bottle of the hard stuff, which was readily available on any Sam Peckinpah film set." Photo courtesy of ABC Pictures.

Sam certainly drank his share of alcohol. His going-away gift to me was a bottle of 100-proof Smirnoff Vodka. At the time of filming *Junior Bonner*, Sam was a big drinker, but he wasn't out of control. A few years later his drinking did get out of hand, and led to his early death. The alcohol eventually cost him everything, including what he loved to do most: direct films. Sam was unemployable for about five years, then in 1983 he directed the disappointing *The Osterman Weekend*. It was a sad ending to a great career. Sam never worked again, except for a couple of Julian Lennon music videos, and died a year later.

Every year on the Fourth of July, Prescott hosts an annual parade through downtown that's tied in with the annual rodeo at

Prescott Downs. All the major cowboys who competed in the rodeo participated in the parade, because it was a big show on the rodeo circuit. Casey Tibbs was the reigning champion that year. He was a small man, but a giant cowboy.

This was my first experience with cowboys, and I found them to be fascinating and very sexy. Steve fit right in with the cowboy look and mind set. I think there's a little cowboy in most men, but with Steve, it suited him well.

My character's first appearance was at the rodeo parade, which was about halfway through the film. I didn't have a large speaking part, but I was the love interest. Whenever I wasn't filming my scenes, I watched the other actors perform their craft, especially Steve. He liked it when I stood by his side, which is exactly where he wanted me to be.

His style was unique from most actors, and that's what separated him from most movie stars. He was a reactor instead of an actor; he didn't initiate action, he reacted to it with his facial expressions and body language. It's a skill most actors don't have, and Steve was perhaps the most talented reactor in the movies. Most actors fight for lines; Steve fought for the shot. Where he placed himself was a lot more important than what he had to say. Watching him perform was a trip; he didn't appear to be acting at all, but that was his gift. You didn't see his acting.

I ate lunch that first day on the set with Steve in his small trailer. His personal cook, Jimmy, made all of Steve's meals to his liking, especially breakfast, which was usually scrambled eggs with salsa. Steve liked it simple, and demanded privacy.

With wardrobe and lunch out of the way, I studied the script and watched Steve shoot his scenes. It would be another four or five days before they'd get to me.

When we finished work, Steve and I headed for his house. It was perched on the side of a hill that had a view from the living room of the Prescott mountains. We often sat out on the porch with tea or beer, relaxing and talking. Sometimes taking a puff of pot.

But the moment we arrived at his house that first night, we tore our clothes off and made wild love. We had missed each other.

I spent the night snuggled next to him just where I wanted to be. The next morning we made love again, then got dressed and had tea on the porch, a nice view to wake up to. Steve was very quiet in the mornings as it took him time to wake up. He wasn't what you'd call a morning person. Some might even call him grumpy.

After we finished our tea we headed for a new day on the set. This became habit; arriving and leaving the set together. There was no doubt we were a couple. The word made it back to Los Angeles—Rona Barrett talked about us on her gossip show. One publication in particular, "Young Romance," a movie gossip magazine, also picked up the story and featured me on its cover. The article claimed that I was "the other woman."

Every morning in Steve's trailer, we shared breakfast while he went over his lines, and I went over mine if I had any scenes for that day. Sam was always waiting for us to arrive. Things started to happen whenever Steve walked onto the set; he was the real boss and everyone knew it.

After Steve changed into his wardrobe, he had his morning discussion with Sam, and then the picture would roll. Steve kept an eye on me to make sure I was nearby, walking over between takes for a hug. We were enjoying the newness of our romance. The sparks were flying on location, which made it all the more exciting.

I especially enjoyed watching Steve with the cowboys. He liked talking to them, and they admired his guts as an actor; you could tell by the way they crowded around him, the way they studied him.

One of the funniest scenes we filmed was of Steve riding a mechanical bull. It embarrassed him to no end that he had to ride a machine instead of a real bull. He hated to be thought of as a "candy-ass actor," but for insurance purposes the production company wouldn't let him ride a bull, even though he wanted to. When Steve had to ride the mechanical bull, he allowed only a skeleton crew to film him. He let me on the set, but I had to watch with a straight face—which was difficult. I wanted to burst out laughing, but I knew that wouldn't have been wise.

Junior Bonner was made eight years before *Urban Cowboy* popularized the mechanical bull. Steve made the best of it, even nicknaming the mechanical bull

"Baby Sunshine" in honor of the mean, nasty bull in the film named "Sunshine." His character in *Junior Bonner* must conquer Sunshine and ride him for eight seconds. He rode the mechanical bull well, and in the final cut of the film you could swear Steve really was riding Sunshine. At the very least, he made the scenes look authentic.

The first time you see my character in the movie is in the parade, but like most films, *Junior Bonner* was shot out of sequence. The first scene I shot was my reaction to Steve riding a bull. I was in the stands watching Steve do his thing in the arena, and Sam was screaming directions at me. I must admit, I was still an ingenue and learning the craft as I went along.

"OK, act concerned, he's fallen now. He might be hurt," Sam yelled through a megaphone. "Look concerned," he repeated over and over, berating me in front of the crew. Sam couldn't control his spitefulness, so Steve took over the directing when it came to these scenes. This was the one and only time he directed me in the whole film. Steve was head honcho on the set, and his word was law. Sam never interfered again, relaxed and finally accepted me. Besides, he was a star in his own right. Everybody in the business knew the tremendous talent Sam possessed.

Steve and I enjoyed one particular scene with co-star Robert Preston. It was a tag-team event with milk bottles. In the scene, the two men had to rope a cow, milk her and bring the filled bottle back to the starting point. It was a very tiring scene. That night I drew Steve a hot bath, then gave him a rubdown. It wasn't something he liked or was comfortable with. He seemed more comfortable being a little rough. Steve's touch and approach was not soft or slow, but more like a teenager's—rough, wild and aggressive. He was a good kisser, but was not into foreplay like Elvis or James were. They could kiss all night long, whereas with Steve, it was just a prelude to lovemaking. Steve was just as attentive as the other two, but in his own bad-boy way.

Filming the Prescott Rodeo Days Parade was a hoot. The locals made their own floats. Some were grandiose and impressive, while others were simple and modest. You could tell by the expressions on the locals faces that the floats were made with pride. The cowboys and cowgirls who participated in the parade were all decked out in their Sunday best and authentic costumes. It seemed as if the entire town was in attendance. It's an annual event, and well-known throughout the state as a great parade.

My scene takes place while I'm with my wealthy cowboy friend and his group of cohorts. We're standing on the side with the crowds of people, enjoying the parade, when Steve walks by and notices me. We're attracted to each other at first sight, and that's when our romance begins. He doesn't care that I'm with a date; he makes up his mind right then that he wants me, and he finds a way to achieve his goal. Actually, Steve was exactly the same way in real life. He wanted what he wanted when he wanted it, and he usually got it. The same went for Elvis and James who usually got their way as well.

The parade moved from the center courtyard down main street to the rodeo grounds. It was an easy scene with no dialogue, just a lot of flirting with someone I wanted to flirt with. It was fun for both of us.

The script was written by Jeb (*The Black Hole*) Rosebrook. It was especially good, if not a little melancholy. Steve liked it because he identified with it on many levels. It was about a person fighting for his dream, but not always attaining it. Sound familiar?

Junior's dream was to ride Sunshine for eight seconds; he went so far as to fix the drawing, so that he could come up with the bull's number. Robert Preston, who played Ace Bonner, Junior's father, is an alcoholic who wants to go to Australia to chase his dream of panning for gold. Curly Bonner, Junior's brother, portrayed by Joe Don Baker, is a successful real-estate broker who's working on his first million, and most likely, will get it. His dream is to get Junior to quit the rodeo circuit to sell real estate for him. Ida Lupino, Junior and Curley's mother, is Ace's estranged wife, who's still in love with him but won't allow him back in her life because of his years of drinking and womanizing. Her dream is to find a solution to their problems.

At the end of the movie, Junior rides Sunshine, is pronounced the winner of the rodeo and buys Ace a first-class ticket to Australia. Junior heads out the door of the travel agency, leaving the audience guessing where he's going. It wasn't an upbeat, happy movie, but it was real.

One funny moment during filming was when we were shooting at Ida Lupino's house on the outskirts of Prescott. Next to her house was a vegetable garden. On the day of filming the family scene, some members of the crew noticed some very tall stalks of trees, but these tree stalks happened to be marijuana plants. The stalks were pulled up and carted away by the local police, but not before Steve reacted with cat-like reflexes and grabbed one for himself. Steve smoked marijuana daily when I was with him. He especially loved the home-grown stuff. He got a big kick out of the fact that it was grown under everyone's noses, going undetected for so long. The fact that it took a film crew from Los Angeles to find it made him chuckle.

After a few weeks, I asked Steve if Gerry could visit with us. Despite his current marital status, Steve was a family man. He thought it would be a terrific idea if we enrolled Gerry in a summer camp in Prescott. He offered to find the camp himself. Gerry enrolled in Shadow Valley Camp, and it was wonderful to have him with me. Steve liked him, paying him a lot of attention. Steve was a natural with children, almost like a Boy Scout leader.

The camp worked out perfectly. Gerry would attend camp during the week and would spend the weekends with Steve and me. If Steve was with his children, Gerry and I would stay at my room at the Prescottonian.

On our weekends, Gerry and I explored the surrounding towns, one in particular, the mining ghost town of Jerome. Gerry got a kick out of the place, because it was as if an old cowboy town had been brought back to life.

That same weekend, Steve bought Gerry a cowboy hat, shirt, boots and jeans and I got him a toy gun and holster. Gerry was ecstatic. He didn't know who Steve McQueen was (Gerry was only 7) but liked him a lot. He saw Steve as a man who paid a lot of attention to him and was good to his mama.

Steve had his personal cook fly to Los Angeles and drive my Mercedes to Arizona, so that Gerry and I could drive back to California.

On a weekend halfway through the shoot, Steve and I decided to get away from the set, making reservations to stay in Scottsdale. We made the two-hour drive together, stopping at a neighborhood bar, or I should say, a real dive, for a beer. When we entered the establishment, the locals were drinking and playing pool. Of course, everyone knew who Steve was, but they treated him as they would anyone else, which Steve liked. He didn't like to be pampered; he just wanted to be a normal guy. Stardom gave him the freedom to be normal or eccentric or whatever he desired.

He played a few games of pool with a couple of locals while I sat at the bar. He'd walk over in between shots for a kiss and a drink of his long-neck Budweiser. It was fun to relax with no pressures. These people were cool. No one asked for an autograph or pestered him with questions.

Once he got tired of playing pool, we moved on to the hotel.

I didn't know that much about Scottsdale, but being there with Steve lent it a magical air. We checked into the luxurious Camelback Inn. The bungalow he reserved for us was secluded and private, so charming. We would spend most of our time there, leaving only to eat and shop.

Steve wanted to buy me a new outfit. I think he got sick of my customary blue jeans, and he wanted to see me in something more feminine for a change. "Baby," he announced after we had lunch, "I'd like to buy you a present." This was not an everyday event with

Steve. He was tightfisted—just like James—but when you least expected it, he'd surprise you. We drove past the Fifth Avenue shops in the heart of downtown Scottsdale, and went into the first women's boutique we spotted. The saleswoman who waited on us was beside herself, and couldn't stop staring at Steve, flirting with him outrageously in front of me. I thought it was funny. I didn't mind sharing him a little in those types of situations.

Steve picked out some clothes he wanted me to try on for him. I settled on a pair of slacks and a print blouse. Even though Steve was a casual dresser himself, preferring blue jeans and T-shirts, he had great tastes in clothes. I was so happy with my new clothes. Elvis would have approved—no blue jeans!

Sunsets in Scottsdale are spectacular. This particular night, the sky was an extraordinary shade of orange-purple that put the two of us in a very sexy mood. Steve rolled a joint and we smoked it as we lay naked on the cool, white sheets of the hotel bed. A portable radio played romantic music, and we made love with the suntan cream mingling in with our sweat. I absolutely loved Steve's hairy chest; it was the biggest turn-on. I teased him, because the suntan lotion made his chest hair knot up into little curls.

We showered, dressed and decided to take a drive into the desert, taking the ever-present joint with us. Steve loved the desert. We drove a few miles to Camelback Mountain and climbed to the top. We settled down on a flat rock, lit up a joint and looked down onto the valley. It was so peaceful and romantic. We talked about life and laughed a lot, acting like we were very much in love. We wouldn't have cared one iota if the world had stopped—at least, I wouldn't have minded.

Back in our room, Steve grabbed me and we started playing around again. Afterward, both exhausted, he ordered room service. It was fun to relax, kick back and watch a little television, before falling asleep in each other's arms.

Back in Prescott the next day, I picked up Gerry at camp so that he could have dinner with us. He enjoyed the precious time we had together, especially when Steve gave him so much attention.

Steve decided that after dinner he would take Gerry for a walk, and talk to him "man to man." Gerry was having nightmares to the point where he would get up and walk in his sleep. The camp counselors were worried about him, so Steve wanted to pick his brain and find out what was bothering him.

Steve thought Gerry was a bit of a mama's boy which he probably was, but I think his real problem was that he wanted to live with me instead of his father. Steve was firm but gentle with Gerry, feeling sorry for him in his own way. I think Steve could identify with him as a small boy.

The next day, we were shooting the scene where everyone meets at the Palace Bar for a drink and ends up in a barroom brawl. Drinking and fighting go hand in hand in the cowboy lifestyle.

Locals and rodeo cowboys alike met at the Palace to drink, dance, shoot pool and listen to honkytonk music. Naturally, there was always a fight going on.

The Palace Bar has an interesting history. It was built in the early 1900s and the original owner's wife had an itchy trigger finger—she shot him five or six times. When the bar owner recovered, he and his merry wife remained married and acted like two lovebirds on their honeymoon. Just a little misunderstanding, that's all.

Before this scene, Sam had the bar lined with drinks. All the main actors were positioned, and then the extras arrived. Everyone had a drink to loosen up; then the scene began. Junior tricks a friend of his into asking me to dance to make my date jealous. Junior's ploy succeeds, and my date works himself into a frenzy and throws a punch at Junior's friend. From there, all hell breaks loose. Even the women get into the action.

Once the fight is well under way, Junior walks over to Charmagne and they begin to dance, flirting outrageously while everyone else is busy defending themselves. Ducking punches, the two excuse themselves to the sanctuary of a telephone booth, where they begin to kiss. They leave the bar together and Charmagne's with Junior for the rest of the movie.

That scene was a little too real for my blood, because everyone was literally smashed by the end. Sam made sure the booze in the glasses was real, not the customary iced tea. Only in a Sam Peckinpah picture could that have happened!

One of the extras in this scene happened to be a local, who was the town lush. This guy loved to drink and chase girls. Sam loved him because he was such a character, and encouraged him to chase any girl he had the hots for. Sam gave him free rein, and the guy was like a dog in heat. At one point, the local came up to Steve and me while we were dancing and Sam yelled out, "No, not that girl!" Everyone on the set burst out laughing, knowing Sam's advice had backfired on him. It was all in good fun, but by the end of the scene, it got out of control. The bar was trashed, and the owner and his wife were not amused. It took the crew some time before the place was restored to normal. By the way, the scene with the local made the final cut, and it was one of the highlights of *Junior Bonner*.

Almost 30 years later, the Palace Bar is still the place to go in Prescott. In the back, there's a wall-sized mural commemorating Junior Bonner dancing with Charmagne. I recently saw the mural for the first time and it brought back a flood of memories of my time with Steve McQueen and Sam Peckinpah, all of them extremely happy.

Steve was aware of my relationships with James and Elvis. Whether or not it was smart, I made it my credo to try and tell the truth to all three men if they had the guts to ask me. I was a free spirit who did whatever I pleased with my life, just as each of these three men did. It was a lot easier if I told the truth, because I didn't have to worry about keeping my stories straight.

Being somewhat up front kept these guys on their toes; it let them know in no uncertain terms that they didn't "own" me. They all had big egos, and were extremely competitive. James, Elvis and Steve all had other relationships with other people at the same time. If they could do it, then so could I. The hard fact is we were all using each other. The plain truth is, it was fun.

Strangely enough, James felt threatened more by Steve than

by Elvis. I think he got a kick out of that Memphis country boy; he liked his music and his manners. James wasn't very enthused when I got *Junior Bonner*. Sure, he feigned, "That's great, Indian," but he knew that I was having an affair with Steve in Prescott. James never asked me how things were going, he never asked me about my part or my experiences with Sam Peckinpah, Robert Preston, Ida Lupino, nor of course, Steve McQueen. My affair with Steve led to our eventual breakup.

All through *Junior Bonner* I kept in touch with both James and Elvis, when I had a few moments away from Steve. Both men would leave messages at my hotel or with my answering service in Los Angeles. It drove them nuts when they couldn't get in touch with me at their convenience.

Unlike James, Elvis wanted to know every detail about the movie and my stay in Prescott. He was so unselfish in his interest and concern for me. I spoke of the charming little town, the parade, the rodeo circuit and the cowboys. From what I could tell, E sounded genuinely interested in everything I had to say. He stayed away from direct questions about Steve, but hinted just a tad.

"How's your co-star?" he asked in a manner that told me he was trying to play it cool.

"You mean Steve?" I asked, searching for the right words.

"Yeah, Steve McQueen," he shot back.

"He's really nice," I said trying to downplay the situation. "He's a good actor, too." I was praying that would be the extent on the subject of Steve McQueen. Thank goodness it was.

Elvis asked me to meet him in Las Vegas after filming was done. It was hard to give him a straight answer and extremely difficult to say no to the man, so I told him that I would have to check my schedule.

"I want you to promise me that you'll do your best to make it," E said. "Can you let me know by tomorrow?" Elvis wanted everything, and he wanted it *now*.

I didn't tell Elvis about Steve at that moment. Elvis didn't like competition and didn't want to hear about other men—other than perhaps James Aubrey. Elvis' ego got a boost every time he was reminded that he had "stolen the Smiling Cobra's girlfriend." Elvis looked up to James, as did I. He recognized James' sophistication and the way he carried himself, his education and silver-spoon background. I think he was also intrigued by James, and it made him feel more manly that he was able to take a girl away from a powerful movie mogul.

On the other hand, I wasn't going to say anything I didn't have to.

I hung up the phone, and wondered how I would go about seeing Elvis without telling him about Steve. Oh well, I would face that when the time came. Why stress over it now?

Things between Steve and me were great, but I wasn't ready yet to move on. I was really starting to like this bad boy.

I found out that my part was set to finish shooting around August 13, Steve's a little later, so I could leave Prescott by August 15.

I called Joe Esposito the next day, and he put Elvis on the phone.

"What did ya find out, darlin'?"

"I can leave Arizona on the 15th, but first I need to take my son home to Tennessee, then I can come to Las Vegas." His answer surprised me.

"I can't wait that long, baby," he said with impatience. "I'm missing you badly." Wow, I couldn't believe what I was hearing. I was astounded. Absence does make the heart grow fonder. Looking back, I realize that Elvis probably couldn't schedule another girl at the time. Time was important to Elvis. He either had too much or too little. Never anything in between.

There was a long pause on the other end of the line. I didn't know what to say or do. I couldn't change the production schedule, so this was pretty much written in stone. Elvis, being a fast thinker, came up with a solution to his little problem.

"I know," he said, "I'll come to Prescott. I've always wanted to see a real cowboy town." He must have really been bored.

Oh boy, here comes trouble.

My heart began to pound as if it were going to jump out of my chest. A sinking feeling came over me.

There was no way I could have Elvis come to Prescott while I was living with Steve at his house. But when Elvis made up his mind, nothing could stop him. He wasn't going to wait another day, or accept any more excuses from me. He was ready to pack his things and high tail it to Arizona. I had to tell Elvis about my affair with Steve.

Busted!

It took me a few seconds to muster the courage to come clean. I chose my words carefully.

"Elvis," I said wincing, "I don't think that will work out."

"Well, why not darlin'? I want to see my baby and if I have to come there, well, so be it," my romantic sweetheart said with the utmost sincerity. This wasn't going to be easy.

I was cornered, and there was no way out for me now.

"E, the reason I don't think it would be a good idea is, well . . . um . . . I'm . . . a . . . kind of dating Steve." Dating, that was a nice way of putting it. There was dead silence on the other end of the phone. I couldn't think of a good lie fast enough, but I didn't want to lose Elvis either. I was greedy, and I wanted to keep all three these relationships going. Finally, Elvis spoke.

"Well, that does make things difficult for me," he said diplomatically. "Do you think we could meet in Phoenix?" The guy was something else! He wasn't very familiar with the word "no."

"E, I'm living with Steve here in Prescott. There's just no possible way I can do that, and maintain my friendship and stay with the movie."

Silence once again.

When he next spoke I could tell that he was mad.

"Let me think about things and I'll have Joe call you." Here he was, willing to see me and I turned him down cold. He was hurt. It was a wonderful gesture on his part, but his timing sucked. Before he handed the phone back to Joe, I blurted out, "Elvis, please don't be mad at me. I love you, and after this movie I'll work my schedule around yours."

"I'll be in touch," he said coldly.

Then he hung up.

CHAPTER TEN

I sat stunned for a couple of minutes, still holding the receiver. I felt awful. I loved Elvis and didn't want to stop seeing him, but he'd pushed me up against a wall. I was forced to level with him and tell the truth. I thought about calling him back, but what good would that do? He was probably thinking about the next girlfriend he'd call to replace me. Joe would confirm this later.

I didn't have the power to change things and I didn't want to, either. I wasn't sure if E would ever call me again, but I decided not to let it get me down. I was having too much fun.

Steve greeted me with a big hug when I walked back on the set. It boosted my ego, helping me to forget the phone call with Elvis.

"Be here now," I told myself, mimicking the 1970s logic of Ram Dass.

After Steve finished on the set we went to the Palace Bar, where an art show was being held.

Surprisingly the show had some wonderful paintings and local arts and crafts. I didn't know anything about art, but Steve did. He surprised me when he told me to pick out a present as a souvenir of *Junior Bonner*.

I was touched. He smiled and squeezed my hand while we walked around looking at the art. I spotted a watercolor of a cabin in the woods; two men fishing and in the background a beautiful rainbow. It wasn't very expensive, but it gave me a happy feeling to look at it. I still have it, and cherish the memories it brings back whenever I look at it.

Knowing our time together was limited, Steve was even more attentive than usual. I had a couple of small scenes to film, and within a week I was finished. I stayed an extra week at Steve's house to be with him, and to let Gerry complete his camp.

Near the end of filming, Sam Peckinpah began to warm to me. It took a while for us to connect, but we eventually became friends and stayed in touch until he passed away in 1985. He would call me in Los Angeles periodically to catch up on our lives. It certainly was a switch from that first day when I read for him and Steve. I think he had a change of heart about me once he got to know me, and maybe it was obvious to him that Steve really liked me. I'm glad we eventually became friends because deep down, Sam was a sweet guy once you got to know him. He sometimes was that fun, bad boy, much like Steve.

"Me, a bare-chested Steve McQueen and maverick film director Sam Peckinpah checking out the Prescott Rodeo grounds in *Junior Bonner*." From the Barbara Leigh Collection.

A week before I left Prescott, Sam gave a small going-away party for the cast. He was wonderful. He gave me a beautiful mohair poncho, which I think Katy Haber presented to me along with a bottle of vodka. Katy was the script girl and Sam's girlfriend. She was a beautiful English woman and a great sport. Katy ignored things good-naturedly, accepting Sam's faults. She was great for Sam, and was one of the few stable forces in his life. Sam toasted me many times and toward the end of the evening, he was hugging and kissing me a little too much for Steve's liking. Steve gently but firmly took Sam's arms off me, and pulled me closer to him. As smashed as Sam was, he knew to let things drop and didn't pursue it.

Finally, the day came to leave Prescott and Steve. The whole experience with Steve, Sam and *Junior Bonner* had been such a rewarding experience. Having my son there was icing on the cake. I was so sad to leave. Looking back, it was the most exciting movie, location and star cast of my career.

Our last night together was sexy and romantic. Steve and I had dinner, smoked a joint, drank a few beers, had some tequila and then sweated the night away with nonstop sex. Steve usually slept in the nude, and insisted that I do the same. It was something I wasn't comfortable with. When I was about five years old I had to sleep naked, because my only set of clothes were wet. It was so humiliating to me that I cried all night. Even to this day, I can't sleep in the nude.

The next morning we had our tea. We sat on the porch talking and enjoying the beautiful view of the valley below. Steve promised to call me as soon as he could figured out his schedule. Maybe we would meet in Palm Springs. We kissed for a long time, then I got in my car and headed for the hotel to pick up my things. As I drove away I watched him in my rearview mirror waving goodbye.

I picked up Gerry at camp, and we hit the road for LA. We had a ball driving back, stopping along the back roads and seeing the sights. Years later we made that same drive together, stopping at all of his favorite places. It was very emotional for us, as we reminisced over that earlier trip. Gerry later became a photographer, and took a lot of pictures of me. There's one picture of me from that weekend, posing as an Indian woman gazing at the majestic mountains. I was feeling high on life. Once I was out of Prescott, I started thinking about getting my son home to Tennessee, which made me think of Elvis. God, I had so many things to think about and plan for.

I stopped along the way to check in with my answering service, and made a couple of phone calls. One was to Elvis. I left a message asking him to please call me at home the next day. I wanted him to know that I was thinking about him. I didn't know if he would ever call back—only time would tell. I hadn't spoken to him since I told him about Steve. I didn't think about James much, but he was also there in my head.

I drove into LA after dark, with Gerry sound asleep in the back seat. Just six hours later there was a message from Joe Esposito. Elvis had called! He cared! I was still in the game, and was ecstatic. I would have to call back after I put Gerry to bed. There were also several messages from James. Once Gerry was in bed, I dialed E's number in Memphis. Joe got on the line and as usual, was seemingly glad to hear from me.

"Hi, Barbara, I'm glad you called back. E wants to talk to you, but he's tied up right now. Can we call you back?"

"Sure Joe, I'm at home. Call me when you can," I cheerfully replied.

I hung up the phone, put on my nightgown and fell into bed.

The next morning I made arrangements with the airlines to fly to Tennessee with Gerry. Elvis still hadn't called back—he'd call me when he got around to it. He was paying me back for Arizona, and probably didn't have an open weekend. I'm sure, however, there were many others ready to replace me. He needed time to rearrange his busy schedule, time to make a plan.

Next, I made plans to have dinner with James that night. He sounded happy, and wanted to see me as soon as possible. My girlfriend Jessica St. John was staying with me while she looked for an apartment, so she would stay with Gerry for me. They were really close and adored each other.

Steve called to make sure I had gotten home safely, and to say that he missed me terribly. He still had a few weeks of filming in Prescott, and would call me every day while he was on location.

Elvis still hadn't called back. This was his way. If I wasn't available when he wanted me, I had to wait until my number came up again. That was OK with me because I wanted to see him, but I wasn't going to sit by the phone waiting for him to call.

As the evening rolled around, I got dressed and headed up the hill to James' house. He was waiting for me with arms wide open, and a big smile. The moment I saw his face I melted. How could I forget that I loved and missed this man? I flew into his arms and we kissed passionately. We stood at the door holding each other—and then passion took over. At that moment, Steve and Elvis didn't exist. Our clothes came off, and we were in bed in no time. James seemed genuinely happy to have me back. He asked no questions. He was only interested in loving me at the moment.

We decided to stay in that night. James was so nice and attentive all evening, telling me how beautiful I was and how much he had missed me. I was falling so in love with him all over again, falling deeply under his spell. I was only 24, but being pursued by three powerful and exciting men, which made me feel like I was definitely one lucky girl.

We sat in front of his fireplace drinking wine and making small talk. After a few glasses of wine James finally worked up the nerve to ask, "Well, Indian, how was Steve to work with?"

Bingo! There was that million-dollar question. I knew this was what he really wanted to know all along, but I wasn't going to volunteer any information. He never told me about his other women, and I was gracious enough never to ask.

I gave him a very noncommittal answer about Steve, but of course, the affair was already widely reported in Hollywood by Rona Barrett. James let it drop, because he missed me.

We snuggled for the rest of the night, and I fell asleep in James' arms. I felt as if I were home. My clothes were hanging in James' closet, my slippers in his bathroom, and I had my drawer in the bathroom as well. What more could a girl want?

James didn't like it if I didn't sleep over. Because I was an actress and not a 9-to-5er, it was easy enough for me, but on days of filming, I usually wouldn't go out at all. The next morning I got up early with James, and when he hit the shower, I hit the road.

"Honey, I'm leaving. See you," I yelled as I was walking into his bathroom. His shower was large and open. It was very easy for him to stick his head out and kiss me goodbye.

"I'll call you later, Indian," my lover assured me. "Glad to have you back."

As I drove down the hill, my mind wandered back to Steve. When I left Prescott we were lovers. How did he really feel about me? Did he miss me? I know that at that moment I really began to miss him.

With Elvis, it was all a matter of timing. Even though he had other girlfriends I knew I could see him more often if my schedule would have allowed it.

When I arrived back at my apartment, Jessica was up with Gerry. She told me that Steve had called, and wanted me to call him back immediately. I gave Gerry a big hug and kiss, grabbed some coffee and sat down to return a few calls.

I knew Steve liked me, but I also knew that he was still trying to make a go of his marriage to Neile for the sake of his children. At 41, Steve was at an age when he needed some excitement in his life; he needed to feel young, handsome and desirable, which was probably why he lusted after young women. I was that young woman.

When Steve and I managed to connect by phone later in the day he let me know that he missed me terribly. He was wrapping up production in a week, and was going to spend some time with his kids, Terry and Chad. After that, he wanted me to meet him in Palm Springs, so we made tentative plans.

Elvis finally called several days later, which led me to believe that he had a girl in Las Vegas keeping him company. At least we were finally able to connect.

I heard that unmistakable southern accent, "Hi darlin'! It's been a long time. Sorry we kept missing each other."

"Hi Elvis, I'm so happy to talk to you. I've really missed you," I said.

"I've missed you, too," E replied. "What's your week look like?" There was my cue. *Oh God, please don't conflict with his schedule,* I thought.

"I'm taking my son home to Tennessee tomorrow, and then I'm off to New York for a commercial and some print work," I said gingerly.

Luckily, that didn't dissuade Elvis. "I was thinking you could fly into Vegas for a show, but I guess that won't do. What about meeting me in Palm Springs? I'm taking a rest before I go on tour."

I didn't want to upset him again and not be available, but it looked like our schedules were going to conflict again. I couldn't think of anything to say, so I said whatever popped into my mind.

"Elvis, yes, you must be exhausted."

He laughed and answered with, "All I need is a couple of days in Palm Springs and to see your pretty face." He probably did need some rest.

"Maybe I could see you when I get back from Tennessee, before I head to New York." I didn't know how I was going to make the time, but I would. One more disappointment on my end would finish us. Elvis didn't like to hear the word "No." There was only so much he would take.

"Great, I'll put Joe on and you can give him your dates. I sure do miss you baby," Elvis gushed.

Poor Joe. I'm sure it was nerve-racking, but he never seemed to get confused with all of E's girlfriends.

"Hi Barbara, what's going on?" Joe asked.

"Well, I'm off to Tennessee tomorrow but will be home in a couple of days after I take my son home." Although Joe and Elvis knew of Gerry, we never discussed him. That made things too real for Elvis. He lived in his own fantasy world and children weren't a part of it, with the exception of Lisa Marie.

"Call me when you get home and we'll know more about our schedule," Joe said.

Great! A new beginning. Soon, I'd be home and back in the arms of Elvis.

The next morning Gerry and I flew to Tennessee, where I stayed with him for the next two days, then headed back to Los Angeles. It was always sad to leave my son.

Messages from my agents and from Steve were waiting when I got home. I had landed another national ad campaign, and would be leaving for New York in a week to work on a major Clairol Loving Care hair project.

When in New York, James would give me the lovely MGM apartment, where I could stay in style. After making flight reservations and travel plans, I called Elvis. I had a week to work out a rendezvous. He wasn't in, so I left a message for him. Then I called Steve.

This was a rough time in Steve's life. He was torn between his family and his ever growing urge to be wild and free. I think Steve needed time to deal with his guilt about what he was doing to his family. He also needed time to figure out what he really wanted in life. He was looking for the romance he once had with his wife, Neile. It was hard for Steve to transition from boyfriend to husband. Relationships change when marriage and children come into play. Elvis had the same problem with Priscilla after a few years.

Steve answered the phone and I said, "Hi, it's me. I miss you!"

"I miss you, too, Barbara," he said playfully. He knew my voice immediately.

We got caught up on the last couple of days' happenings. I told him about my upcoming trip to New York and my big commercial. He was happy for me. He said he would be back in LA by the time I finished shooting my commercial, and we made tentative plans to get together the last week of September or the first week of October.

I spent most of the week with James, truly enjoying all the attention he was giving me. He seemed to have genuinely missed me, and it was nice of him to loan me the MGM apartment during my trip to New York.

Elvis' schedule didn't allow us to get together before New York, so we planned on the first weekend of October. We'd confirm our plans for Palm Springs when I was in New York.

James and I spoke on the phone every day while I was gone. He was reeling me in more and more firmly than before. Not only was he the only eligible bachelor of the three men I was seeing, but he was by far the most intriguing.

The next two weeks working on the Loving Care commercial were so hectic I didn't have time to miss anyone. It was hard work being a model, and it certainly wasn't as glamorous as most people would like to believe. But my biggest complaint was my aching feet; all that walking did me in. After two weeks in the Big Apple, I was ready to go back to LA.

James picked me up at the airport, something he didn't often do. I guess my not being available to him at all times made me more appealing. That first night home with James was special, and I felt like we really belonged together.

Meanwhile, Steve wanted me to meet him in Palm Springs, which I thought would be a great idea, since it was easier to make an excuse to James about where I would be. We made arrangements to meet again.

I loved Palm Springs, and visited every chance I had. Steve's house was on a hillside in an enclave of five homes called Southridge. A private road led to the homes and a guardhouse protected the entrance. The enclave included Bob Hope's mushroom-shaped house with panoramic views, and his other neighbor was Frank Sinatra. Steve's house was very modern, with wonderful views and a lot of garages. I was met at the door by my rugged movie star.

"Hi baby, glad you're here," he said as he greeted me with a hug and a kiss. He was smiling from ear to ear, and so was I. It wasn't long before we were fooling around on his king-sized bed, beneath which he kept a loaded sawed-off shotgun. Steve had been traumatized by the Manson Family's murder spree in August 1969, when two of his friends were killed: actress Sharon Tate and hairstylist Jay Sebring.

I met Jay shortly after I arrived in Los Angeles. He was a gentleman, and loved women. He once took me to a party at Roman Polanski and Sharon Tate's home—the same house where Sharon and Jay and others were murdered.

It was later discovered that the Manson Family had a hit list of celebrities they intended to kill; Steve's name was on that list. We spoke a lot about the price of fame. In one way, fame afforded Steve many luxuries. The flip side of the coin was that fame brought with it many atrocious things. Steve had numerous threats made on his life.

We stayed in bed for what seemed like hours, making love, laughing, cuddling, settling back with a joint and a beer. Later, Steve took my hand and led me stark naked to the pool. We jumped in. We were happy and in a playful mood. The water felt great in the heat.

Steve later gave me a tour of the house. I liked it. It was tastefully done—more beautiful than Elvis' or James' homes. It was professionally decorated in a modern style, with floor-to-ceiling windows and sliding glass doors. The house had beautiful art and furniture, which surprised me. I expected a more masculine-looking place from Steve. The house had two bedrooms upstairs, one downstairs and a separate guest house. Steve's bedroom had a porch, which looked out onto the courtyard and pool area below.

The two of us were getting hungry, so we hopped on Steve's big motorcycle and went to a great little Mexican restaurant in nearby Cathedral City.

After lunch, Steve drove me by his friend's motorcycle shop to catch up on the latest gossip. "Have you ever ridden a bike by yourself?" he asked.

"No, but I'd like to try." My answer brought a smile to his face.

He borrowed two dirt bikes from his friend, Bud Ekins, and we were off in a flash into the desert. Steve was a seasoned rider, absolutely fearless. I was trying to keep up with him and not let my little bike stall, which it often did, because I didn't know how to operate it.

Finally, after Steve had to circle back several times for me to restart the bike, he said in defeat, "OK baby, this is the last time I'm coming back for you. Don't keep letting the bike die. If you think it's going to die, rev it." The thought of being stranded even for a second terrified me. Steve had told me that he was once chased across the desert by a bitch coyote protecting her babies. That thought came to mind and from that moment on, I never let the bike die on me. Nothing like a little fear to keep you motivated.

When we arrived back at Steve's house, we were covered in dust. We tore off our clothes and jumped into the pool, and settled back with a beer and some quiet time together. It was wonderful to be with him. I truly enjoyed Steve's company, and didn't have a care in the world while I was with him.

I could tell that his faltering marriage lingered in the back of his mind, but I never questioned him about it. He was still weighing things, and trying to come to some sort of decision. Steve was basically a one woman man. Yes, he had his affairs and one night stands, but he loved having his main woman, Neile, at his side. Neile was Steve's security blanket. Knowing she was there felt good to him, and he didn't want to share her with anyone.

Everyone knows the temptations movie stars have with beautiful women constantly throwing themselves at them. The adulation and propositions get to them eventually. "You can only say 'no' so many times," Steve used to say.

Steve was genuinely happy to be with me, and he showed it by showering me with affection. That night we just hung out at home, loving and talking. We spoke specifically about *Junior Bonner*, and our experience together on the film. He liked the movie and was looking forward to seeing the finished product. He bragged to me a little, making me feel very special. We cuddled and finally fell asleep, content to be in each other's arms.

The next day we awoke early, sipped tea and looked at the

view from his balcony off the living room.

"What would you like to do today?" he asked me.

"I'd love to explore the mountains," I said without a moment's hesitation.

He was game, immediately suggesting that I put on my swimsuit and sandals so we could go for a sunny bike ride in the mountains. It sounded thrilling!

Steve produced a large Harley Davidson, and off we went. We headed up the mountain to Idyllwild, where we parked and smoked a joint while sitting on a big rock. We rested for awhile, then got back on the bike and headed to a town on the other side of Palm Springs, Desert Hot Springs, which is famous for its natural hot springs. The heat was beating down on us pretty good. It must have been around 110 degrees. Steve was handling it a lot better than me; several times he had to find water and hose me down. I was getting heat stroke.

We stopped at a local bar to grab a beer. Only one or two cars were parked in front of it. The place might have been dead outside, but inside it was jumping. It was packed with patrons swilling booze, dancing, laughing and having a real good time. Everyone stopped in their tracks and stared at us as we stood there in our bathing suits, with the sweat pouring off of us. We were quite a sight!

Steve and I were in complete shock. We did an about face and closed the door behind us, laughing.

"Baby, can you make it home?" Steve asked me.

The thought of his pool would have to carry me all the way home.

We made it back to the house, but both of us were exhausted. We chugged down several beers. Steve rubbed lotion on my sunburn, and I returned the favor.

Steve hinted about the possibility of our living together when we got back to Los Angeles. When we were together, it felt so right.

And yet, I preferred James' manners and social grace. I think I learned more from James than any other man about how to behave properly. James also led the kind of lifestyle I wanted for myself. In some ways Steve could have been my brother, we were so much alike. We were both P.W.T., affectionately known as "poor white trash." (Those words never ruffled my feathers; I'd heard them often growing up.)

Slowly but surely Steve was falling for me, even though he was aware of the other men in my life. He seemed a little bit more jealous of Elvis than of James, and referred to E as a "guitar hick." In retaliation, Elvis called Steve a "motorcycle hick." The two men were very alike in some ways.

I knew if I decided to live with Steve, that there could be no other men in my life. Maybe I could give up James and Elvis for Steve. Could Steve give up every one else for me? I doubt it. Steve was going through a restless time in his life, and he became increasingly more withdrawn as he got older.

But even though I adored Steve, there were a few things that bothered me about him. He could be crude, boorish and coarse. He would eat with his feet on the table, spit whenever he wanted to and cussed like a sailor when the mood hit him. His manners were rough, bordering on vulgar for lack of a better word. Elvis wasn't perfect either, but his polite Southern charm overshadowed any bad manners he might have had. James, however, was refined and was a breath of fresh air compared to the other two. He rarely lost his cool, and was in control most of the time. One of the few times he did lose his cool was when I discovered I was pregnant with Steve's child. The pregnancy was to be the back breaker in my relationship with James, even though we remained together on and off for another year.

But that last year was hellish as James Aubrey became obsessed with me, and gave into a get even mentality with me. The *Love* in *The Love Machine* was replaced by just the opposite: *hate*.

CHAPTER ELEVEN

Looking back, I think the fact that the three men in my life knew about each other made me more appealing—maybe more of a challenge to each of them. It's all in the way you play it, and I was the willing pawn.

Not that I used the fact that I was dating these three powerful men to make them jealous of one another. It wasn't something I planned on doing, but it definitely worked in my favor. Who wouldn't have done the same thing in my place? I was having fun.

I followed Steve from Palm Springs all the way into the downtown area off Interstate 5. The last thing I saw was his hand waving out the window, then he disappeared into traffic. I sure would miss him.

Once home, I kicked off my shoes and made my way to my lifeline: the telephone. I checked in with my answering service, and began returning my calls. I dialed MGM and asked for James. When he got on the phone, he sounded annoyed. Actually, he sounded pissed off. This was one of the few times when he wasn't his usual calm, in control self. His emotions seemed to be running high.

"Hi, Indian. What's up?" he said in a flat, abrupt tone.

He knew I was returning his call, but he wanted to show his displeasure. James was dying to know more intimate details of my life, but he wasn't going to give me any satisfaction by asking. He once told me the bird-in-the-hand story: If you close your fist too tightly, the bird will die trying to get free; if you allow the bird some room to breathe, some freedom, it will stay. That was James' philosophy, but he didn't like it to be mine.

Miffed or not, James asked me to have dinner with him at La Scalla in Beverly Hills, a favorite hangout for the rich and famous. I dined there frequently with Ed Garner and his Beverly Hills brat pack friends. The staff knew me by name.

That night when I walked into La Scalla, I was greeted with a big smile and handshake by the maitre'd, then led to James' table. After being seated, I spotted my friend, Freddie Fields, and he came over to say hello.

Freddie was one of the first super agents in Hollywood, and he was a living legend. He represented Steve McQueen, Paul Newman, Dustin Hoffman, Sidney Poitier, James Coburn and Barbara Streisand. Later he would become a successful producer, making *Victory* with director John Huston, and the Oscar-winning *Glory*.

James and Freddie were good friends, and in time, Freddie would become a friend of mine. He hosted a wonderful 31st birthday party for me at his house on the beach in Malibu. He and his first wife, actress Polly Bergen, would spend Christmas with James, Skye and me in Acapulco. Freddie taught me how to water ski. A man of many talents, that Freddie. Women especially found Freddie sexy.

He came over to my table to give me a hug and kiss, and the two of us waited for our dates. James arrived 10 minutes later, and the three of us sat there having a drink until Polly showed up. Freddie and Polly went to their table, leaving James and me alone. Having a drink with Freddie helped break the ice, and we warmed to each other without referring to our awkward telephone conversation earlier in the day.

James seemed as happy to see me as I was to be with him. We caught up on small talk while stuffing our faces. The wine kicked in, and the two of us began to relax. His hand was under the table, and he calmly let his fingers do the walking from my knee and slowly headed North. I smiled and squirmed a bit, feeling slightly embarrassed. He smiled back. It was a sign that he was ready for some lovin'. We ate quickly, paid the check and said our goodbyes. I followed him up the hill to Seabright.

We parked our cars side by side and entered the house the

same way. There were no more questions, and he didn't care about anything else at that moment. His mind was focused on one thing: sex! We quickly undressed each other and fell onto the bed.

Sex was always great with James. He had a trait that's rare in a man: His priority was always to satisfy me first.

"Jim Aubrey and me comparing raffle tickets at an MGM studios function." From the Barbara Leigh Collection.

When I got home the next morning, it wasn't long before the phone started ringing. It was Steve asking me to have dinner. I didn't have any definite plans, so I answered in the affirmative.

How could I keep things straight with three men in my life? I could easily live in the now, without a commitment to or from any one of them—credit Ram Dass for that. I was as free to do what I wanted as they were.

The 1970s were a time period for female independence. Many women in the country had romantic adventures without having feelings of guilt. In a way, it was our first taste of personal power. We didn't have to marry to experiment and enjoy sex.

Of course, with Elvis, I had Priscilla to think about, but she was having her own affair with her karate instructor. Steve had Neile, but he was legally separated and getting a divorce. James was single and it all made sense to me. I have a few regrets, though I would handle some situations differently now. I was having the time of my life because I loved all the attention. We were all juggling romances and playing the dating game.

Unlike James, Steve came to my apartment to pick me up. He arrived promptly at six, with a six-pack of Budweiser in hand. We started for Malibu, to his favorite restaurant. After dinner, we headed to his place, which was only a few minutes away. Once again, Steve brought up the subject of our living together. I gave the idea some thought, but I wasn't ready to give up Elvis or James. With Elvis, his being still married kept our relationship in perspective. With James, even though I knew he was committed to staying single, deep inside I hoped that marriage was possible. With Steve there was a feeling of "this is my old man," but there was something missing. I couldn't quite put my finger on it, but we were too much alike. I preferred the challenge James represented. I was young and naive, with no direction. I was living in a fantasy world.

I got home in time to receive one of Joe Esposito's late-night calls. "Hi Barbara. Elvis wanted me to call and set a time aside for tomorrow so he could talk with you."

"I'll be home all day," I said. "Call me anytime that he can talk."

Joe asked if I could go to Palm Springs in the morning.

"Jim Aubrey and me dressed up for another night on the town." From the Barbara Leigh Collection.

I told him I had the whole weekend open.

"I'm not sure when we can get back to you, but be prepared to leave at a moment's notice," Joe said.

That was the way it was with Elvis. Sometimes you had an elaborate plan, other times it was at a moment's notice. I hung up the phone and relaxed for the rest of the evening. I drew a hot bath, lit a few candles and enjoyed some quiet.

While I was in the tub, the phone rang. It was late, and I wondered who it could be. I jumped out, water pouring off me, and ran into the bedroom. It was Steve.

"Hi, I just wanted to say good night and that I miss you, baby."

"I was in the tub," I said, and we both laughed. He made a joke about coming over to wash my back.

"I'm not sure I'm up for that," I joked. We both knew very well it wasn't my back he wanted to wash. Besides, I was tired and wasn't in the mood for company, regardless of who it was.

"Get a good night's sleep and I'll call you back tomorrow," Steve said.

As soon as we hung up, I got back into the tepid tub. I got out and literally fell into bed, exhausted. My body and mind cried out for rest. From the time that I first met James until the end of our relationship, my life was a whirlwind; a nonstop merry-go-round.

The next morning I woke up feeling refreshed. What a good night's rest won't do for the body! I put on a pot of coffee, turned on the radio and sat back without a care in the world.

It was still early morning, and no one had called yet. I could drink my coffee in peace. I wasn't sure if Elvis would call, but I was optimistic because Joe told me so.

The phone rang as I finished dressing. It was Joe. Perfect timing.

"I've got E here for you," Joe said.

"Wow, you're up early," I commented. "I'm surprised to hear Elvis is up, too." We both laughed and he put Elvis on the phone.

Never one to beat around the bush, Elvis got right down to business, "Hi honey, can you make it to Palm Springs?"

Right at that moment, my front doorbell rang. "E, can you hold on for a moment?

Someone's at my door."

"Sure, darlin'," he said politely.

I ran to the door, not wanting to keep The King waiting. When I opened the door, my roommate Jessica stood there looking as if she wanted to die.

"Come in," I said in hurriedly, "I've got Elvis on the phone." As a quick afterthought, I asked her, "What happened to you? You look awful!" I couldn't put it any other way.

"I broke it off with Freddie," she said in tears. Freddie was Fred Amsale, a Beverly Hills celebrity agent.

She looked so sad. I ran back to the phone and picked it up.

"Thanks for holding, Elvis."

"That's OK, darlin'. Can you be at the airport and ready to go in two hours?" he asked.

"Yes," I replied. Then I looked over at Jessica, who was by now in a shambles. "Elvis, can I bring my girlfriend Jessica along? She's in a bad way. She just broke up with her boyfriend."

"Sure darlin', but I don't know where we'll put her. All of the guys are here with me." He thought for a second before speaking, then said, "Don't worry, Barbara. We'll manage. I can always put one of the guys on the couch."

"E, thank you so much. You are too kind," I had to tell him.

"Now, don't you be late OK? Hurry, cause I can't wait to see you!" he said, then put Joe back on the phone to arrange the details.

I walked back into the living room to give Jessica the news.

"Guess what?" I said, trying to contain my excitement.

"What?" she said with a sniffle.

"I'm flying to Palm Springs to spend the weekend with Elvis, and he said I can bring you." Her face lit up like a Christmas tree, the tears replaced with a huge smile. There wasn't anything I could have said that would have made her feel better.

Jessica was so excited, she instantly forgot about Freddie. "What shall I wear? What should I take?" Her excitement was contagious.

"You look great in anything. Whatever you'd like, but no jeans. Elvis hates jeans on a woman," I said.

Jess was a huge Elvis fan, having met him once years earlier by actually knocking on his front door in Bel Air. Surprisingly, he let her in. She had a great Elvis collection of records and memorabilia.

We were both in a state of euphoria, and Jess wanted to smoke a joint to settle her nerves.

"Elvis doesn't permit smoking marijuana so we can't take any with us, but I have some mescaline. Do you want to share some?" We both decided it might add some adventure to our journey, so we split the half and took it. Like LSD, mescaline is a drug used to induce hallucinations.

We hurriedly packed our things and headed for the jet. The pilot was waiting for us. Once in the air, I caught up with Jessica on her breakup with Freddie. The mescaline had us buzzing pretty good. In hindsight, I realize it wasn't a good idea to have taken drugs, knowing how Elvis felt about them. The guilt began to take effect, and I asked Jessica not to mention to Elvis that we had taken anything.

"He's dead set against drugs," I said to her. That was a laugh, because Elvis was hooked on prescription drugs. Because they were prescription, he never considered them addicting, but Elvis' prescription drugs were far more potent than most street drugs.

Joe and Charlie Hodges were waiting for us at the air strip in Palm Springs. I introduced Jessica to them and we piled in Elvis' big black Mercedes. The car reeked of gas fumes, which made Jessica and me feel slightly nauseated. By now, Jessica's mind was completely off Freddie. She was ready to meet The King. October 2, 1971 was a day that Jessica St. John will never forget.

A few minutes later we were at Elvis' house. We jumped out, barely waiting for the car to stop. Jessica and I headed for the front door, with Joe at our side. Joe opened the door with me following closely behind, bouncing with excitement into the living room where E was waiting. He stood up with a big smile and outstretched arms. I ran into those beautiful arms for a much-needed hug.

"You look beautiful, darlin'" he commented, making me feel so happy and important. We embraced and kissed gently on the lips. Then I introduced him to Jessica.

"Elvis, this is my good friend, Jessica. She also happens to be your No. 1 fan."

It was quite an introduction.

Elvis held out his hand to her, "Hello Jessica, welcome to Palm

Springs. I'm glad you could make it." Jessica was between cloud nine and heaven.

There was something odd about Elvis, but I couldn't quite put my finger on it. His hair looked different, as if he'd been given a very bad haircut. Even so, he still looked like a million bucks. He was dressed in his usual attire, all decked out in his black pants, high collared shirt and precious medals hanging from his neck. He had added something new to his normal wardrobe, though: four-inch leather cuffs on both wrists. I thought it was odd, but with Elvis, anything went. He was also fidgeting with an enormous flashlight. He liked having something in his hands; I guess it helped alleviate his nervous energy.

After introducing Jessica to the guys, we settled down on the couch next to Elvis. I noticed a gleam in a member of the Memphis Mafia's eyes as he ogled Jessica. I chuckled inside, because I knew he didn't have a prayer. She was a one man woman, and even though she had just broken off with Freddie, there was no way she would switch her emotions so rapidly. No, the guys could just wish for now. They would once again be forced to watch Elvis and me romance each other. Years later after Elvis died, Jessica met up again with Joe and they had a brief affair, and remained good friends.

I wasn't too concerned that Elvis might be attracted to Jessica. Even though she was beautiful, she was too tall and too much of an intellectual for him.

He needed someone he could mold into a sweet, unassuming pupil. After all, Elvis saw himself as a Svengali, and strong women were a threat to him. Jessica could be combative, speaking her mind when she felt the need to, and that was something Elvis would not accept. Not that she would have displayed this behavior with E, but the possibility was definitely there. Actually, they got along great. Elvis recognized her admiration for him, which was exactly what he wanted.

Elvis was happy to see me. We sat and talked, neither of us pursuing the topic of Steve McQueen or *Junior Bonner*. The whole time we were talking, Elvis kept tugging on his hair, and I kept wondering what it was about him that was wrong.

Our conversation switched to E's new karate moves, and since Charlie Hodges was in the room, he was the perfect demonstration partner. Sweet Charlie. By this time, Charlie was so used to the routine that he just went along with the program. He seemed to be a little bored by it all, rolling his eyes when Elvis first mentioned sparring with him. Oh well, he was a good sport, if not a well paid sport, and a friend.

Elvis and Charlie excused themselves to don white gees for one of E's famous demonstrations. Jess was outside with one of the guys, looking at the view, but they both came back just as Elvis and Charlie began the exhibition.

Elvis was good at his karate moves, and executed them with precision. He was very limber back then—before he put on the pounds. His hands were beautiful and graceful. He was a natural. If he had been serious about the sport, and I don't mean in the way he thought he was, he could have been a heck of a fighter. He bragged about his black belts, but they were mostly honorary. I know, because a few years later, I married a great karate champion, Joe Lewis. I had the opportunity to watch real black belt competitors.

For Elvis, though, karate was mostly a fun thing to do to pass the time. He laughed up a storm, giving Charlie a good scare with close kicks to the face.

During one of Elvis' high kicks, something flew off his head. There was dead silence. Now I knew what was odd about him: He had been sporting a wig all day. For a couple of seconds, we all panicked. Everyone was afraid to say anything. Elvis calmly walked over to the wig, picked it up and laughingly put it back on his head to continue with the demonstration.

We all laughed after we got the cue from Elvis that it was OK to do so. I'd seen everything now! There was no doubt about it; the man was unique. The wig was just a new toy for him, along with the wrist guards and flashlight. He got bored easily, and picked up new hobbies to maintain his interest in life.

Another hobby he picked up while I was around was collecting guns.

After E exhausted himself with his karate moves, he decided he would go to his favorite gun store and show off his knowledge of firearms. He changed from his gee back into his regular clothes, and we all piled into the smelly Mercedes. Elvis, Joe and I were in the front while Jessica, Sonny and Charlie filled the back. The rest of the entourage followed in another car.

The thought that a gun was dangerous and could kill someone never crossed Elvis' mind, except when Priscilla left him for Mike Stone, and E wanted someone to "knock Stone off." To Elvis, a gun was a toy. Guns were macho—something to collect and display.

Our cars pulled up at the Palms Springs Frontier Gun Shop, which was a little house off the main street in Palm Springs, very close to where Elvis lived. The owner, a man Elvis nicknamed Tiny, actually was a huge man with a big belly and a hearty laugh.

Tiny was introduced to Elvis by Dick Grob, a Palm Springs police officer. Tiny was very taken by Elvis, but then again, who wasn't? Tiny would open his shop to Elvis at all hours to accommodate him, and not just because he wanted to sell Elvis guns, but because he genuinely enjoyed visiting with him. The King, with his elaborate clothing and his entourage, was a show all its own.

We piled out of the cars, with Elvis leading the pack. Tiny was waiting for us with an outstretched hand and a warm, toothy smile. He recognized dollar signs when he saw it.

"Glad to see you, Elvis," bellowed the huge man.

"Hi, Tiny. Did you lose any weight?" Elvis asked teasingly. As soon as Tiny laughed, the rest of the guys laughed as well.

"Well Elvis, let me show you some of the new merchandise I think you're gonna like," Tiny said, letting the show proceed.

The first handgun Elvis was shown was a Berretta, which he immediately fell in love with. He fondled and caressed the weapon as if it were a woman. He acted as if he knew what he was doing, loading and unloading the magazine clip. It was quite impressive. The gun would end up in his huge collection, never to be fired.

A few other customers were wandering around inside Tiny's. One couple stands out in my mind. They were young and, by their appearance, obviously didn't have much money. Actually, they were quite shy. The young man must have been in his late teens or early 20s and he was holding a rifle, peering through the scope with one eye open. It was clear that he was only going to look that day, not buy. However, with Elvis Presley in the building, anything was possible.

Out of the corner of his eye, Elvis noticed the young man as he showed the rifle to his bride.

"Do you like the rifle?" the calm, composed rock star asked the young man.

A little stunned, the young man responded, "I love it," and proceeded to show Elvis the rifle's features.

When he finished talking, Elvis said, "It's yours." The young man's mouth fell open; he was at a loss for words. Elvis yelled out, "Tiny, I'm buying this rifle," and Tiny dutifully added the rifle to Elvis' growing list of guns.

"Hey, thank you, thank you," the young man said, fumbling to shake Elvis' hand.

He repeated it over and over again, unable to believe that Elvis Presley, the man, the legend, The King, had bought him this incredibly expensive rifle. Elvis liked making people's dreams come true and to E's credit, he always did it with class. How could you not help but love a man like that?

E walked over to me and asked, "So darlin', did you find something you like?"

Elvis obviously wanted to buy me a gun. "Thanks Elvis," I said, "but I really don't know the first thing about guns." Actually, I hated guns, but I couldn't tell Elvis that. They scared me, but if Elvis Presley wants his girl to have a gun, she was going to have a gun. What the heck, I thought, make him happy. He bought me a Colt that he thought could protect me, yet was small and simple to use. He also purchased a pair of Dueling Derringers that he thought were cute.

Whenever Elvis was in a buying mood, he spent his money until he got bored. Whoever happened to be in his presence usually ended up with whatever the object was that Elvis wanted to buy. After presenting me with the two Derringers, he tired of the buying spree and bid Tiny farewell. Joe settled the bill, and we all piled back into the Mercedes and the other cars with our new guns in tow. The way Elvis held his gun when we came out of that store, you would have sworn we were the Clyde Barrow Gang ready to knock off another bank!

Once again, Joe, Elvis and I sat in the front while Jessica, Sonny and Charlie rode in the back. I snuggled close to Elvis as he fondled one of his new guns. Joe looked over at me and winked. He got a kick out of watching Elvis' childlike enthusiasm.

E was happy. He had a new toy gun, and he'd gotten to play Santa Claus. And to top it off, he had me and Jess to show off for. What more could he want?

When we got back to the house, Elvis and I headed straight to the bedroom.

Although in many ways he was shy, there were times when Elvis could be aggressive. Once the bedroom door was closed, we went into a lover's embrace, kissing passionately. It was something I adored doing, and Elvis was a legendary kisser. Those pouting lips gave him an edge that no other man could touch.

Elvis excused himself to freshen up in the bathroom. Knowing him, that meant he was probably taking a "little upper" to help him through the rest of the evening. I didn't understand why he needed a lift, because he was naturally energized. Looking back, I think a lot of it was out of habit. He thought that by taking uppers he could control his energies more effectively.

We didn't get around to making love. The night was young and we would end up back in the bedroom, so why rush things? Besides, Elvis was on a roll. He had a "new girl" and he was going to do his Elvis thing and teach, preach and have some fun. I didn't mind sharing him with my friend. I even enjoyed watching the play.

By this time in my relationship with Elvis, I knew the routine; I had it down pat. It was pretty much the same with Steve. Both of them were simple men when it came right down to it—simple, and yet complex. Their routines were easy to figure out; what went on inside of their heads was a different story. James, well, he was altogether a different story.

James was the wild card of the bunch, totally unpredictable. He liked going out in public. He liked to interact with the entertainment world, not keep it away. Elvis and Steve had very private inside worlds apart from entertainment, private worlds that revolved completely around themselves.

Elvis came out of the bathroom with a big smile. It was show time. We headed for the living room, where everyone was waiting.

Charlie got up from the couch and put on the album *Where Does Love Go*, by Charles Boyer. Yes, Charles (*Gaslight*) Boyer, the actor. I'd heard Elvis play the album in Las Vegas, and he gave the title song his own interpretation, complete with grand gestures, but I had enjoyed it so much then that I loved hearing him do it again. Elvis had even given me a copy of the album, so I knew it by heart. Once the song began, Charlie started clowning around, lip synching to the words and acting silly, which made Elvis crack up. Elvis even got into the act. Jessica and I laughed aloud with the two of them, which encouraged them to continue.

Once the song was finished, someone mentioned that he was hungry and we ordered a quick dinner. The major effects of the mescaline were long gone, but I could still faintly feel it. After dinner, Elvis continued showing off for Jessica. He talked briefly to her about her boyfriend. Freddie was twice Jessica's age, and also was a confirmed bachelor. He was a lot like James in that regard. Elvis, the voice of reason, offered her some simple advice.

"Dump him, honey," E said, mincing no words. "He's not the man for you. You can get anyone you want, and you deserve better."

Hearing that from Elvis was just what she needed. Jessica wiped the tears from her eyes and managed to say with a smile, "Thanks Elvis." He talked with her awhile and his genuine concern, voiced in his soft-spoken way, helped her to see the light. Plus, if Elvis Presley tells you to dump someone, that's a pretty good impetus to go through with it.

Elvis excused himself and went off to his bedroom.

He wasn't at his best this weekend. He had started putting on weight from his prescription drugs, and appeared bloated. By this time, Elvis had discovered the book, *The Physician's Desk Reference,* a huge encyclopedia of medication and its effects.

From the day he first laid eyes on the book, it never left his side.

It was a book that changed his life forever, and sadly, it was a change for the worse. The book made Elvis believe that he was in control of his drug usage, because he knew the causes and effects. For Elvis, it was the beginning of a road that would end in tragedy.

CHAPTER TWELVE

I want to make something perfectly clear as I saw it: Elvis felt he was in total control of his use of prescription drugs. He believed he knew and understood the effects of the narcotics he took. He gave his "girls"—including me—prescription drugs because he wanted us to be on the same level as he was. He didn't do it to get us high and take advantage of us, he just wanted us to be 100 percent with him in whatever he did. His intent was good. Unfortunately, the effects were not. Which leads me to what happened next.

When Elvis came back from the bedroom, I was still sitting on the couch where he'd left me. He discreetly slipped something into my hand. It was a gray capsule. I had a slight headache, and had casually mentioned this to Elvis.

"Here, honey," he whispered, "take this for your headache."

As was the norm in our relationship, I never asked Elvis why or what, I simply obeyed whatever he said, trusting him completely. Knowing that I still had mescaline in me, I was afraid to add the mysterious pill to my already drug-laden system. So when E wasn't looking, I stuck the capsule in between the pillows of the couch, and faked swallowing it.

Elvis brought out his prized collection of police badges, along with a photo of himself and then President Richard Nixon in the White House. The picture is famous today, and Elvis was extremely proud of it. Elvis had wanted Nixon to know that he thought drugs were ruining the youth of our country, and if there was anything Citizen Presley could do for President Nixon, all he had to do was ask.

If you look closely at the picture, you'll notice that Elvis' eyes are glazed over from the many drugs he had ingested that day. If only Elvis would have taken his own advice.

Elvis had also wanted to meet President Nixon because he wanted a special governmental badge that was extremely rare. Elvis proceeded to tell us about his special trip to Washington, D.C. The guys had heard the story about 10,000 times before and were bored to tears, but E had a captivated audience in Jessica and me and that was all he needed. At some point, Jessica went outside with Sonny, who was definitely showering some much-needed attention on her.

The night was getting late and I was fading fast. An involuntary yawn from me brought Elvis to attention.

"I've got something for that," he offered, and he proceeded to go to his bedroom for another gray pill.

"Oh, Elvis, I'm fine. Really, I don't need it," I said in my most convincing tone. My words had no effect on him, and he handed me the pill and his bottle of Mountain Valley Spring Water. Like a good doctor, he watched me take the dose, and this time I couldn't fake it. He was watching me with owl eyes.

I washed the pill down. Again, I took it because I thought Elvis would never give me anything that would be bad for me. I had blind trust when it came to Elvis.

We settled back down on the couch and played a game in which we whispered into each other's ear, purposely not talking to anyone else. It was a game for just the two of us; a game for lovers. I wanted this night to end so that the two of us could retreat to his bedroom, where I would have him all to myself. I couldn't believe that he wasn't tired yet. Elvis usually wore out everyone else, and was the last person to call it a night.

Jessica and Sonny came back in from the patio and, because she was the new person in the group, Elvis went through his usual repertoire of showing off, exhausting everyone else in the process. I began feeling dizzy and nauseated. At first, I tried to hide it from Elvis. He couldn't deal with adversity like a normal person. Everything and everyone had to be upbeat and positive. Elvis was not good at noticing other peoples' problems, and even worse at handling them. That's where Joe came in. Whatever the problem, Joe stepped in and took care of it, which was why he was indispensable to Elvis. Joe knew Elvis better than anyone else, and usually was there working the problem before Elvis even took notice.

As the night wore on, it became harder for me to breathe. My palms were moist and my face was flushed. Elvis took notice of my worsening condition and asked, "Darlin, are you OK?"

"Elvis, I'm not feeling very well." I was honest with him, knowing that he wasn't going to like my answer, but I felt like death warmed over. I'm sure I looked the part, too.

By this time, Joe had also picked up on my color.

"You need to lay down," Joe said. Laying down sounded great. That was, if I could make it to the bedroom.

With my last bit of strength, I asked E's permission to be dismissed. There was still a protocol that had to be adhered to.

"Elvis, do you mind if I lay down for a few minutes?"

"No darlin', go ahead," he said with concern. However, I could tell he was a bit annoyed. He wanted his woman next to him, no matter what. It was as if he was in complete if there wasn't a woman by his side. But at least he had Jessica, and her undivided attention.

Joe graciously helped me to the bedroom. Once my head hit the pillow, the room started to spin. God, I felt sick! Joe was wonderful, putting a wet wash cloth on my forehead. He turned out the lights and closed the door, coming back every 20 minutes to check on me.

Elvis, on the other hand, went on with the show.

He did keep tabs on me through Joe, though. Whenever Joe visited me in the bedroom, he would report back to E—who perhaps was feeling a little guilty about giving me the pills. It's not uncommon for people to have reactions to medicine, but Elvis fancied himself an expert when it came to doling out prescription drugs. However, since he didn't know about the mescaline in my system, my worsening condition baffled him.

After the third trip to the bedroom, Joe asked me if I had taken something in addition to the gray pill. I came clean, and confessed to him about the mescaline. I also made him swear on his mother's grave not to tell Elvis.

As sick as I was, I knew the night was shot. Making love was out of the question. I couldn't even hold my head up, so how could I concentrate on making Elvis happy? At this stage in his life, Elvis' sex drive was beginning to wane from all the drugs in his system. I felt totally depressed. Another obstacle.

Jess, on the other hand, was having the time of her life. She was the only female, a true fan, fitting right in with this group of playful guys. Now she could have Elvis all to herself. One door closes, another one opens.

The evening lagged on, and Elvis began to check on me himself. He was very sweet, but I could tell he wasn't happy. I had let him down. When Elvis finally came to bed, I mustered all of the energy I could to pretend that I was better. But believe me, I wasn't. We talked for a bit while we waited for his sleeping pill took to kick in, then we both fell asleep. I wasn't in the mood for cuddling or anything else; I just wanted to stay warm, which wasn't an easy thing to do because Elvis' room was, as usual, ice cold.

"Morning darlin'," Elvis said sweetly the next morning. "Feeling better?"

"Kind of, but I feel a little hung over. Do you mind if I stay in bed a little longer?" Once again, my honesty took over, but only because it was so early and I was caught off guard. If I had had my senses about me, I would have lied about my condition.

Elvis tried to fake a sincere reply, "No, you rest and I'll send Joe to look after you."

I knew that Elvis already had Joe on the phone making arrangements for my replacement to fly in, to take care of The King in the manner to which he was accustomed. At this point it really didn't matter to me, because I was too sick to care. I just wanted to get back to Los Angeles.

Jessica and the guys were already up. Elvis persistently quizzed

Jess about what I had taken the day before, denying to himself that what he gave me could have brought this on.

It was decided (by Elvis, I'm sure) that it was best for the two of us to cut our trip short and fly back home. I was relieved, because I didn't want Elvis to remember me like this. A woman always had to be at her best for The King. Elvis sent Joe in to give me the news, and I accepted it graciously. Joe helped me pack my things and as we opened the bedroom door, Elvis was there to say goodbye. He kissed me sweetly and said he'd call me later in the evening. Fine, I thought, please just get me home.

Joe drove us to the waiting plane, and I must confess, it looked awfully good to me. It would take me to where I wanted to be—home. I realized something amazing on this trip—life with Elvis Presley, the most exciting entertainer to have ever lived, could be boring. Elvis had a routine, and after awhile it became tiresome. I could pretty much predict what was going to happen before it actually did. It was a full-time job to keep Elvis Presley happy, and on this particular trip, I had let him down. My appeal had diminished in his eyes.

This was the turning point in our relationship. I had allowed myself to become a downer, and that wasn't tolerated in the Kingdom.

The flight home was uneventful. Jessica was ecstatic, rambling on and on about the weekend. I wasn't listening very closely, because I was still sick. Luckily for me, Jessica was there to drive me home. When I arrived at the apartment, I headed straight for the bedroom.

It took me the rest of Sunday and Monday to fully recover from my escapade in Palm Springs.

On Tuesday night, I met James for a drink at the famous Polo Lounge in the Beverly Hills Hotel. It was an exciting place to meet. In those days, business deals were struck between studio executives and agents on cocktail napkins. Stars were in abundance, and it was a great place to bump into someone who could do wonders for your career. After drinks, the two of us headed over to Chasen's for dinner.

At Chasen's, we were seated in a big leather booth. The trick was to tip the host or hostess so that they would seat you in a booth where everyone coming and going could see you.

That evening, William Holden strolled by and said hello to James. The two were friends, and James asked him to join us. I was thrilled, because I had adored William Holden. He was so handsome, manly and polite, and I couldn't take my eyes off of him. We ordered a round of drinks and I just sat there taking in every word he uttered, remembering him as he was in *The World of Suzy Wong*.

The two talked about a movie project in which they were both interested. During dinner, Bill spoke about his ranch in Africa, which he had just started to develop. The ranch became a labor of love that he worked on together with his girlfriend, actress Stephanie Powers.

Bill was wearing an elephant hair bracelet, the likes of which I had never seen before. I couldn't get over the fact that it was elephant hair, because it felt so fine and smooth. Later, Bill remembered how taken I was with his bracelet and sent me one from Africa via James. Although I thoroughly enjoyed his company, Bill Holden was a sad man who drank too much. Ten years later when I heard about the horrible way he died—bleeding to death alone in his bedroom, after falling backwards in a drunken stupor and hitting his head on the night table—I couldn't help but think of that night in Chasen's with James, and how sweet he was to me.

After we finished with dinner, James and I spent the night at a motel. Earlier that evening, James had locked his house with the keys inside. Since it was too late for a locksmith, and he wasn't about to break a window, we agreed to spend the evening in a motel down the street from Chasen's. In a way it was exciting because it wasn't the same old routine, and all I really cared about was being with James. He never once asked me where I had been all weekend, even after leaving several messages with my answering service. "Don't ask, don't tell" was our policy long before Bill Clinton made it a national catch phrase.

The next morning, James went up the hill to meet a locksmith. I went back to my apartment and spent the next couple of days auditioning for commercials. I was cast for ads for Kleenex tissue and for Modess feminine hygiene products.

"James Aubrey and me during a movie premiere. James was quite a catch, but also quite a challenge." From the Barbara Leigh Collection.

My hard work kept my mind off the embarrassing incident in Palm Springs. I later found out from other books that similar incidents had happened to a couple of Elvis' "girls." No wonder he distanced himself from me. After reading other people's accounts,

I can better understand how he must have felt some fear and responsibility about the consequences he might have faced, had anything serious happened to anyone to whom he had given drugs. He was lucky that none of the girls died, although there was one very serious life threatening incident in Las Vegas that has been well documented.

Steve called, and we made a dinner date for Friday. When he arrived he produced his usual joint and six-pack of Budweiser, which we managed to consume before going out for dinner.

Steve was still struggling with his dilemma as far as his marriage was concerned, but he wasn't willing to give me up. Surprisingly, we were closer than ever. That went for James and me as well. As for Elvis and me, we needed time to forget the unpleasant weekend in Palm Springs. Knowing Elvis as I did, something would have to happen to put me back into his good graces, but that would only happen on his terms.

As a couple, Steve and I became more comfortable with each other, but things got complicated again when he brought up the subject of our living together. I definitely didn't say no, but I didn't say yes, either. He was a hard man to turn down, especially because he usually got his way. We were also extremely compatible sexually and I could be myself around Steve. I felt secure knowing that he truly wanted me. We played around and joked in the same manner, and his humor was very dry and corny, but endearing. Elvis possessed a wonderfully funny and often child like sense of humor that I adored. And then there was James, who had *no* sense of humor at all. His sophistication wouldn't allow him to be anything but arrogant.

Steve and I liked to do many of the same things, and I think he was as comfortable around me as I was with him. We had a lot going for us, but he was putting me in the uncomfortable position of having to pick between him and James.

"Steve, I enjoy living alone, I need my space. Living together is not something I'm ready for right now," I told him in a tone that was sympathetic, yet firm. Living alone has always been a luxury to me.

I'm the first one to admit that I'm not easy to live with, chiefly because of my compulsion to have things clean and sparkling. It was something ingrained in me at the orphanage, where it was a daily chore to deep clean. I have carried this to an extreme at times.

Luckily, he didn't press any further, and we spent the rest of the evening hanging out at his tiny guest house.

I left Steve's place early the next morning. I had plenty of things to do on Saturday before I was to meet James for a dinner party being given for Dolly and Dick Martin at producer Bill Blasco's house. Dick was a friend of James, and a very funny man in real life as well as on television. He co-hosted *Rowan & Martin's Laugh In*. The television show was very hip and popular in the late 1960s and early 1970s. Dolly Martin was formerly Dolly Read, a 19-year-old *Playboy* bunny. Her Playmate pictorial appeared in the May 1966 issue titled "Bunny from Britain." She later starred in Russ Meyer's controversial cult film *Beyond The Valley of the Dolls*.

Before the dinner, I helped Jessica move into her new apartment in West Hollywood, and we also spent a good part of the day shopping. By the time we finished around 5:30 p.m., I finally had my place all to myself again. It felt good. I showered, dressed for the party and drove to James' house. He was already dressed and drinking a vodka on the rocks. I declined his offer of a drink and we drove to Stone Canyon.

Bill Blasco was a gracious and flamboyant host, and he made sure that all of his parties, large or small, were memorable. He served only the best wines and food to the Beverly Hills elite.

Months later Bill and James would have a falling out, because of an intimate dinner party that Bill had invited me to when James was away on business in New York. This dinner party was cleverly disguised as a prelude to an orgy. Even though James had tried in vain to involve me a few times with himself and other women, he became furious when I told him of the events that unfolded at Bill's party. What I had witnessed shocked me—a menage a trois with two men and a well known singer/actress. They invited me to join them, but I declined.

Bill was a little out of control that night. He produced some high quality drugs, such as cocaine and marijuana, for his dinner guests. I don't remember doing cocaine at his house, but it was definitely around. He lived a very wild life. Sadly, a few years later, he died in a car crash while in his beloved white Rolls Royce.

Steve and I got together a few more times during the following week. He had moved from his guest house in Pacific Palisades into a small house on Mulholland Drive near Coldwater Canyon. This is where he lived when he started dating Ali MacGraw, who also had a place nearby. Only a large field separated their homes, which were just a few hundred feet away from each other.

More and more, Steve began showing his irritation with me when his phone calls weren't returned promptly. Once I had my evenings or weekends planned, I didn't always return calls. I discovered it was easier to call back afterwards, ready to plan the next date, without having to make excuses for a date I couldn't make.

Although he knew about James, he was getting fed up with being "worked" into my schedule, and he let me know it.

When Steve and I got together on the weekend of October 23, he once again gave me the dreaded ultimatum: Was it him or James? His mind was made up; he was splitting up with Neile for good this time. It wasn't a marriage proposal, but it was a big step for him. It must have been a horrible decision for him to leave Neile and the kids, because Steve was always happiest when talking about his children. Unfortunately, they couldn't help him with his personal demons.

Steve and I went back to his new place on Mulholland. I thoroughly enjoyed dating all three men and, I must admit, I was greedy. I didn't want to give up any of them. After all, what woman in her right mind would? The sex was more passionate than ever. Steve knew that it would be difficult for me to leave James, but he had enough confidence in himself that he would be able to talk me into it, and he was right, I said yes. My answer made him so happy—for the moment. He hated to be alone.

I spent the rest of the night in his arms, cuddling and feeling very needed and wanted. I loved looking at Steve's rugged face and examining his character lines. He loved my looks, too. I think I reminded him of Neile, and later, Ali MacGraw and Barbara Minty. The four of us are dark brunettes with exotic features. We all had the look that appealed to him. Even though he liked fooling around with "chippies"—that's what he called young, beautiful blondes—he married brunettes. I had never heard the word "chippie" before, but it was one that he liked using. I didn't like the sound of it, and obviously it made an impression on me because I've never forgotten it. To me, it was a put down. I don't think that Steve had a lot of respect for women in general.

The next morning I headed home for Westwood, skipping our usual morning tea. I needed coffee, and a lot of it. The thought of breaking up with James made me sick to my stomach. I got home just in time to be violently ill.

After I recovered, I checked with my answering service. There was a call from James, but my stomach needed to settle down before I could call him back. I made a pot of coffee. It didn't sit well with my stomach, but my body craved it. I went into the bedroom to lie down for just a minute, and slept until noon.

Finally, I made the dreaded phone call to James at his office. His secretary left me on hold for what seemed like an eternity, and I didn't know what to expect when he got on the line.

"Hi Indian, do you want to catch a movie later on?" he asked, sounding as pleasant as I had ever heard him. It only made it harder.

"I'm not sure. I'm feeling a little sick," I replied. I knew that I had to see him in person and break it off, just as I had promised Steve. It had to be done, soon. James, once again, threw me a curve ball by being so accommodating.

"That's OK, we'll stay in and have a quiet evening at home. How's that?" God, he was really making this so hard.

"I'd love that," I said, faking enthusiasm.

"See you at seven."

Seven o'clock seemed more like high noon.

By mid afternoon, I was beginning to feel better. I made some soup and sipped it slowly, thinking about what I was going to say to James, and how I would say it. I decided that I would tell him as soon as I walked in, so there would be no way he could work his magic on me and change my mind. Just the thought of packing up all of my clothes and loading them up in my car gave me a stomach ache all over again.

After several hours of worrying about my strategy, I was totally spent. This wasn't going to be easy. James always knew how to win in any situation.

It was time to get dressed and head up the hill to Doomsday. I dressed in a mini skirt, high heels and sweater. I applied James' favorite perfume, "Joy," to my neck and cleavage. I looked smart and confident and I was dressed for the part, but I was still uncertain as to how I should approach the situation. As I drove up the hill, I decided that I would just have to trust my instincts, and let things happen as they may. Be here now—oh, how I wished I didn't have to be here now.

Being with James had its moments, more often than not. Life with him was never boring. I saw him as my knight in shining armor, and that became clearer to me every day. How could I leave this man I loved so much, my dream lover, my father image? After all, he was what I had waited for my whole life, or so I thought.

As I pulled into James' driveway, I thought of the many times I had driven up that hill. I felt a little sad that this would be my last trip. His door was open; he always left it open for me. I took a deep breath and mustered all of my courage as I stoically walked in. There he was in all his splendor, sporting a big smile with arms wide open.

"Indian, come here. I've missed you so much," he said with sincerity and warmth. I could feel that he was genuinely happy to see me. He embraced me. My knees buckled, and I could hardly stand up. He knew what to say.

"James," was all I could manage to get out before his lips were on mine. Before I knew it, we were entangled in the most passionate lover's embrace. I could feel my body tingling and in an instant, my head was in the clouds.

"Indian, would you like a glass of wine?" he politely asked. His was already on the coffee table. In the background, I could see the flames flickering in the fireplace. The mood was set for romance, not for ending a relationship.

James went into the kitchen to pour my wine, while I walked into the bedroom to look around and take a fast peek in his closet. There were my clothes as always—lots of them, too. I turned around to see James standing behind me with my glass of wine in his hand. I took it and we clinked our glasses. I'm not sure why we toasted, other than the custom of "to you," but it was a romantic gesture on his part. A calculated move on his part? Perhaps.

He was smiling at me and telling me how beautiful I looked. He kept saying and doing all the right things, and I was trying to remember why I was there.

My birthday was approaching, and James told me that he had made reservations in Palm Springs for November 13 at our favorite hideaway, the Sierra Villas. He was excited, a rare display of joviality, which in turn got me excited about our trip. Then it hit me: If I were in Palm Springs on November 13, I wouldn't be with Steve. I needed to make up my mind once and for all, and to stop playing games with all three men. I was on a roller coaster flying through the air. Someday, that ride would have stop. Of course, it did.

Instead of his usual coldness, James was different on this night. He treated me decently, and I believe I brought out a softer side of him, a more affectionate side. The bottom line was that he didn't come with the baggage that the other two men still had in their lives.

I realized that I truly loved James Aubrey. Good or bad, he was the man I most wanted of the three. He was the only man in my life whom I had ever pursued. I should have run in the opposite direction and never looked behind me, but I was thinking with my heart, not with my head.

James never knew what my real intentions had been that night. My clothes remained in his closet. By spending the night with James, I was in effect giving up Steve. I felt a little saddened that I had broken my promise to Steve, but when it came right down to it, I didn't want to leave James. In the end I chickened out, and my decision had to be final. There was no turning back.

The Smiling Cobra had struck again.

CHAPTER THIRTEEN

Once I had made my decision, the pressure was off, I was able to relax and enjoy the rest of the evening with James. His housekeeper Anna had prepared a casserole, which we shared in a romantic candlelight dinner together. When James was in a good mood, he could be terribly charming and attentive. Charming and attentive described him perfectly this evening.

After we finished our meal, we crawled into bed, snuggling up close to each other. The warmth of our bodies was the only excuse we needed to make love for the rest of the night. Right then, there was no doubt in my mind: I had made the right decision.

After making love, I showered and put on the white cotton button-down shirt James had worn that day. I loved wearing his shirts to sleep in, because they smelled like him.

There were moments that night when I thought of Steve, but I quickly put those aside. I would think about Steve later, but not while I was falling asleep in James' arms.

The next morning, I stayed with James while he got ready for work. I slowly sipped my coffee in the bathroom, hanging out while he showered and shaved. I think I was avoiding going home to face the inevitable with Steve.

I began feeling a little nausea. I decided to head home as soon as possible. I threw on my clothes, kissed James goodbye and drove home. My stomach was churning. I poured myself a glass of Coke to settle my nausea, plunked myself down on the sofa and reached for the phone. The first call I made was to my gynecologist. I had begun to suspect that there was a reason besides stress for my frequent nausea. I made an appointment for the following week.

My second call was to my answering service, to retrieve my

messages. I had a few calls to return, but decided to put them off. Every time I thought of calling Steve, my heart started pounding and I would get sick all over again. No, I decided, I would wait for him to call me. Knowing him the way I did, it would be a matter of time.

By lunch I was feeling better and at last, I was hungry. I fixed myself a sandwich and returned my calls, but I wouldn't answer the phone. I still couldn't face Steve. Part of me didn't want to stop seeing Steve, because I loved and adored the man, but I also loved the freedom of seeing who I wanted. I knew I would miss him and our friendship tremendously, but I also thought that I had made the right decision. I felt that I had picked the right man for me. Actually, *none* of them proved to be right for me.

I took a bath, plotting what I would say to Steve. Would he be upset with me? I so hated the thought of anyone being angry with me that I went out of my way to avoid confrontations. It's something that I grew out of as I got older, I'm happy to say. It's a big responsibility always trying to be liked by everyone, and constantly trying to stay in other people's good graces. I'm sure my upbringing had a lot to do with my being a people pleaser.

I was mustering up the courage to call Steve when the phone rang. This time, I answered it.

"Hi baby, what are you doing?" Steve asked pleasantly.

"I'm just finishing my bath," I said just as politely.

"I'll be over in one hour," he stated, as if I had no say in the matter.

"OK," I said obligingly.

Well, that was easy. Too easy. Knowing the time was at hand, I felt slightly better. He was bright as a fox, that Steve. He didn't give me an opportunity to say no to him; he had already taken control of the situation. I think he must have known what was coming because he didn't ask, he just demanded to come over.

One hour later, Steve was knocking on my door. I took a deep breath, said to myself, "Tell him and get it over with," and opened the door.

There he was, standing with his hands on his hips and a big smile on his face—that wonderful boyish, crooked smile. He walked in and grabbed me, holding me in a very long embrace. As we let go, he asked me, "Well, what happened?"

I was caught. Nowhere to run and nowhere to hide. "Well," I stammered, "I couldn't do it, Steve. I tried, but I guess I'm just not ready yet."

He looked disappointed, but he didn't yell or come down hard on me. He simply said in a sullen voice, "I know it's difficult. It's OK, Barbara."

That was it. I was completely exhausted from the stress I'd put myself through, and he was letting me go so easily.

"I guess 'you're not ready yet' is an understatement." He paused for a moment and asked, "Do you need more time to think about it?"

"Yes," I almost shouted back. Damn! Why didn't I just say no and end it? I couldn't believe what was coming out of my mouth. What a little chickenshit I was!

In my head, I thought it was settled. In my heart, well, that was another story. Seeing Steve really threw me off guard and confused me. I still wanted him, but I wanted James, too.

In the past, when I wanted to break up with someone, I tried to create a situation where the man would have to be the bad guy. It demanded some well thought out strategy and was often tiresome, but very effective. My situation with Steve was totally different; I didn't really want to break up with him. How could I get him to see things my way? To let the sexual relationship end, without having to break up a friendship?

We sat on the couch drinking beer, feeling a little awkward with each other. I must have looked pretty sad, because Steve reached over and pulled me to him. We embraced and I let out a big sigh. He kissed me ever so sweetly, and asked if I would like to have dinner.

We phoned for a pizza. By this time, Steve was feeling a little down himself. He was under a lot of pressure in his tangled personal life. We really did like and respect each other and I couldn't believe he was being so sweet about the whole thing. Actually, I didn't know what to expect from him, but he was definitely making things a lot easier than I had anticipated.

We were starving by the time our pizza arrived and gobbled it down, catching up with each other's work projects. Steve was going to make Jim Thompson's *The Getaway* with Sam Peckinpah again. While we were filming *Junior Bonner*, Steve had given me a copy of the novel to read, hinting that perhaps we could do the film together. Of course, we all know what happened when he made that movie with Ali MacGraw.

After dinner, we both felt much better. We began necking on the couch, and before I knew it, we were in the bedroom making love.

Steve stayed the night, and left early the next morning, something he didn't normally do. We didn't make any definite plans, but we would be in touch. I would continue seeing Steve for a couple of more weeks. I guess you might say that I was reluctant to give him up. He wasn't ready to give me up, either, but our relationship had come to a close. It had become too real, not the fun, romantic, carefree, fantasy relationship we had enjoyed in Prescott.

The rest of the week was uneventful. I had a few interviews, and some acting classes at Jeff Corey's. James and I got together a few times as well. Over the weekend, I watched football with James and a group of men. He bet $100 for me, but if I lost, I had to pay up myself—nice guy! If I won, my good friend Nicky Blair had to pay me. Often, I was one of very few women at these football Sundays, sometimes the only one. I honestly enjoyed the game, and I must admit, I enjoyed the attention I received from James' friends. But having a bet riding on the game made it even more fun to watch.

Tuesday, November 2, came. I had an appointment with my gynecologist, Joe Marmet, a good friend of mine today.

The nurse instructed me to put on a gown and leave a urine specimen. Shortly after, Dr. Joe walked in.

"So what's wrong with my patient, today?" he teased.

"I'm experiencing some nausea," I explained.

Joe always had a funny joke to tell; it was his way of putting me at ease. He proceeded to examine me while telling his latest joke. When he had finished, he told me to get dressed. The nurse came back to draw some blood.

A little later, Joe walked back and closed the door. He sat down, looking straight into my face, and smiled.

"Well Barbara, you're pregnant."

Oh boy.

I was stunned, even though the thought had occurred to me.

Now my being so sick with Elvis in Palm Springs made sense to me. My hormones were changing and introducing any foreign substance, like drugs or alcohol, was not only dangerous but stupid. I'm certain that if Elvis had known that I was pregnant, he wouldn't have given me the pills. On the other hand, had he known I was pregnant he wouldn't have wanted me there.

In my heart, I wanted it to be James' child, and so this is what I kept telling myself. Stupid as it seems, the thought of it being Steve's never dawned on me. And it certainly wasn't Elvis' child.

One reason the pregnancy took me by surprise was that when I was 20 I had a cyst removed from an ovary. The ovary had to be removed, and my doctor told me it would be extremely difficult for me to get pregnant again. I accepted the news, and was grateful that I was alive to see another day. From that point on, I believed that birth control was no longer necessary. Since I hadn't gotten pregnant in five years, I didn't worry about it.

Today, a lot of women have children out of wedlock, often successfully suing the father for child support. Some women genuinely want to have a child regardless of how the father feels, even forfeiting financial support obligated to them. It certainly could have been a financial gain for me to have Jim Aubrey's or Steve McQueen's baby, but I never thought that way. To trap a man by getting pregnant without his consent, and then sue him for child support, was never my style.

"Joe, I'm not sure what to do. I want to talk to my boyfriend, and I'll call you tomorrow."

The moment I got home, I picked up the phone and dialed MGM, and made plans to meet James for dinner.

For the rest of the day, I could only think of how I was going to break the news to him. He had let his dislike for kids be known from the start. He already had two grown children, and there wasn't any room in his life for another child. I knew it, but I thought, "There's always hope."

All sorts of fantasies ran through my head. Who knows? He might just surprise me. And he did!

We arrived at his house at the same time.

"Want me to pour you a glass of wine?" he offered.

"That would be great." Even though it wasn't a smart thing to do, I needed a drink.

It was the first time in my life that I had to tell a man other than my husband that I was pregnant. I was praying to God that he would take the news well. After taking off his tie and jacket, he opened the first couple of buttons on his shirt. He sat down with his wine for a moment's rest. Deciding it was best not to wait or play games, I just blurted out what was on my mind.

"James, I'm pregnant."

His face lost some color, and he stared icily at me for a moment before answering. I really did love him, and whatever he wanted to do about the child was fine with me. It would be his call. He finally spoke and when he did, he broke my heart.

"Well, who's is it?"

It was as if he had slapped my face. I was more stunned at that moment than when Dr. Joe broke the news to me at his office. I was crushed by his remark, but angry at the same time.

"It's yours!" I said. He sat there completely still; the room was in total silence, a thundering silence. He reached over and took my hands.

"No, Indian, it's not mine," he said very sweetly.

I was in shock.

"What do you mean? I said in an irate tone.

"Indian, as much as I would like to make you happy, I can't. You see, many, many years ago I had a vasectomy," he said with cunning satisfaction.

Oh, my God!

I was crushed. I was embarrassed. I was at a loss for words. The tears streamed down my cheeks. I had chosen the man I loved, but not the father of my child.

I cried a lot. Finally I calmed down and James and I talked it over. With his financial help, I decided to abort the pregnancy. I then told him about Steve and the choice I had made. He was unusually sweet and wonderful, stroking my hair.

Some might say that I made such an important decision much too hastily, but under the circumstances, I felt I had no choice. If I wanted to remain with James, there was no way I could keep the baby. My decision was made that night, and there would be no turning back.

James was very tender and loving that night, but later he would make me pay dearly. I stayed at his house, and we cuddled all night. We didn't make love; we both needed time to get over this most unexpected development in our relationship.

When I left James' house, I was at an all-time low. I wanted another child, but not like this. I hurried home and called Dr. Joe's office.

"Listen Joe, I've decided to have an abortion." God, did that sound horrible!

"Are you sure this is what you really want, Barbara?" Joe asked.

"Yes, I'm sure. I've talked it over with James, and it's our decision," I said. I then took a breath and added, "Joe, I'd like to do this as soon as possible."

"I'll see what I can do with the scheduling," Joe promised. "Call me this afternoon and I'll let you know when I can do it. And Barbara?"

"Yes, Joe?"

"This is a really big decision. I want you to be sure, I mean, really sure. Think about it, OK?"

"Thanks for your concern Joe, but I don't have to. My mind's made up," I said.

I did practically nothing but stare at my clock all day, waiting as long as I could stand before I picked up the phone and called Dr. Joe back. Moments later, Joe got on the line.

"Well, I had to pull a few strings," he said, "but we can do it on Saturday, November 6th."

God, that was quick. But I had to get it over with. I was in love with one man, and carrying another man's child.

I hung up, feeling exhausted and depressed. I didn't see James for a few days. He needed time to pout, and I gave it to him. Even though I wanted to call him and be with him, I didn't.

Steve called, but I was out when he phoned. When I got his message, I felt a twinge of excitement, the most excitement I had felt in days. That wasn't good because I couldn't turn back now, even if I wanted to. I dialed Steve, leaving him a message, and was a little glad that I didn't reach him.

I would have to tell him about my pregnancy, but I wasn't going to tell him the whole truth, that the child was his. I didn't want to upset or confuse him any more than I already had, considering the turmoil going on in his personal life. Instead, I would tell him it that was James' child. That would seal our fate, once and for all I thought, and then I could move forward with my life with James.

In hindsight, not telling Steve was a rotten thing to do. He had every right to know that I was carrying his child. I'll regret forever my choice not to tell him. I should have given him the opportunity to have a voice in my decision. Instead, I let another man help me make up my mind; a man who didn't deserve to be a part of a life or death decision. I know now that he tried desperately to have another child with Ali MacGraw, but sadly, she miscarried. He always felt that had she not miscarried, they would never have gotten divorced.

It totally amazes me that I loved James as much as I did. This ardent love for him caused me to make so many wrong choices.

Steve got back to me by early afternoon. He was perky but uncomplicated and easy to understand. He invited me out for dinner.

We decided on 8 p.m., which was a little late for me, but it didn't matter. What I had to tell him would finish us anyway, so why rush to give him the bad news?

I still hadn't heard from James by the time Steve picked me up. I was feeling awfully hurt by his actions. He was being incredibly mean, but then again, he had excessive pride. I knew that my affair with Steve had deeply hurt his ego, and I would just have to be patient with him.

Steve walked in with his usual six-pack of beer. It didn't really interest me at the moment. I needed something a bit more potent, more relaxing, like a joint which Steve faithfully produced. We hugged and kissed, giggling as we smoked. Looking back, it was not a very smart thing to do, since I was pregnant.

I dreaded dinner. I knew that I had to tell him and dinner would most likely be the right time to come clean. Steve kept grabbing me, kissing me, trying to get me in the mood for later on. I almost gave, knowing there probably wouldn't be a later. I had to tell him tonight that I would be in the hospital on Saturday.

We drove to his favorite hideaway on the beach in Malibu. How ironic—it was the same restaurant where we had our first date, where we started and would end our relationship. It was a little sad, and not my first choice of where to go, but I wasn't going to say anything until I had a glass of wine to help bolster my courage. It would take a lot of courage to tell Steve.

He was in a jovial mood. I wasn't. He talked the whole way as he drove. I was so preoccupied, I hardly listened to what he said. Once we got to our table and our drinks arrived, I let out a big sigh of relief. I was sighing a lot lately.

"OK, come clean. What's troubling you, babe?" Steve asked. It didn't take a rocket scientist to figure out that something was bothering me. I took a big gulp of my wine and laid it on the line.

"Steve—I'm pregnant." There, it was finally out! He had a strange look on his face, but before he could answer I continued, "It's James' child." His face tensed and looked almost melancholy.

We sat in silence for a few minutes, each of us taking in what had just transpired. Steve broke the silence.

"What do you want to do about it?" he asked. He then took my hand, looking straight at me, right smack square in the eyes. It was hard to return his stare. He was being so wonderful, so decent, so understanding.

"I'm having an abortion on Saturday," I told him.

"Is that what you want, Barbara?"

"I think it's best, under the circumstances," I said. He didn't ask me what that meant specifically; he had his own thoughts swirling around in his head.

My problem wasn't what he'd expected to be the topic of discussion over dinner. To hear that the woman you're having an affair with is carrying another man's child is a little shocking, to say the least. I don't believe he ever thought for a moment that it might be his child. I was convincing. He trusted me, I'm sad to say.

All the while, he tried to calm me—I was on the verge of breaking down, and he knew it. Little did he know the real reason.

We ate our dinner, or should I say, he ate and I attempted to eat. Steve held my hand the whole time. He was so kind and gentle. I felt so close to him. How could he be so nice to me under these circumstances?

I looked at him, studying his weather-beaten face. I loved his looks, especially his mole. I teased him about the mole quite a bit, calling it a beauty mark. I loved his soft, baby fine hair and his strong, powerful hands. I really did love him as a man, a friend and a lover. How lost I would be without my dear friend. Had I made the wrong choice?

When we finished, both of our moods were mellow. Steve had a gentle side, a side that was not the image he portrayed to the public. He allowed this soft side to emerge that evening, making me feel even more like a heel. I had envisioned that when I told Steve about my pregnancy he would get upset, storm out and leave me to spend the rest of the evening alone. Once again, he surprised me by how well he took it and how loving he was. We left the restaurant and headed back to my place.

"Do you want to come up?" I asked him.

"Sure, babe," came his reply.

We held hands as we walked up the stairs to my apartment. Maybe I was giving him the wrong impression. Maybe he was thinking that this meant I was getting rid of the baby and James. I'll never know what was going through his mind. I didn't ask him. He was holding back, protecting his feelings and emotions. This was just one more problem for him to deal with, and God knows he'd had enough of them in his life.

He held me for a long time. It's amazing how men treat women like china dolls when they know they're pregnant. That's the way he treated me that night, as if I were going to break. He stayed for a few hours, taking precautions to make sure I was all right before he left. We didn't make love that night, or ever again. We felt it was best. He was such a gentleman, caring about me as a person and not as the object of his desires. That night Steve McQueen became my good friend. He would always have a special place in my heart for his kindness to me when I was down.

It was late, and I encouraged Steve to leave. We both needed some rest.

"I'll call you tomorrow, babe," he said sweetly.

"Thanks," I responded and then closed the door.

I was confused. What I needed most was some good advice. It needed to come from someone who greatly cared about me, and had my best interests at heart. I didn't have the confidence and self-esteem to make the right decisions at the moment. If only I had a father to go to for advice, or a mother who could guide me. I was lonely, frightened and certainly in no position to make life altering choices.

When Steve left, I slipped into a nightgown and immediately fell asleep. Telling Steve and getting that out of the way was a tremendous relief for me. I was temporarily taking a vacation from my thoughts, knowing my troubles would be waiting for me as soon as I woke up. Sleep was my only escape.

Both Steve and James would call the next day, lifting my spirits for a little while. James was somewhat aloof, while Steve was surprisingly considerate and sweet, asking me if I needed anything.

The next few days just flew by. I saw Dr. Joe one more time for a quick examination and some moral support. He assured me that everything would be fine, and I felt safe in his hands. I didn't allow myself to dwell on the reality of what I was doing to my body and my baby. I had blinders on; my decision was final, and I was ready to go forward with this ordeal. I just wanted to get it over with.

On Friday, I had the required blood test, registered for my hospital stay and began mentally preparing myself for the abortion. The surgery would be early on Saturday morning at Cedars Sinai Hospital. I would be released on Sunday. It didn't seem like such a big deal. How wrong I was.

I had arranged for a friend to drive me to Cedars Sinai Saturday morning. Before I left, Steve called to wish me his best. James did not call and his thoughtlessness made me feel horrible. I put it out of my mind, knowing that he would come around after the problem was solved.

The hospital was cold and sterile. My thoughts turned to the birth of my son, Gerry years before. How happy I had been then. Boy, did I miss him! Dr. Joe was there talking to me, as the anesthesiologist placed an oxygen mask over my face. The last thing I remember before I went under was Dr. Joe's face.

When I awoke, the first thing I saw was Dr. Joe. He was sitting next to me, holding my hand to console me.

"Barbara," he said in a strained voice, "there were some complications during the abortion. You're going to be fine, but I had to do some repairs, and that means you're going to have to stay in the hospital for a couple of days." He was visibly shaken. Without going into all of the medical details, I will simply say that if the nurse had not watched me as closely as she did, I could have died that day, along with my child. I believe that God and my guardian angel was on my side and forgave me, allowing me to live.

Having an abortion is an enormously heartbreaking decision for a woman to make. It brings out all sorts of emotions and guilt. Those feelings, plus the hormones in my body, gave me a gigantic case of postpartum depression.

When I looked down at my pelvic area, I saw a huge incision. It was supposed to have been a simple procedure, requiring one night in the hospital. Now I had this huge incision, and was required to stay for five more days. This was turning into a nightmare.

On Monday there were calls from Steve and James. I called James back first, even though he had been a shit to me.

"Indian, where are you?" he asked. "I've been worried sick about you!" He was worried sick? Like hell he was!

"I'm in the hospital, and there were complications. I'm staying here for a few more days."

"Do you need anything?" he asked. I wanted to say, "Yes, I need *you*," but my pride wouldn't allow it.

"I'm fine," I said with false bravado, "I'll be OK."

"Indian, you call me if you need anything," he made sure to say, covering his ass.

When he hung up, I put the receiver down and had my first good cry in the hospital. It wasn't just over James; it was about the whole ordeal. I also cried for my son Gerry because I missed him. James' phone call, and the fact that he didn't want to visit me, brought on a flood of tears and sad thoughts. James didn't visit me once during the whole time I was in the hospital. He sent flowers and called a few times, but he was still pouting and keeping a safe distance. A colder man I have yet to meet.

James took care of all the expenses. He kept his promise, and never mentioned the money to me. The pregnancy was a different story. As time passed, he became even angrier with me, as if he were trying to punish me, until he got the poison out of his system. The pregnancy was a reminder of my affection for Steve.

When I called Steve back, he was much more giving and loving. He hated hospitals with a passion, but as much as he hated them, he came to visit me twice, bringing a burger and a milkshake. It was such a lift for me. I started to cry, but quickly stopped. The postnatal blues, I'm sure.

"Here, here, none of that," he said sweetly, wiping away my tears. It was so good to see his smiling, crazy, wonderful face. I didn't feel so alone for the moment.

Steve even took the time to meet with Dr. Joe to discuss my condition, asking all sorts of questions. He was concerned for my well-being. I needed that, and that was the irony of it all. It made me feel sadder and guiltier. Would he have been so wonderful had he known that it was *his* child I had just aborted? I'll never know. Probably, yes.

He crept in at night so that no one would see him, always aware that the media was out for a juicy story. James wasn't there for me, but Steve was.

I cried when Steve left my hospital room that night. His being there, and James' absence, left me with a horrible feeling of "what have I done?" Through the years, I've wondered what my child would have been like, and the differences he or she might have made in my life. It's a decision I've thought about many times during the last three decades. If there is a spirit world beyond this Earth, I pray that the child's spirit I aborted and Steve's spirit are together again, and I'm forgiven.

CHAPTER FOURTEEN

Being in the hospital is never pleasant. As I lay there alone, thinking about everything, it gave me the opportunity to reflect on the past. I was specifically thinking of Elvis. He had no idea where I was or why; we hadn't been in touch for some time. The last time I had been in a hospital was earlier that year on March 16, 1971, in Nashville, Tennessee, when Elvis had been the patient.

When Joe Esposito called, there was an urgency in his voice I had never heard before. "Elvis needs you. Can you visit him in Nashville at the hospital? He's staying at the Nashville Baptist Hospital. I'll make the arrangements." Joe rarely had time for small talk or long conversations. He was usually brief and to the point. As Elvis put it: taking care of business.

"What's wrong with E?" My pulse quickened, accompanied by a moment of panic.

His hospitalization was a secret, and he wanted me by his side to hold his hand. He was suffering serious pain in his eyes, with blurred vision. He had a tremendous fear of going blind.

His doctor, David Meyers, treated him in secrecy at the Nashville Baptist Hospital. Both the prognosis and outcome were positive, but when I look back on what the outcome might have been, I marvel at Elvis' bravery during his frightening ordeal.

I didn't question why Elvis wanted me there, but I wanted to be there for him. "Don't get upset, Barbara," Joe placated me. "It's not life threatening, but it's serious. He has glaucoma."

I didn't know what glaucoma was. I had never even heard the word before. Was Elvis going to be OK? I was alarmed.

Joe remained positive. "Nothing's going to keep E down, but here he is and he wants to talk to you."

"Hi, Barbara," said the voice on the other end of the line. It was Elvis, but boy, did his voice sound weak. "Can you visit me in the hospital? I miss you, baby. I just need to see my girl." He could be the sweetest guy in the world sometimes. He didn't want to upset me, and so he downplayed the situation. Elvis always made me feel special, as if I were the one and only woman in his life, even though I and everyone else knew otherwise. He had a real gift in that department. Who knows what number in the pecking order of his girls I fell into? Timing, they say, is everything.

"You're going to be staying with me here in the hospital," Elvis informed me. I was a little stunned, but I took the news well. Life with Elvis was always interesting.

I hurriedly prepared for my trip, my escapade, with The King.

My life was very busy at this time, but when the opportunity arose, I tried my best to fit in a couple of days with Elvis. Most of the time it worked out well, but there were occasions when I couldn't afford to leave in the middle of a job. My finances dictated my life. No matter how generous Elvis was with cars and other gifts, he didn't offer to pay my rent or my bills, so there were times when I couldn't afford to break away. Luckily, this time I could manage to spend a few days by his side. Just to be in his presence made me feel alive. He had that kind of magic.

When I arrived in Nashville, Joe picked me up, as usual, and promptly took me to E's hospital room. As I walked into his room, he was sitting up in bed with the television on and the clicker in his hand. He loved that darned remote control. He quickly turned off the TV and motioned for me to come to him. I ran into his arms for a warm embrace.

He was like a big, overgrown kid, and played the hospital patient role to its fullest. He milked sympathy for all it was worth.

"Hi baby, glad you're here," he said with a big smile, and he pulled me into the hospital bed and began to kiss me. The last thing I expected was a bedridden Romeo who wanted to play doctor.

"Elvis, we'll get in trouble."

"Who's going to punish us, baby?" he laughed. I knew he was joking, but he was also serious. Who was going to say 'no' to Elvis Presley?

We got under the sheets, undressed and made love undisturbed. I kept nervously looking at the door, wondering who was going to pop in, but Joe stood guard outside, ready to rebuff anyone, including the hospital staff. Joe never failed to amaze me. He was forever taking care of business!

Elvis wanted me to lay in bed and continue holding him when we finished making love. I was giggling with embarrassment when a nurse came in to check on him. He told me in front of her, "You're staying here with me in the hospital."

"Where Elvis? I can't possibly sleep in this bed. It's for you, and it's too small for the two of us."

Elvis laughed, "No silly, in the doctors' guest quarters. They have a whole apartment set up for visiting surgeons." The news was a great relief to me.

Later that day, Dr. Meyers checked on his favorite patient. Elvis introduced us, and the doctor didn't seem to care that I wasn't Mrs. Presley. As I recall, Dr. Meyers was a tall, thin, strikingly handsome man—very much a gentleman.

Dr. Meyers explained glaucoma to Elvis, to what extent it had progressed, and the procedure he would use to fix it. He would need to administer a shot directly into Elvis' eyeball; the thought of it made my skin crawl. Elvis took the news well, just shaking his head and pretending that it didn't bother him. I'm sure the thought of a needle going into his eyeball gave him the willies, but he never showed his fear to me or the doctor. When Dr. Meyers gave Elvis the shot, I wanted to leave, but Elvis wouldn't let me.

"Come here, honey. Sit next to me and hold my hand," he said. I was trapped. Dr. Meyers told him not to move. E obeyed and squeezed my hand tightly. I thought he was going to break it.

Elvis was a real trooper, though. When the doctor left , Elvis became a little boy again, wanting me to baby him and love him. I stayed with him for the rest of the night, lying beside him in the hospital bed. When he finally fell asleep much later, Joe escorted me to the doctors' quarters, where I fell onto a bed, thoroughly exhausted.

The next day was a repeat of the first. Elvis made me watch the injection again. "If I can do it, so can you," was his reasoning. And so I watched. It wasn't quite so bad. Once again, Elvis didn't flinch or make a sound. I think he was scared that if he moved or cried it might do something to make him to go blind.

This may sound selfish, but two days of Elvis in the hospital was not my cup of tea. The whole experience was draining. I loved being with Elvis, but two days was long enough. Luckily, I had to be in New York, and since Elvis knew that up front, he didn't lay a guilt trip on me for leaving. He scheduled another woman to take over when I left. That's our boy!

Joe and I laugh today about all of his close escapes—and he had several. Elvis couldn't be without a woman for a day. I believe the women filled the void left by his mother's death.

When the time came to depart, we hugged and said goodbye. As I left, I blew him a kiss.

Now *I* was the one lying in a hospital bed. It had been only eight months since that visit with Elvis. And in that time, Elvis' sex drive had waned and there wouldn't be any sex in a hospital bed, or rarely, for that matter, in any bed. It's amazing how things can change so dramatically in such a short time. How I wished my man was lying next to me in my hospital bed, when I needed him most.

Five days in the hospital gave me a lot of time to think. My last visit from Steve was brotherly; the romantic feelings weren't there. We bonded in a different way. Through this dilemma, we grew stronger as friends, and he accepted my choice of James as the lover in my life with grace. He could have easily moved on to his next conquest much sooner, but he chose to honor our friendship with his loyalty to me. I think his seeing me in a hospital bed helped him move on.

Through my harrowing hospital stay, James remained calm and cool, hiding his emotions. The day before I checked out, he called to remind me of our upcoming weekend together—my birthday weekend in Palm Springs. The thought of being out of the hospital and in the sunny desert gave me something to look forward to.

I was released from Cedars on Friday, in time for the weekend. My girlfriend, Judy Baldwin, brought me home. Shortly after I entered my apartment the phone rang. I rushed to the phone to hear James' voice.

"Hi, Indian! How are you feeling?" I was still sore, sad and blue, but I wasn't going to show him my true feelings. I gave him the most upbeat tone that I could, and played his game.

"Hi, James. I'm feeling good, thank you."

"Are you up for our little trip?" he asked. I couldn't believe that he thought I was up for a trip so soon after major surgery, but I was happy he finally wanted to be with me again.

"Yes," I answered. "I'm looking forward to a little sun and rest."

"Good, I'll pick you up at 7:30 and we'll grab a quick bite at Nicky's. Traffic will have died down by the time we're through." This was the second time I recall James picking me up at my apartment.

I moved timidly and slowly. Even though I was only in my early 20s, when your body goes through what mine did, it takes its toll—not only physically but emotionally.

It would take another week before I could comfortably put on my jeans. It would take years for me to recover from the emotional surgery.

I returned five day's worth of phone calls, and packed for my weekend with James.

I wanted to put everything behind me and start fresh. Steve and I were now officially platonic friends; we were both allowed to move on with our lives. I would continue to see him from time to time. I even gave Ali MacGraw the thumbs up when she asked me about Steve, at the beginning of their affair. Sadly, once Steve and Ali's romance was sealed, we would go our separate ways. What was most important to me, however, was that we left the relationship as friends.

I hoped Elvis would call again; it would just be a matter of time. Something would remind him of me, jar his memory, making him call. And, if he didn't call, I could handle that. I now felt that it was time to move on, whatever came next in my chaotic life.

I was ready and waiting for James as he picked me up on his way home from the studio. I buzzed him in. Seconds later, he was knocking gently on the door. I opened it to his smiling face.

"Hi, Indian. Are you ready?"

"I am," I answered We were both vulnerable and quiet at that moment. James grabbed me. We hugged and kissed, then he held me for a long time. I felt so happy to feel his arms wrapped around me. He was being so nice.

He loaded my things in his car, then headed to his house, where he had his bag packed. Grabbing it, he locked the house and we were off to Nicky's for dinner and an adventurous weekend. Nicky's was always a delight. He spoiled us with his specials, along with a nice bottle of wine. I was starving for a real delicacy and tired of hospital food after almost a week, with the exception of the delicious burger and milkshake Steve brought. That night, I didn't worry about calories!

During dinner we ignored the past week. James never brought up the abortion. I didn't either. I had a lot of emotions welling up inside of me, and I didn't want to spoil our weekend. This was to be a new beginning, and I wanted everything to be perfect.

It turned out to be just the opposite. It was a weekend from hell.

James' mood changed during the 120-mile trek to Palm Springs. The several glasses of wine he'd consumed at dinner was part of it. He became quiet, so I tried chatting with him to keep up some semblance of happiness. Unfortunately, his mood worsened the further we drove. The happier I appeared, the more annoyed he became. After a long period of silence, I asked James why he was acting this way.

"Indian, if you want to talk, I have something for your mouth," he said foully, with much disdain. He then reached over and grabbed the back of my head, seizing a handful of my hair and yanking my head violently down toward his crotch. I was stunned.

The pain shot through my body; my stitches were still very sensitive. How could he be so cruel? He was mean, nasty and spiteful. I felt like I'd given up a lot for him. He should have been more aware of my feelings. But, he either didn't have a clue or didn't care.

After a few seconds, he let go of my head and I sat up. We drove toward Palm Springs. I didn't say another word for the rest of the trip, nor did he. There was nothing but silence in the car. I was miserable and wanted to go home, but I was too scared to utter a word. James showed no signs of remorse or concern for my condition. He was vengeful and pouting. This was just the start of our horrible weekend together.

We arrived at our villa in Palm Springs in a bad mood. How could an evening that started off so well become so dreadful?

After an hour of silence, James started to talk. I didn't reply and left him to stew. That was the only way I could handle his quiet temper.

Once I came back in the room, James lit the fireplace. He became more subdued, like his usual in control self.

"Indian, come here," he commanded. His famous last words.

I moved near him. He reached out and took me in his arms.

"You know how much you mean to me," he said, flashing that infamous Cobra smile.

"I know," I answered him softly.

I accepted his statement as a form of apology; it was the closest thing to one he could offer. I'd been through so much with him that I decided not to react quickly, but I was now a bit more careful with my emotions around him. We snuggled in front of the fire, drinking Almaden wine.

His anger and frustration turned to a slight case of remorse. It was almost like I could read his mind. Then he said something strange.

"If I want to make love with Indian, maybe I should be nicer," James said. His statement was revealing; he knew what he had to do to get his way. Nothing came from the heart; it was all mechanical. I was beginning to see James as I'd never before seen him.

I felt as if we'd made up without really discussing the issues. I talked myself into believing that he was sorry for his despicable behavior in the car. He was getting even with me in his mind, and once the incident in the car was finished, I thought the rest was water under the bridge.

I was wrong.

Even though we had technically made up, I wasn't ready to jump into bed with him. My feelings were still too raw and hurt, not to mention my body. After holding each other in front of the fireplace, we moved into the bedroom. I went into the bathroom first, taking the shirt he wore during the day to put on as a nightshirt. James burst through the door while I was changing. He wanted to brush his teeth, he said. He stripped completely naked and stood next to me, acting as if nothing hostile had passed between us that evening. What he said next was beyond cruel.

"Let me see your scar." The blood rushed to my face. It was the first time in my life that my body was an embarrassment to me. He used it against me.

The scar was from the complication I endured after the abortion. Dr. Joe had to cut into my stomach to repair a tear in my womb.

Acting as nonchalant as I could, I lifted my shirt to show him the scar. To me, it was the ugliest thing in the world, but it was more than that. It was a permanent reminder about my abortion. It was a scarlet letter that was hidden beneath my clothing. No matter how much I covered it up for the public, I always knew that it was there and would never go away. At the time, I remember thinking that it would ruin my chance to model bikinis—the shallowness of youth! James surprised me. His face softened, and I could see all kinds of emotions going through him. It made everything more real to him. It was probably the first time that he truly understood the pain of what I had endured in the hospital. My scar didn't repulse him. In fact, it sensitized him to my misery. From that point on, he became a little more humble, if that's possible, feeling some remorse over how he had treated me. He gently touched my new incision.

"They did a good job," he said encouragingly. "They did a really good job." That was his idea of a compliment, I guess. "Does it hurt? Are you sore?" At last, he was acting like a concerned lover. Of course I was sore, of course I was hurt, especially if I moved the wrong way or coughed, but nothing hurt more than his dirty little act in the car. He hurt my soul. Get over it, I thought. Live in the now.

James laid down next to me. It would be the first time I'd slept with anyone since my surgery, and it wouldn't be easy. Needless to say, we didn't make love. I had to sleep on my back, without turning on my side. Wine helped me sleep a little, but unlike Elvis, James didn't have any little "helpers" to put me in la-la land.

"You look tired, Indian. I want you to rest tonight," James said. What a switch! Hours before he was a tyrant, now he was the concerned boyfriend.

"I am tired," I said. "I'm sure I'll feel better tomorrow." I was trying to tell him that we would have sex, or make an attempt to, later. I was relieved that he let me off the hook so easily. It was late and we'd fall asleep shortly. Tomorrow would be a new day.

The next day in Palm Springs was a perfect 84 degrees and sunny. We went out for breakfast, and strolled down Palm Canyon Drive. James walked with me at a slow pace while we window-shopped. Things were beginning to feel normal again. He was showing signs of affection. I was starved for his love and warmth.

My birthday on November 16 was approaching. James asked me if I wanted anything special. The question came from left field, and it surprised me. I was at a loss for words, and answered, "Nothing, just you." I was his kind of gal—low maintenance, lots of sex and little money. James laughed and I blushed. I was in for a surprise, a nice surprise.

Before we went back to the villa, we stopped at the liquor store to pick up a bottle of vodka for James and bottle of water for me. We headed for the pool the minute we got back. I wore a one piece bathing suit that covered my incision, and we both settled back on the lounge chairs. James had a pile of scripts to read, while I had a paperback copy of Truman Capote's *In Cold Blood*.

When the cocktail hour arrived, James poured himself a stiff vodka. I enjoyed my usual glass of white wine.

"Indian, are you up for Mexican food?" I knew what that meant. Our favorite Palm Springs restaurant was a place called Las Casuelas, on North Palm Canyon Road. It's famous for the many celebrities who frequent it. The food was superb and the atmosphere friendly. A three-piece mariachi band serenaded the diners, which lent a romantic air to the place. We made reservations for 7 p.m.

We sat in our room enjoying our cocktails while the conversation got a little deeper. James rarely discussed my career, always leery that I might ask him for help or for an acting job. On reflection, I realize that there were many important issues we never discussed: the future, old age, marriage. You might say our relationship was superficial, but I didn't see it that way at the time. Maybe a lot of that had to do with my youth and naivete.

Before I knew it, James was starting to get a little physical, kissing me harder than normal. The vodka was hitting his system, making him aggressive and tapping into the anger he harbored against me.

Here we go again, I thought at one point. In truth, James needed to be babied and coddled, if you can imagine babying a snake. I was a good sport about his mood swings, and assumed they were all my fault. And—as always—he was making this my weekend of repentance. My gut reaction was to ignore his innuendoes, and try to win him over with love. Luckily, we had reservations at Las Casuelas, and we had to go if we wanted to eat. That stopped any physical contact for the time being.

Once we arrived at the restaurant, we ordered drinks at the bar; a margarita with salt for me, another vodka for him. I wanted to tell James that he'd had enough to drink, but that wasn't possible. I never dictated to him in our relationship. He was the boss, and that was that. I could tell that his dark side was emerging.

We sat at the bar for our first round, and the mariachi band approached James. He requested his favorite song, "Saborame," which he proceeded to sing along with the band. The song's title means, "A little taste of you," and I've never forgotten the tune. Hearing it always makes me think of James. When the band finished, he gave them a tip and we sat down for dinner.

While we were eating, we talked of a planned trip to Acapulco for Christmas. That put me in a festive mood. He told me that we were going to stay in a villa at the world famous Las Brisas Hotel, in the hills of the rich and famous. James was being manipulative; he was using his glamour and influence to control me, enticing me with gifts of wealth, not love.

Our dinner was fine, but as James continued to drink, he became more belligerent as the night wore on. He hadn't completely processed his anger. He still harbored a lot of resentment and hostility. There was no place for me to hide or run, while he twisted the knife. James Aubrey was a mean drunk. He rarely lost control, but when he did—stay clear. Like a tray of fresh fruit left in the sun too long, the evening was going bad. It had lost its sweet, fresh fragrance and aroma.

It started when the mariachi band approached us to sing another song. While they played, the lead vocalist sang directly to me and smiled. I returned his smile, thoroughly enjoying the music. Big mistake. James mistook my appreciation for flirting and dismissed them without a tip, making all of us feel awful. I wanted to hide under the table, because I was so embarrassed.

I started to get mad. How long was he going to keep up this nasty, immature behavior? James paid the check in silence, and we headed back to our villa. By the time we arrived I was livid, and couldn't keep quiet any longer. James parked the car and stumbled into our room, with me following closely behind. Once the door was closed, I spoke my piece.

"Why did you treat the band so horribly?" I asked in anger, my voice louder than he had ever heard. "They did nothing wrong, and neither did I." That didn't sit well with him.

"You *bitch*!" he hissed at me. "You were flirting with the whole band, and they were out of line."

I stood my ground.

"No, James, I wasn't flirting," I shouted. "All I did was smile and tell them that I liked their music. You're the one who is out of line!" He didn't like what I had to say. He wanted me to be my sweet, gullible old self, the person he could take advantage of, the person who usually gave into him. He didn't like this independent woman who spoke her mind. All I wanted was a quite weekend to recover from my surgery. James wasn't going to let me. He was doing everything in his power to torment me.

I confronted him. "James, why are you treating me this way? You're acting like a spoiled brat, like a monster. What have I done to make you behave so badly?" I felt like saying, 'God help me, I've made a terrible mistake.' I just wanted to hurt him like he had hurt me, but I was afraid to make things worse by angering him more than I already had.

He grumbled under his breath, and began to let me have it full force. "You're the one who got pregnant. I didn't tell you to have the abortion. That was your decision. You got what you deserve, Indian."

Well, there it was. The abortion was eating him up inside.

He also brought up my affair with Elvis, and the weekend I had left him hanging around the house waiting for me.

What about all the times I had waited for him? But, I suppose those didn't count. I couldn't believe what I was hearing. He was turning vicious, and he was angrier than I had ever seen him. He looked like an ugly, old man.

"You're being unfair!" Those were my last words before I ran into the bedroom and slammed the door, trying to escape his rage.

I lay down on the bed. It was all catching up with me. I was tired, and didn't want to play this game any longer. Seconds later, James barged in and started ranting and raving some more.

"You'll do anything to get out of having sex, won't you Indian?"

What was that supposed to mean? Did he really think that I was capable of having sex with him right now, with my body in the condition it was in? The nerve of the man! Sex was the farthest thing from my mind, especially when he had been so mean to me. You want to have sex when someone shows you love, not when they're degrading you.

"James, I don't know what you're talking about. I haven't done anything," I said, my voice a little quieter, almost defeated. He was wearing me down. I knew he was drunk, because he was slurring his words and he was unsteady on his feet. I spoke again.

"I want to go home, James," I said abruptly. The words just came out of my mouth.

James, on the other hand, had something to say about that.

"You're not going anywhere!" he said loudly. Then he tried to grab me, but I rolled over to the other side of the bed. I cried out in pain, as I rolled on my stitches. I got up and slowly made my way back into the living room, with James following closely behind. If at any time in our relationship he was going to hit me, this was it. Although I had never seen him hit a woman, he had a reputation for it. I knew he was a hair's breath away from hitting me.

He grabbed my shoulder, spinning me around so that I could meet his eyes. There was fire in them.

"James, stop this. You're hurting me," I pleaded with him. To his credit, he stopped and regained his composure. We sat down on the couch; there was no way I was going back into that bedroom with him unless he calmed down. James got up to pour himself another vodka.

"Don't you think you've had enough already?" I asked. It was the wrong thing to say.

"Don't *ever* tell me what I can or can't do! Do you understand, Indian?!" He was yelling again. Instead of being scared, my blood boiled and at that moment I hated him. He poured the vodka into a glass and gulped it down.

I sat on the couch, planning my escape. Once he went into the bathroom, I would make a break for it and grab my bag and his car keys. I couldn't take his abuse for another moment. My world was crashing down, and I had to get out of there. When he went to the bathroom, I made a mad dash for the car. I drove off in his car, leaving the bastard to fend for himself.

Once safely behind the wheel, I started to cry. I was feeling sorry for myself. I drove out of Palm Springs by myself, and when I got 15 miles from home, my guilt kicked in and got the best of me.

As much of a bastard as James was that night, how could I leave him all alone? Begrudgingly, I turned the car around and drove back to Palm Springs. I didn't know what to expect, but I never expected to see a lonely old man sitting in a chair in the middle of the living room, crying. I was in shock. James looked so sincere, and yet so helpless. When he saw me, he looked surprised.

"Indian, I'm so sorry. I love you. I don't know why I behaved the way I did," he said apologetically. I forgave him instantly. This wasn't a mean man who stood before me; he was was drunk, that's all. Oh well, a little drama never hurts to put the fire back into a relationship. I moved toward him and put my arms around him, hugging his head to my bosom. Then I kissed his cheek.

"It's all right," I whispered, rocking him gently, "I'm here, and I won't leave you." As strange as it may sound, his mood changed before my very eyes.

"I thought I'd lost you, Indian," he said quietly.

"No, James," I reassured him, "you won't lose me." We then went to bed holding each other, and soon fell asleep. The next morning we immediately went for coffee; James was extremely hung over.

When we finished with our morning coffee, he asked me to drive us back to Los Angeles, because he was feeling "less than perfect."

The drive back was a far cry from our drive to Palm Springs. James was loving, and paid me all kinds of compliments. He regretted his behavior, and it showed. I forgave him and put the weekend behind me. He never brought up the incident again, and he never got outrageously drunk or out of control like he did that weekend.

I think James needed to get rid of the poison inside him regarding my abortion. Blowing up at me was a release for him. He was so used to keeping things inside. This time he just couldn't contain it—which combined with the alcohol—made it easier for him to act out what had been in his heart for a long time. Stone cold sober, he would never have shown his emotions.

"I love you, Indian," he said on the drive back.

"I love you, too, James."

We drove back to Seabright, and everything fell back into its normal pattern. Once inside his house, feeling safe and secure, we undressed and made soft, sweet love.

I had my man back.

CHAPTER FIFTEEN

The following Tuesday was my 25th birthday. James planned a lovely dinner at Nicky Blair's, surprising me with cake and champagne. That would be one of my most memorable birthdays with him.

After dinner James drove me to his house, where we completed the evening with more champagne—and a lot more loving. James didn't give me a gift, but I didn't say anything, partly because I felt a little hurt. I was so happy to have him back, and I didn't want to do anything to spoil it. We ended the evening making love for hours, then falling asleep, totally spent.

The next morning, James woke me up with am unusual statement.

"I guess you're not the princess and the pea, Indian." I didn't have a clue about what he meant.

"I'm not what?" I asked, still half asleep.

"Here," he said, and gently moved the pillow from under my head, where he had placed two ring boxes from Cartier. Astonished, I looked at him.

"Happy birthday, darling."

I squealed with delight.

"I'll bet you thought I didn't get you a present, hmmmm?" he asked

"The thought had crossed my mind, but I considered the birthday party my present," I replied. I felt like jumping up and down on the bed out of sheer joy.

I opened the first one. It was the classic Cartier signature "Rolling Ring." It was three rings intertwined; one yellow, one white and one pink gold. It took my breath away.

"Now open the second one," he said excitedly. I could tell he was liking this. I opened the second. Wow! It was another ring like the first, but with a new look. Cartier called it the "Rolling Engine Ring" because the ring had grooves in the gold. The Rolling Engine is discontinued today but the Rolling Ring is as popular as ever.

Now I understood what he meant by "the princess and the pea."

"I guess I'm not a princess after all, James," I murmured playfully.

"You will always be a princess to me, Indian," he assured me. We hugged and I was overcome with joy. Even though these rings weren't a promise of an engagement, I loved them just the same. My Rolling Engine Ring was stolen a few years back, to my dismay, but I still wear the Rolling Ring.

* * * * *

Steve and I spoke on the phone every now and then. He confided to me that he was considering Ali MacGraw for the female lead in his new movie, *The Getaway*. I thought she was a terrific choice because she lent an air of class to any film. She also was one of the hottest actresses on the planet, since her previous movie was the mega hit *Love Story*. In addition to being so popular, she was beautiful and sweet natured, just Steve's type. Although I didn't know Ali at the time, I later met her when James and I attended a dinner party hosted by Ali and her then husband, Robert Evans.

Bob Evans was a very nice man, and so was his brother, Charles. The Evans brothers were handsome, charming and well connected. At that time, Bob was the executive vice in charge of production at Paramount Pictures, and had supervised *Love Story* as well as the classic, *The Godfather*. He was a powerful man who hosted wonderful dinner parties.

I first met Bob when I was 20. We were introduced by a mutual friend. A lot of stories were circulating in Hollywood about Bob, not all good, but I found him to be a perfect gentleman. That is, until I incurred his wrath later on.

The time came for dinner at Bob and Ali's. We arrived dead last. It was an enjoyable feast, and after dinner everyone headed to the theater overlooking the tennis courts. Ali knew that I had just completed *Junior Bonner* with Steve, so she pulled me aside and discreetly asked about him.

"What's he like?" she wanted to know.

I had only glowing things to say about Steve: He was wonderful to work with, he was extraordinarily nice to my son, and so on. I never spoke of our affair or my pregnancy. As I was talking, I was thinking about how much they would like each other, knowing that she might be taken in by his persuasive blue-collar charms. The two were complete opposites, but as we all know, opposites attract. She was refined and elegant. He was a down home good old boy. What sparks they would create both on screen and off!

My talk with Ali made me feel guilty, because she later left Bob for Steve, making it the most torrid and talked about affair in Hollywood since Elizabeth Taylor and Richard Burton ignited on *Cleopatra*. I became even more involved when Steve asked me to call Ali, to relay messages to her on his behalf. Foolishly, I agreed, because I felt beholden to Steve, who was my only real friend while I was in the hospital during my abortion.

Unfortunately for Bob, Steve and Ali's relationship took off from the first time they set eyes on each other.

"Sparks were flying all over the place—and it was definitely mutual attraction," Steve confided to me. I believe that their love affair was in the stars, with or without my involvement. Once they made their romantic connection, Steve and I would lose touch. Actually, that was fine with me, because I didn't want to be caught in the middle by relaying any more messages.

I was happy for Steve and Ali, because it seemed that Steve had finally found the woman he was searching for. I thought they'd be together forever, but as it turned out, neither their relationship nor mine with James would last. Steve and I would reunite five years later for dinner, when he confessed to me that he and Ali were having marital problems.

I have found "time heals all wounds" to be a true statement. Eventually, all would be forgiven between Bob Evans and me. We moved on in our lives, and our paths occasionally crossed. Years later when I was working as a social director for the St. James Club on Sunset Boulevard, I ran into him again. He was still his charming old self.

Things were back to normal with James, or as normal as they could be. In fact, our relationship was better than ever. We spent Thanksgiving with Dick and Dolly Martin.

I then spent five days with Gerry in Tennessee, during the Christmas holidays. I was to meet up with James and Skye in Mexico after Christmas. It was always wonderful to be with my son, but leaving him after our visits became increasingly more difficult. I knew that Gerry was in the loving, capable hands of his dad and stepmother, which gave me peace of mind. Nevertheless, I missed him terribly. We had a very loving and affectionate relationship. We were close, even with 2,000 miles between us.

After five days with Gerry, I left for Acapulco. James, Skye and I would spend 10 days in Frank Sinatra's villa in Las Brisas, the place to be, with views overlooking Acapulco Bay. Frank wasn't there, and he was gracious enough to lend it to James. I needed this vacation after the last few months.

For my Acapulco trip, I packed a lot of shorts, T-shirts and bikinis, along with my best dress for New Year's Eve. I had sun and fun on my mind. James would be all mine for the next 10 days and nights.

I boarded the plane for Mexico on December 26. My flight gave me a lot of time to reflect over the past year. Thoughts of Elvis began to creep up on me. He had called me on November 27 just to catch up on what had been happening in my life. It was great to hear from him again.

It had been a few months since our Palm Springs disaster, and he had been on tour since the beginning of November. Elvis sounded tired. He didn't bring up my last visit, which was fine with me.

Elvis asked me if I wanted to meet him in Texas and take in a few of his shows. I told him that I wasn't sure I could make it because of work, but I promised to leave word with Joe Esposito regarding my schedule. While Elvis was pleasant, he seemed a little annoyed that I couldn't commit to him. He confided to me that things at home weren't good: He and Priscilla were splitting up. The news came as a big surprise, although I knew something of their problems and her affair with Mike Stone. I always felt deep in my heart that they would never divorce, despite their problems. I didn't say much to Elvis about his breakup with Priscilla, but I could feel his pain.

To be honest, I wasn't dying to join him, because I was already familiar with the routine. In September 1970, Elvis had asked me to go on tour with him and I was ecstatic to be able to tour with the King. Yes!

At first it was exciting to see how his show was produced and all the behind-the-scenes how it all happened, but the excitement quickly faded as the everyday routine kicked in. No sleep, bad foot and too much partying. Well, you can imagine . . .

Staring out the window of the plane, I gazed at the cloud formations and thought about a trip I had taken with Elvis the previous September. We were flying in Baron Hilton's gorgeous Lear Jet, which he rented to Elvis at a reasonable price. It was the first luxury plane I'd ever seen. I felt rich just sitting inside.

We played silly games to pass the time, and one was making out figures in the clouds. Most of the band and backup singers flew in a separate plane from Elvis, Joe, Charlie Hodges and E's most trusted bodyguards.

Wherever our plane landed, the fans were there to greet Elvis. They waited hours upon hours just to get a glimpse of The King. I found it amazing that the fans knew E's schedule, and were usually one step ahead of him.

Elvis and I always got into separate limousines at the airports, because he was afraid the press would be able to identify me from my movies, commercials and print ads. Once we were away from the airport and the paparazzi, the driver would pull over and I would climb into Elvis' limo. We were never caught.

Touring isn't easy—crowds of people always around, strange cities, a different bed almost every night, hotel food, odd hours—nothing is familiar. It's hard on you physically and emotionally, and get's boring after awhile. Airplane to hotel, hotel to auditorium, auditorium back to hotel, a quick party and a little sleep, then back to the airplane to start it all over again. What a glamorous life!

Touring made Elvis weak, because he didn't get the proper rest or nutrition. His nervous system was out of whack, which made him pop more pills. He was more content to be at home in Graceland. Many times he simply couldn't handle the effects of the travel.

The stewardess interrupted my reverie by asking me if I wanted a drink. What the heck—I was on vacation—so I ordered a rum and Coke.

I rested my head against the seat while my thoughts drifted back to my glory days with Elvis. I missed him, and almost felt that if I turned my head he would be in the seat next to me, making me laugh with his jokes.

Maybe I should have agreed to meet with him in Houston. Part of me wanted to, but I would have to face James' wrath again. I wasn't prepared to do that—not yet. So I called Joe and blamed my absence on work. I didn't know if my relationship with James could survive another weekend with Elvis. Besides, James and I were starting fresh, and I didn't want to be the first one to deal out the infidelity.

My drink arrived and I sipped it slowly. The alcohol relaxed me, and my mind wandered back to that first tour with Elvis. We arrived in Miami on September 12, 1970. That night's show is my favorite, because it was my first. His show on tour was not as glamorous and exciting as his Vegas shows, but the touring shows were more intimate in a way. Being in Miami was exciting for me because

I had lived there, and my mother still lived in the city. In some ways, Miami was home. We stayed at the famous Fountainbleu Hotel, located on the south Miami Beach Riviera. I had always wanted to stay there as a kid and now, many years later, I *was* staying there—and with Elvis Presley, no less!

Once security saw us safely to our rooms, Elvis left to rehearse. The most difficult part of the show was making sure that the sound was perfect. Elvis, being a perfectionist, lost his cool if the sound production was faulty. I witnessed this once in Mobile, Alabama. He exploded at his sound man, because he couldn't hear his voice over the echo that reverberated from the speakers. He stormed off like a child. When Elvis showed his temper, people tended to get busy. It didn't take long before the problem was solved and The King went back to rehearsal.

Elvis demanded organization. If things didn't go right, the people who were responsible would be dismissed, and replaced by others who would take the job seriously. [His private life was a bit more spontaneous, but not much.] His professional life was meticulously planned.

Elvis had butterflies in his stomach before his shows, but once he strode on stage, all his shakes subsided. His shows were sold out long before his arrival in town, and he made sure his fans got a great performance every time. A lot of E's fans would save all year to buy their concert tickets, and The King never let them down. Every performance was worth the price.

I'm sure there were many times when Elvis tired of being Elvis, but he was a consummate showman and the song "I Did It My Way" fit him perfectly. His costumes were so much a part of who he was—flashy, overdone, sparkling—yet when you put it all together, it spelled "The King."

My favorite was his white outfit, beaded jumpsuit, although one might have identified it more with Liberace. Elvis may even have borrowed the look from the great pianist. I think he enjoyed the jumpsuits because they were easier to perform in, with all of his karate moves. Besides, they were just plain sexy.

The crazy outfits worked for him, because he totally believed in himself. He loved being outrageous in those clothes, and judging by the reactions of the women in the audience, they loved him in them, too.

Elvis preferred his women to wear long, sexy dresses and a lot of make-up, so I brought along the gowns he'd bought me at Suzy Creamcheese. I must admit, I did enjoy dressing up for Elvis. I felt like a princess. I always had the best seat in the house—the booth in the middle of the room. I could see the spit fly from his mouth as he belted out songs. Of course, E always made me feel as if he were singing only to me. I'm sure all of his women felt the same way.

As long as I knew Elvis, next to being home at Graceland, he was happiest when he was performing live in concert. He especially got a kick out of his ever attentive female fans. Part of his show included frequently bending to plant kisses on the adoring women in the front row. Without missing a beat, he'd throw one of his colorful sheer silk scarves to some screaming fan. He went through hundreds of them on every tour.

It was during this tour that I met the infamous Colonel Tom Parker. He definitely left an impression. He was a man of few words, and always seemed to sport a large cigar. The Colonel—he wasn't really a Colonel—usually traveled to the next town ahead of Elvis, to make preparations. He knew the music business and took good care of his only client. He was surprisingly messy and disheveled, and certainly didn't have the appearance of a man with a lot of money, but then again, he was a "carny" at heart.

I was in awe of him because of his reputation, but that changed when I met him. If you didn't know who he was, you wouldn't give him a second glance. He rarely came around, and the few times I did see him, he'd grunt a hello to me, barely acknowledging anyone except "his boy Elvis." The only time he paid me any attention was in Mobile, Alabama. As usual, he was at the bottom of the steps on the runway, waiting for Elvis, greeting him like a father. He actually said "Hi, Barbara," to me and added a slight wave and then went about his business. I guess that was as good as I was going to get. I don't think the Colonel approved of Elvis' lifestyle or his many girlfriends, including me.

The Colonel's life was simple and uncomplicated. It mainly consisted of taking care of Elvis, and gambling whenever he could. Elvis rarely spoke of Colonel Parker, but when he did, he'd inevitably make some joke. One thing was for sure: The Colonel and Elvis never socialized together. I think Elvis had mixed feelings about him, but out of sheer loyalty, he made no attempt to change their situation.

The guys often speculated about the Colonel's true identity; where he was from, why he was called "the Colonel" and so on. It later became known that he was born in Holland, came to the United States illegally, and never bothered to become a citizen. Colonel Parker died on January 27, 1997.

The concert in Mobile was our last stop together on this tour. Mobile was hard to forget, for reason's other than E's tantrum regarding the sound check.

It started like many nights on tour—with a call to room service. Elvis ordered everything he could get his hands on. I think that the menu and its down home cooking reminded him of Graceland. My favorite sandwich was a bacon, lettuce and tomato—you can't go wrong with that. Most hotel food, with the exception of the Fountainbleu, was not very edible. It usually arrived cold and undercooked. I once saw Elvis throw his fries at a couple of the guys, yelling, "Get me some *fresh* fries, not these cold limp taters." A second batch of fries arrived shortly, and they weren't much better than the first batch, but Elvis ate them anyway. Elvis and the guys were much more used to the lousy food than I was.

The Mobile show was held on September 14 at the Mobile Municipal Auditorium. The crowd was bigger than the crowds in Miami, and was more out of control. A lot of people tried to push their way into the show. It was just short of a riot.

During the show, Elvis stopped singing and said in a barely audible voice, "Barbara, I'm glad you're here, baby." My hair stood up on my arms. It was such a kick to hear him say my name in front of all of those people, even though he said it very low, from the back of his throat. Then he sang my favorite song, "It's Now Or Never." My body went numb when his velvet voice came out of that gorgeous, pouty mouth. It was a combination that was too much for any woman to resist. His smile is one of the things I miss most about him. E's smile always had a way of making you smile back.

"My Winston ad which was a big campaign in the 1970s." From the Barbara Leigh Collection.

Once the show concluded, we headed back to the hotel. That night our suite was filled with the usual after concert crowd: the regular guys and their girls, Joe and his current girl, Darlene, along with Elvis and me. There was some serious partying going on—lots of drinking, dancing, laughing and talking. The room was wall-to-wall people. We didn't always have so much happening, but for whatever reason, this night we cut loose like never before. We drank a lot more than usual, getting loud and rowdy.

I was sitting on the couch next to Elvis. Darlene was next to me. She was very attractive, in her early twenties, with light dirty blonde shoulder length hair. She was doing her damnedest to befriend me. It's my nature to be friendly, and I was no different with Darlene. That was a big mistake.

Darlene started asking me some very personal questions. At the time I didn't know that she had a serious crush on Elvis, nor did I know that she had already "chatted" with some of Elvis' other girls. We talked like two old girlfriends. When Elvis got up to use the bathroom, she made her move.

"You know, Barbara, Elvis has lots of girlfriends. I wouldn't get hung up on him, if I were you. You mean nothing to him, you're just another girl," Darlene said very matter of factly.

I was taken aback. One minute we had been laughing and carrying on, and the next minute she delivered a left cross to my chin.

I was used to women hating me. They usually liked me once they got to know me, and saw that I was basically a very down-to-earth person. Darlene was a witch, however.

When Elvis returned, I tried to act as if nothing had happened. The party was still in full swing, and I wasn't going to ruin the evening. So, I sat there sulking. Someone had brought in some vodka and orange juice, and I asked Elvis if he would mind if I made a drink. I rarely had anything to drink around Elvis. He was a little surprised by my request—because he rarely drank—but I needed something.

The party went on for several more hours. Finally, Elvis called it a night. As usual, no one was allowed to leave until The King proclaimed that the evening was over. The suite thinned out, and the guys escorted their girls to their rooms. As Joe and Darlene said good night, I noticed that she had a glint in her eye. It only reinforced my insecurities. The minute the door closed Elvis kissed me, and as much as I wanted to proceed, Darlene's words echoed in my head. I excused myself to the bathroom, to change into my nightgown. Even this far in our relationship, we never undressed in front of each other.

When I came out, Elvis was on the phone with his doctor. He hung up, and laid me on the bed to make soft, sweet love. Even though I was emotionally wounded, I loved Elvis, and nothing was going to keep me from showing him how I felt about him. In those days, Elvis was still strong and into sex. It would change as the drugs took away his energy. Afterwards, we held each other for a few minutes, until someone knocked on the door.

"Elvis, who's at the door?" I asked suspiciously, wondering who could be knocking at that hour.

"It's the doc, baby," he said innocently. I got up and answered the door and there stood Dr. Nick with his little black bag of goodies.

"Come on in," E yelled to Dr. Nick.

This was my first meeting with Dr. George Nichopoulos. I would later bump into him again at Graceland. I had no idea what Dr. Nick was doing there, but I sensed that they wanted privacy, so I excused myself and went into the bathroom. Once there, I brushed my hair, and stared at my reflection in the mirror. I was feeling melancholy. Darlene's trap was setting. I stood there for a long time, before Elvis knocked on the door.

"Barbara, honey, come out here. I have something for you." I opened the door still in my nightgown. Elvis and Dr. Nick were standing at the foot of the bed.

"Doc's going to give you a shot to help you sleep," Elvis said soothingly. "I've just had mine, and you're going to get the same thing." I hated needles! The thought of a stranger giving me a shot—I didn't care if he *was* a legitimate doctor—frightened me to death.

"I don't need a shot, Elvis. I'm already so tired that I'll fall right to sleep," I said in my most convincing words.

"Don't be a 'fraidy cat, it's not going to hurt you. It'll just put you to sleep with me," my man told me. He looked so sincere and trustworthy. Who was I not to believe that what The King said wasn't Gospel Truth? Again, I gave in—a very dangerous thing to do.

"OK, Elvis, if you say it will just put me to sleep." Foolish girl! Dumb, silly girl! Dr. Nick prepared my injection and I lifted my gown. I was a little embarrassed showing him my bottom, because I had just met the man. He administered the shot, and before I could open my mouth to protest, the drug was in my system. Once Dr. Nick left, my mood became more apparent to Elvis. I was still reeling from the Darlene incident.

"Baby, are you OK? You're awfully quiet," Elvis observed.

"I'm fine, Elvis," I said with a touch of impatience. But I wasn't fooling him one bit. He was too perceptive.

"What's wrong with my girl?" he demanded to know.

I started feeling woozy, and a little out of control. Before I knew what I was doing, I blurted it all out.

"Darlene told me I'm just another girl in your harem, that you really don't love me." Her words, spoken through my mouth, made the veins on Elvis' forehead stand out.

"*What*?" he yelled. He got up on his knees, grabbing me, and demanded to know what else Darlene had said.

"Elvis, please don't say anything to her," I begged. "I don't want to cause any more trouble." But it was too late.

"Tell me everything Darlene said." Elvis was visibly irate.

Sniffling between my tears, I told him exactly what she had said, and how much it had hurt me. Elvis became madder and madder the longer I went on. By the time I had finished, he was dragging me down the hallway to Joe's room. He pounded on the door with his fist.

BOOM! BOOM! BOOM!

"Open this door right now," Elvis yelled. He was pissed. Joe was asleep, but the pounding on the door woke him in an instant. I was feeling guilty, because getting Joe involved was the last thing I wanted to do. Elvis started in on Joe, telling him word for word what Darlene had said to me.

I saw Darlene sneak into the bathroom and I followed, with the intention of apologizing. We were still in our nightgowns. What I saw startled me: Darlene was standing in front of the mirror trying to glue her eyelashes back on. The sight of her put everything into perspective. She was putting on her eyelashes so that she could look good for Elvis! I was blown away. Any feelings of guilt I may have had vanished.

I quietly walked back to where Elvis was standing. Joe was trying to calm Elvis down, and began to apologize profusely to me.

"Barbara, she didn't mean what she said. She was out of line, and probably had too much to drink," Joe said, trying to sooth my feelings. Darlene came waltzing out of the bathroom with an innocent smile, eyelashes intact, looking as if she were ready for the show.

Elvis glared at her.

"What the hell were you telling Barbara those lies for?" I had never seen E so livid before.

"I, I, uh, uh, I'm sorry Elvis," was all Darlene could stammer. She wasn't so smug now.

Elvis raged at Joe.

"I don't ever want to see her again, Joe. You got it?" Elvis said.

"Got it boss," Joe said, taking his orders like a soldier.

Poor Joe was forced to dump her right then and there. It was that way with all of the guys. One misstep, and their girls were gone. It was a good thing most of them had wives at home, or they'd have never had a long-lasting relationship.

Elvis grabbed my hand and pulled me out the door. He calmed down once we got back to our room. The shots Dr. Nick had administered should have put us to sleep, but our adrenalin was pumping. Why would Elvis go to this great length to confront Darlene if he didn't really love me? Elvis grabbed some scratch paper and a pen. He scribbled feverishly, then handed me the paper. The note read:

Barbara,

For what it means, I have loved you and will continue to love you as long as I live. Keep this to yourself. It's yours alone.

The Panther

I've saved that note for all these years, and it has meant more to me than anything else Elvis ever said or gave to me. As long as he lived, I never showed that note to anyone, since he had asked me to keep it to myself.

CHAPTER SIXTEEN

Still lost in my thoughts while at 30,000 feet, I passed on dinner with the airlines. Food for thought was all I needed, with the exception of another drink. Daydreaming about my tour with Elvis the year before made the time pass quickly, and before I knew it the seat belt light came on, indicating our descent into Acapulco. Reminiscing had left me feeling melancholy, and made me miss him. Again, I began to doubt my decision not to meet Elvis in Texas, and at that moment, I wished I had said yes.

My popping ears immediately brought me out of my dreamlike state. I looked out the window, and noticed the runway right beneath the plane. A flash of excitement went through my body, and for the first time that day, my thoughts turned to James.

My heart began pounding at the thought of a whole week with the Smiling Cobra; they were sure to be exciting. The plane taxied up the runway to the gate. I threw on my hat and sunglasses, and ran into James' arms. I saw this trip as a chance to solidify my relationship with him. It turned out to be our last hurrah.

I was greeted at our beautiful rental house by the other guests: James' daughter, Skye Aubrey, and restaurateur Nicky Blair.

Nicky gave me a warm hug and a kiss. Skye was more casual toward me, but pleasant. The two of us were the same age, which made it difficult for her to relate to me as her father's girlfriend.

We toasted each other with banana daiquiris, and began our vacation by getting bombed.

Frank Sinatra's villa was gorgeous. You wouldn't expect anything less from Frank. As if staying in Frank's villa wasn't enough, we also had his entire staff ready and waiting to cook, clean and wash our clothes for us. What luxury!

The villa was open to great views of the bay, and tastefully decorated in Mexican decor. The floors were tile, and southwestern art hung from the walls.

Most of the time we lived in our swimsuits, lounging by the pool. Frank's place became the unofficial Hollywood hangout while we were there. Las Brisas was a trendy small community; everyone was always throwing a party. God, how I miss the '70s!

This part of Mexico was much the same then as it is today: tequila heaven. Tequila was the main poison among the young and beautiful, and the drink was plentiful. There is no better place than Acapulco to sip on a Tequila Sunrise, while watching the sun set on the horizon. Combine that with the waves lapping at the banks of Acapulco Bay, and it made for a very romantic setting.

Backgammon was the rich, trendy sport of the day. There was always a group of men playing for high stakes while the women just played for fun. One of the great players, whom I'll call Russ, was a wealthy Beverly Hills entrepreneur and playboy. I met him at Freddy Fields' place in Acapulco, when he showed up with a pretty blonde French starlet who was leading her miniature poodle on a leash. This lethal beauty happened to be wearing very skimpy shorts, which caused quite a reaction. It was the kind of entry people don't forget. All the men stopped their backgammon game to admire her legs. Naturally, the attention made all of the wives and girlfriends green with envy.

To me, this Beverly Hills playboy was a dead ringer for Neil Diamond and was drop-dead gorgeous. He was bright, charming and flirtatious, but respectful when he did so. It made James nervous when Russ struck up a conversation with me, and it never failed—James and I would eventually end up having a big fight over him. Russ had a magic about him and James felt it.

New Year's Eve 1971 was one of the best days I ever spent with James. We went to a party hosted by Freddie Fields and Polly Bergen. Nothing in the world mattered to me that night but to be there with James. We danced, drank, laughed and were completely lost in each other. We were in love that night.

As is often the case, the romantic New Year's Eve turned into a big hangover.

A few days after New Year's, Russ showed up unannounced at our villa with some friends. This infuriated James, and he later took it out on me. I hadn't thought anything of the playboy's attention, but James was furious. For the rest of our vacation, it seemed as if we ran into Russ no matter where we went. There seemed no way to avoid him.

As far as I was concerned, James overreacted. In public, he kept his cool and made friendly overtures toward this playboy, but once the bedroom door was closed, he accused me of leading him on. The accusation was utterly ridiculous. James was the only man I wanted to be with. Why couldn't he see that?

James was ruining it for us with his jealousy. When he got angry, he acted in one of two ways: He was either silent and cold, or heaved verbal abuse at me. Neither was pleasant. His behavior ruined our vacation. His jealously was beginning to intimidate me, making me afraid to even smile or look at another man. No one in our tight knit little group had any inkling of the anger James was heaping on me, because he was a master at deception.

After several heated battles with James, I began to question our relationship. He was doing his damnedest to push me out the door and into the arms of a stranger.

Being a Scorpio, I have a stubborn side. I wasn't about to apologize to him for something I hadn't done.

By the end of our trip, I knew it was over. Too much had gone down between us. Eventually, I withdrew from him sexually, which angered him even more. I wasn't going to give myself to a man who made me afraid to bc myself.

Once back in Los Angeles, the discontent in my heart grew and I would never feel the same about "The Love Machine." I never recovered from the hurt of my abortion, and he couldn't get over his anger, jealously and damned pride.

Breaking up is never easy, no matter who's right or who's wrong. But once my mind was made up, there was no going back. We were only happy when I gave in to his wishes. My life was back in the hands of the little girl from Georgia.

Our last night together was like the closing scene of Margaret Mitchell's *Gone With the Wind*. My feeling was, "Frankly James, I don't give a damn!"

"Indian, you know I love you. We can work this out," he pleaded, but it was clear. James would never fully forgive me for getting pregnant with Steve's child, and I was only kidding myself to believe otherwise. He picked too many fights.

Even though our relationship had been strained for the past year, when the time came for it to end, it was painful. It was hard letting go of a dream. He was my hero, my Heathcliffe, my Rhett Butler, maybe the dad I never had.

And it was even more painful to find out that there was another woman in James' life.

I confronted him about a certain actress who had been spending a lot of time with him, which James confirmed. It was over. I needed to move on, but I also needed to hear it from his lips. I remember getting into my car and driving to Skye's home.

A surprised Skye greeted me at the door.

"Your dad and I broke up. Can I come in?"

Skye opened the door, and I threw myself into her arms. Instantly, we were two women clinging to each other for support.

Through my tears, I relayed to Skye the night's events. She already knew about Pamela, the new woman in James' life, but being her father's daughter and not yet my friend, she felt it best not to cross her father. Pamela would be James' last girlfriend. After that, he just drifted from woman to woman, without any real commitment.

Skye and I bonded that night. Her feelings of abandonment by her father, plus my feelings of betrayal brought us together. We became close friends, and the friendship continues to this day. I thought I had lost a boyfriend, but in reality, I had only lost a bad relationship. I came out on top, because I won a beautiful friendship.

James and I would never kiss, touch or share another intimate moment together. It would be many years before our paths crossed again and when I did see him, the question on my mind was, "What did I ever see in that guy?"

A few days after James and I broke up, I was invited by director Roger Vadim to go to Paris with him. The timing couldn't have been better. I needed to get out of Los Angeles, and away from any temptation of returning to James. I accepted Roger's invitation. Although James and I were on the outs, he saw to it that people at MGM looked after me. It was very generous of him, but it wasn't necessary. Roger and his wealthy jet-setters took good care of me. I had a ball in Paris. It was the perfect remedy to a broken heart.

"Director Roger Vadim and me during *Pretty Maids All In A Row*." **From the Barbara Leigh Collection.**

Before I left, Elvis called. It seemed as if our schedules were forever conflicting. He was home at Graceland and he invited me to visit him there, but my heart was set on going to Paris.

I loved Graceland and was almost tempted to say yes, but our screwy schedules made it difficult. I enjoyed my visit in the spring of 1971—an experience I'll never forget. Elvis had taken me on a tour of his childhood homes, including the projects in Memphis, Tennessee. He also drove me to his beloved birthplace in Tupelo, Mississippi, with a barricade of the Memphis Mafia following closely behind us.

The house in Tupelo has been described as a shotgun shack, and it wasn't too far off the mark. Vernon and his brother, Vester, built the all white 15-foot by 32-foot room for about $180 shortly before Elvis' birth.

"The place would fit in the living room of Graceland," Elvis remarked. Incidentally, the house in Tupelo has been placed on the National Register of Historic Places.

He even took me to see the first home he bought for his mama. He loved sharing his past with me.

It's hard to describe the excitement I felt driving through the cast-iron gates of Graceland the first time. I'd seen pictures of it, but nothing did justice to seeing it in person. It was breathtaking.

Graceland was purchased by Elvis in 1957, but the house was built in 1939. It was a Georgian Colonial style home, with four huge Corinthian columns in the front portico. The facade of the home was a vanilla Mississippi fieldstone, with hunter green shutters.

Graceland boasted 23 rooms, eight bedrooms, four-and-a-half baths and more than 10,000 square feet. Elvis was more himself, more relaxed, at Graceland; it was home. It represented The King, his career, his family and all of his achievements.

As I entered the hallway through the front door, I immediately noticed the Strauss crystal chandelier overhead. A staircase lined with smoked glass mirrors led to the second floor. The dining room was on the left, and the living room was on the right. The living room was open and inviting. The carpet was white, as were the extra long sofa and two chairs. The drapes were dark blue with gold trim. There was also a fireplace with mirrors above it, and a gold sunburst clock centered above the mantle.

The living room led into the music room. At the center of the music room sat a gold leaf grand piano, given to Elvis by Priscilla for his birthday. The drapes were gold lame with white trim, and the sofa was upholstered in gold and white striped fabric. There was also a white television with gold trim. Elvis liked to have a television in every room, if possible.

After a quick look around the main floor of the house, we went outside to drive go-carts. Elvis was very competitive at whatever he did—playing games, riding horses, driving go-carts. Whatever it was, he wanted to win, and the guys let him. When we were riding the go-carts, Elvis gave me the scare of my life while playing his version of "chicken." Elvis usually made the other drivers move, in order to make them appear chicken. He laughed so hard on those go-carts, which made it all the more fun.

When we tired of go-carts, Elvis took me upstairs. On the second floor were Elvis' bedroom, wardrobe room and office, and Lisa Marie's bedroom and bath.

We spent a lot of time in his bedroom, which looked out over the front yard. The main thing I remember about it was his custom-made bed. It was 11 feet square, and the frame was upholstered in black leather.

The bed was surrounded by TVs: a big one at the foot of the bed, and two smaller ones on the ceiling near the top of the bed. Despite the fact that three televisions were constantly on, Elvis was more interested in talking about philosophy and his books than actually watching TV. I loved E's bedroom; it was our private sanctuary.

Just off his bedroom was the bathroom where he died. I can still see it clearly, and it saddens me. It breaks my heart to think of Elvis lying there with no one to help him. If only someone had knocked on his door, or walked in to check on him. He might have gotten angry at them for disturbing his privacy. But if only they had.

Graceland was a happy place at the time I was there. Meals were shared with whomever happened to be there, and Elvis made sure no one starved. He loved to eat, but he didn't like to eat alone. We had the same taste in food. I was thrilled with the overcooked meat, gravy and biscuits, mashed potatoes and black-eyed peas. He also enjoyed heavily sugared iced tea with fresh lemons.

I felt right at home eating with him in his gorgeous dining room. It was ironic eating down home cooking in a room that looked like it was built in Rome. The room had a black marble floor, and blue drapes with gold trim. Black and gold trim chairs sat around a large table.

After dinner, we'd usually take a stroll on the grounds or through his trophy room, which was simply beyond description, but I'll try.

The "Hall of Gold" stretched for nearly 80 feet. The walls were lined with glass cases that contained Elvis' gold and platinum records, music awards, trophies, certificates and memorabilia of every kind. The contents of that room represented a lifetime of work, and that was only up to 1971. It was overwhelming.

The hallway led into what is known as "The Big Room," which today houses the biggest collection of Elvis memorabilia in the Graceland complex, including movie scripts and posters, scrapbooks and even Elvis and Priscilla's wedding clothes! Also on display are paintings done by his fans, as well as his cherished gun collection and karate outfits.

Outside of the trophy room is the Meditation Garden, which at the time was his private retreat .

The Meditation Garden was a beautiful mix of exotic plants and flowers. It was built in the mid-1960s, and was influenced by Elvis' fascination with Eastern religions and philosophies. Four 19th century Spanish stained-glass windows decorated the rear brick wall, which was supported by white columns. At the center of the garden was a water fountain enclosed by a black cast-iron fence. It was inspiring.

The garden later became the grave site for Elvis, his twin brother, Jesse; his mother, Gladys; his father, Vernon; and his grandmother, Minnie Mae, who managed to outlive them all.

One of the highlights of my trip to Graceland was meeting Minnie Mae. You could always find Minnie in her room, gently rocking back and forth in her rocking chair. She was gracious and sharp as a tack for a woman her age—she must have been in her late 70s when I met her. She loved telling stories about Elvis when he was a boy. Minnie Mae appeared to be a very lonely lady, and her greatest joy was seeing Elvis. He adored her.

The highlight of the trip was when Elvis sat at the piano and we sang "Amazing Grace" together. It was one of our favorite religious songs. We'd both grown up singing it in church. Nothing can bring two people closer than singing, especially when one of them has a voice like Elvis Presley.

Years later, I drove through Memphis with a friend, but I couldn't go to Graceland. I wanted to remember the house as it was when I last saw it—the memory of Elvis living in it, his laughter, his energy—not as a museum open for tourists.

Reminiscing about Graceland left me once again wondering if I had made the right choice in turning Elvis down. One thing was for sure. He was getting fed up with my unavailability. I had a choice: Elvis or Paris.

I chose Paris. Simply put, I'd never been to Paris, and I knew the routine with Elvis. Roger and I were friends at the time. I knew Paris would be exciting, and I wasn't disappointed. He showed me one of the best times I've ever had while in Europe. After returning from Paris, I headed to New York to shoot an ad for Revlon. Once again, I was unavailable when Elvis called me to join him on his next tour. This was the coup de gras—our affair was officially over. When I turned him down, he moved on with his life and other girlfriends. We were no longer lovers, but we remained in touch sporadically. You can only say no for so long, and the newness wears off. The King was onto his next challenge.

Linda Thompson became the new lady in his life. She was good for him, and he needed someone like her. She didn't work, so there were no schedules to plan around and no excuses why she couldn't be with him. He had found the perfect woman to replace Priscilla. His ego had been shattered when Priscilla left him for Mike Stone, and he needed a woman to stand by him and pamper him. By June 1972, they were a couple.

Linda was a beautiful 22-year-old Southern Belle. She was a former Miss Tennessee, but more importantly, she was smart, nuturing and had a great personality.

Their relationship lasted until 1976, but by the summer of 1973 Elvis was calling me again. By that time my career was the most important priority in my life, so I avoided any serious long-term relationships. I wanted to be free to do as I pleased, and not have to live to please a man, as I had done so many times in the past.

After two major studio productions, *Pretty Maids All in a Row* and *Junior Bonner*, I returned to my acting career in an independent exploitation film, *Terminal Island* with Tom Selleck. I did it as a favor to director Stephanie Rothman, who also helmed *The Student Nurses*.

Making the film was fun, especially working with Tom Selleck, whom I had known previously when we shot a commercial for British Sterling cologne and also from *Bracken's World*.

Terminal Island gained a promotional boost from a nude pictorial I did for *Playboy* entitled, "Indian," which was published in their May 1973 issue. *Playboy's* West Coast Photo Editor Marilyn Grabowski had seen me in *Pretty Maids*, and got the idea that I should pose for them. She approached the photographer Charles Bush, who was my dear friend, and had him ask me. At first I declined, but I later reconsidered. We shot a test session at a private home in Palm Springs, because *Playboy* wanted to see how my body looked, and we sent it to them. They accepted it, and Charles negotiated the deal for a full celebrity pictorial.

Charles and I produced the entire pictorial by ourselves, in the summer of 1972. I'm very proud of that, because we didn't have a stylist of any kind. We rented outfits from the Western Costume Company, and used authentic looking Native American garb. We also rented a camper, and mapped out our route. We then headed to the Navajo Reservation at Canyon De Chelly in Arizona, where the cliff dwellers lived, and to Bryce Canyon in Utah and a little into Monument Valley. It was an enchanting experience.

"Photo from the *Playboy* layout 'Indian.'" Photo by Charles Bush, courtesy of P.E.I.

We had a ball shooting the photos. We would find a location, and then haul all the equipment up to the area we chose to set up and shoot. We hiked for a long time to get to some of those spots, where I did my own face and body make-up. At night we stayed at a motel in town because I needed a hot shower to wash off the layers of dirt, and there was plenty.

Our locations were spectacular landmarks and the best that mother nature had to offer. We spent a week shooting more than 100 rolls of film, with 36 photos on each roll. I had agreed to show my breasts and the rest of my body, but not my pubic hair. That was a big issue for me at the time. I wore a robe when we weren't shooting—I didn't just sit around naked. When we had an idea for a pose, and I was trying to provoke the readers' imagination in the photos we were creating, I removed my robe and didn't think about the nudity. I focused on the big picture.

I had picture approval on which photos would be submitted. Charles and I viewed every one with a projector in his studio and edited them. We were blown away by the images. They were incredible photos—visually, artistically and spiritually. We gave *Playboy* the best ones, and the editors made the final selection for their May 1973 issue.

"At the mouth of a cave from my *Playboy* layout titled 'Indian.'" Photo by Charles Bush, courtesy of P.E.I.

I was proud of the pictorial when I saw it in the magazine. Once it was published, I went to Chicago and visited the original *Playboy* mansion where I first met Hugh Hefner. I felt very much at home in that environment. In fact, the people at *Playboy* have always made me feel comfortable and at home. I've never been made to feel that I was being exploited. To me, if someone is happy to pose for *Playboy*, that is their choice. It was never a moral issue for me.

However, my friends and family had a mixed reaction, and gave me some flak. To my surprise, the pictorial also provoked a negative professional consequence. I shot a TV commercial for men's slacks with Linda (*Dallas*) Gray. When the company's executive's discovered that I had posed for *Playboy*, they refused to air the commercial.

On the other hand, Elvis loved the layout, and immediately got in touch with me by phone. He went on and on about how much he loved it, and told me that seeing my pictures made him miss me. Then he asked me to visit him.

"What would Linda say about that, Elvis?" I asked. His response was classic Elvis—sweet and noncommittal. "I knew you first, baby."

That was true. Elvis never liked being questioned. Furthermore, he hated giving answers. We didn't get together then, but we did manage to get together a year later at his home in Beverly Hills while Linda was out of town. By this time Elvis and I had moved way past sex, so I didn't have any guilty feelings about seeing him behind Linda's back. I don't think Elvis was having sex with anyone by then. He had put on a lot of weight, and his daily routine of prescription drugs was out of control. He was lonely, and seemed unhappy and unfulfilled, even with a steady girl in his life.

He stayed in his room most of the time, his head buried in many books. His appetite was enormous and he ate what he craved—sweets and peanut butter sandwiches.

The last time we spent the night together was in the fall of 1974. It was wonderful to see Elvis, but this time it was sad. He was grossly overweight and his once beautiful face was terribly swollen. In just four short years, Elvis had aged physically by at least 20 years. To me, it didn't really matter, I loved him no matter how he looked. I knew that it was the drugs that had taken such a heavy toll on him. But the drugs couldn't completely take his mind. Even when his body was bloated, his spirit was clear. It was his soul that I adored.

I arrived at his house in Beverly Hills, and was met at the door by Joe Esposito. He escorted me to E's bedroom door. I knocked gently.

"Come on in, Barbara," Elvis said in that familiar, sexy Southern drawl. That was rare. He hardly ever called me Barbara; usually it was "darlin'." I should have known something was wrong. What I found when I went in wasn't my Elvis. He was the Elvis I'd heard about—fat and depressed. He sat on the bed with his back against his headboard, surrounded by a dozen books.

"It's great to see you," I said, beaming from ear to ear.

"Great to see you too, baby," he said with a smile.

I kicked off my shoes and jumped on the bed, landing in his loving arms for a big bear hug. We laughed and kissed playfully. Elvis was sweating profusely. His skin felt clammy and sticky.

What the hell has happened to him? I thought. I told myself that I didn't care what he looked like—it was his company that I enjoyed. I still wondered what had happened to the beautiful, sexy and energetic man I had once known.

Within a few minutes, he was citing scripture and philosophizing about the world and current events. I sat there listening to him as any good pupil would—just like in the old days when I took in every utterance—but there were moments when I'd think of something I needed to do. I found my mind wandering, and it was strange—this was my *idol*. I stayed with him most of the night, listening to his every word. He got a kick out of the fact that I was able to recite the books of the Bible, and was tickled when I recited for him verbatim the poem "Deserata." He loved that poem as much as I did.

Later that night I got hungry, and asked Elvis if he was in the mood to grab a bite to eat.

"Not really, but you eat, baby. Help yourself to the kitchen, and could you bring me some cold water when you come back?" It was unusual for Elvis to turn down food at that point, but I must have caught him on a full stomach.

"Sure E, I'll be back in a second."

On my way to the kitchen, I stopped off in the living room

to say hello to Charlie Hodges, Joe and Lisa Marie. I exchanged greetings with Charlie and caught up with Joe. Lisa Marie, Elvis and Priscilla's only child, must have been around five years old. She was sitting on the floor combing her doll's hair, but the doll didn't have a body, just a head. It was an eerie sight.

Next to her was a large music box with flashing colored lights that changed to the beat of the music. Lisa Marie sat there, combing the doll's head and singing to her daddy's record.

"Hi Lisa," I said to her, although she didn't know me. She looked up quickly, then back to her doll's head as she quietly said hello. Her eyes looked so sad. She didn't look like a little girl. She looked like an old soul in a little body, but with a beautiful spirit.

Lisa spent a lot of time with Elvis in those days. I think Priscilla wanted them to be close, and they were. I didn't observe a nanny. Perhaps there was one, but it always appeared to me that the guys were her nannies.

Joe got up and walked to the kitchen. He opened the refrigerator, which displayed every kind of food imaginable. I was hungry, so I made up a tray of peanut butter and jelly sandwiches, milk and bottled water. Joe carried the tray of food and drinks for me back to Elvis' bedroom, and we cautiously entered the room. Elvis was still sitting in the same spot as when I had left him.

"What took you so long?" E asked with a touch of impatience.

"Sorry Elvis, I couldn't make up my mind what I wanted to eat," I said. Actually, I had wanted to be with normal people; to watch Lisa Marie play and talk with Joe, so I had spent longer than I planned away from Elvis.

"Honey, I told you I'm not hungry," Elvis said with a touch of annoyance, as if I didn't listen to him.

"Do you mind if I eat sitting on the bed?" I asked him.

"My bed is your bed," he said sweetly. Then we laughed. I crawled up on the bed with a sandwich in one hand and a glass of milk in the other. He waited until my mouth was full, and then he asked me a lot of questions. When I tried to speak and couldn't, we both cracked up. For that moment, he was his old sweet self again.

We stayed up late, going over all of his beloved books. *Be Here Now*, *The Impersonal Life* and the Bible were books Elvis read over and over again. He was like a child holding onto a favorite toy or blanket.

He was happy that I was there by his side once again; happy to have someone there with whom he could relax. I gave him the attention he craved, and listened to him as he waxed philosophical. Around 4 a.m. he started winding down. I didn't pay much attention to what pills E was taking, but he fell asleep during one of his dialogues. At this point in our relationship, it seemed normal for him to take so many pills.

I held him like a child, then fell into my own deep sleep. There was no need for a little red pill that night. I didn't want one, and Elvis didn't try to give me one. The entire evening had been a soul-searching experience. Everything became clear to me. I realized that no one woman, man, child or thing could have saved The King. It was a scary feeling, but I felt that he was ready to meet his maker.

It was evident to those who knew him that he was unhappy. His career had hit a lull, and sadly, I think, he was still reeling from losing Priscilla.

The next morning I awoke early. I looked at Elvis sleeping so peacefully, kissed him gently on the cheek, touched his face with my hand, and slid out of bed without waking him. I got dressed quietly, closing his bedroom door behind me. The house was unusually still. Trying not to awaken anyone, I tiptoed through the house and out the front door. It would be the last time we spent an evening alone together.

* * * * *

"Harris Comic's Vampirella cover #69." From the
Barbara Leigh Collection.

In 1975, the comic book character "Vampirella" was being cast for a movie to be made by the world famous British company Hammer Films, in association with American International Pictures. *Vampirella*, created by *Famous Monsters of Filmland* magazine editor Forrest J Ackerman, is a female vampire from Draculon, a planet where there are two moons and two suns.

After an unsuccessful worldwide search, especially in Europe, Hammer chairman and producer Michael Carreras came to Los Angeles. Even Lynda Carter, later of *Wonder Woman* fame, was turned down for the role.

As fate would have it, I won the part that changed my life forever.

If any film company could capture Vampirella as she was meant to be, it was Hammer Films. They had brought Dracula to life with Christopher Lee, and had also made many films with the legendary Peter Cushing, who portrayed such memorable characters as Baron Frankenstein, Dr. Van Helsing and Sherlock Holmes for them. Michael Carreras and Hammer also produced *One Million Years B.C.* starring Raquel Welch, in which special effects wizard Ray Harryhausen brought his beloved dinosaurs to life on screen. The company was very innovative, and the leader when it came to horror films.

I had loved vampires as a child, ever since my first viewing of *Horror of Dracula,* which starred Peter Cushing and Christopher Lee. Lee and Cushing were my horror idols. If someone would have told me at the age of nine that I would one day meet these two men, I couldn't have imagined it.

The two much loved British actors starred together in many horror films, and were good friends. Christopher Lee even attended my 30th birthday party, which was catered by Chasen's restaurant. The party was given by Donald Bren, the Irvine land king who lived in Beverly Hills and whom I was dating at the time. Imagine that—my favorite Dracula was among the 250 invited guests sharing my special birthday with me. It was too much!

Christopher Lee took me completely by surprise. He was a gentle giant, nothing at all like the bad guys he portrayed on screen. He was very tall, with broad shoulders and a deep voice. I just adored him. He was kind and engaging, instantly making me feel at ease with him.

After being cast for *Vampirella*, I went under contract to Hammer Films for a three-picture deal, the first of which was to be shot in London. Ed Hookstratten, Elvis' lawyer, negotiated my contract for me instead of my agent, Ronnie Lief, because Michael and Ronnie didn't get along. Ronnie wanted a better deal, and wasn't happy with the contract that was drawn up by Michael. The two had a very heated discussion and finally Michael refused to deal with Ronnie.

For the first time in my life, I was totally consumed with my character. During the year-and-a-half that I was involved with *Vampirella*, I actually *became* her in my mind. I looked very much like her character and I started dressing like how I envisioned she would dress. Gone were my jeans and T-shirts. I started wearing black colors everywhere I went. My hair was unusually long, and I even sported bangs and long red fingernails. The only thing I was missing were the fangs. Eventually, friends would tell me to get a hold of myself, which I reluctantly did.

To me, the ultimate compliment is that old adage, "Imitation is the sincerest form of flattery." I was comfortable in the part of Vampirella, and felt that in many ways I had embodied her spirit. Dressing and wearing my hair like her was a way to connect with her character. If Robert De Niro could be lauded by critics for losing himself in an acting role, why couldn't I do the same?

To me, Vampirella represented a dream come true—the part of a lifetime. She was a strong female who was smart, sexy and vibrant. Her movie came along at the perfect time.

"Harris Comic's Vampirella Cover #76." From the Barbara Leigh Collection.

The long-term plans for *Vampirella* were huge. I sold all of my personal belongings, and looked forward to moving to London. Hammer Films had a first draft of a script (which I still have) ready for production. In November 1975, on the way to London, we stopped in New York City where Michael Carreras, Peter Cushing, Forry Ackerman and James Warren of Warren Publishing—who owned the rights to *Vampirella*—were to be special guests at the *Famous Monsters of Filmland* Convention. We held court at the convention, a popular event for horror film buffs, where people young and old alike gathered. It was a wonderful publicity boon for *Vampirella*.

Promo shots were taken of me in the infamous skimpy, red Vampirella costume, which was made by The Western Costume Company. It was the happiest time in my life, dwarfing all of my relationships with men. This was what I had sacrificed years for, and now it was paying off—or so I thought.

While in New York, Michael, Peter and I were scheduled to do *The Tomorrow Show with Tom Snyder*. When we arrived at NBC studios, and Tom saw me in costume, he refused to allow me on camera. I had not been cleared by the network, and the costume was a little risque for television in the '70s. Ironically, the provocative costume wouldn't raise an eyebrow today. Michael was furious, but he and Peter did the next best thing: They talked about me on the show, and how I brought Vampirella to life.

Elvis happened to watch the show that night, and yelled for Joe to get me on the phone. He eventually found me at my hotel in New York. The first thing Elvis said to me was, "Darlin', I want to see you in your costume." Elvis never got to see that costume, but he did see a cover of Vampirella magazine. Elvis always made me laugh, even to the very end.

Peter Cushing and I spent considerable time in New York appearing at the *Famous Monsters* Convention, giving interviews, signing autographs and shaking the fans' hands. We stayed at the same hotel and enjoyed many dinners together, along with Michael Carreras. I particularly loved dinner alone with Peter, because he was so fascinating. He was my childhood hero, my Dr. Van Helsing who killed Dracula.

Peter was a quiet, slender man with a powerful English voice. He had a penchant for exaggerating his gestures, and was every ounce the actor, even off stage.

One dinner was especially memorable. We were to eat in his hotel suite and the table was already set when I arrived. I noticed it was set for three, so I asked who else was coming.

"It's for my wife, I always set a place for her," he replied.

How odd, I thought, knowing that Peter's wife, Helen, had died in 1971. Then again, what a loving, devoted husband he must have been.

After the *Famous Monsters* Convention, while we were still in New York, a rift developed among Hammer Films, American International Pictures and Warren Publishing pertaining to the Vampirella merchandising rights. After selling all of my things and giving up my home in Los Angeles so that I could move to London, Michael called with bad news: The project was going to be held up, until he and Jim Warren could work out their differences.

"Me with Forrest Ackerman, creator of Vampirella, at the Famous Monsters Convention in New York City." From the Barbara Leigh Collection.

My heart skipped a beat, and then nearly stopped altogether. At that time, the project wasn't dead, just delayed. Trying to keep a stiff upper lip, I hid my feelings from Michael and accepted what I knew I couldn't change. Inside, however, I was seething with anger. My life was put on hold, while everyone else was free to go on with theirs. And they had homes to go back to; I didn't.

Because of my association with *Playboy*, Hugh Hefner allowed me to stay at the Los Angeles *Playboy* mansion for a month, until Ed Hookstratten rented me one of his managed apartments. Ever since my "Indian" layout, *Playboy* had been like a family to me. Hef was and is the consummate host to his celebrity friends and playmates. The *Playboy* mansion still rocks!

It finally became apparent that Hammer Films and Warren Publishing weren't going to work out their differences, and I had to let go of my dream of portraying Vampirella. I felt betrayed by everyone, especially Michael. The last time I saw him was in Los Angeles a year later, when he was trying to get his remake of Alfred Hitchcock's *The Lady Vanishes* off the ground. We went out with a group of people to a jazz show, and as the evening progressed, I did a slow boil. I didn't handle my frustration well. I ended up leaving the table, and sat in the car until the show was over. I couldn't stand being in the same room with Michael, since we had stopped all communication. He never took the time to explain his side of the story to me, or why the project had folded, and he patronized me the entire evening. I felt let down. We subsequently lost contact, but by then my feelings were, "Adios, amigo!"

I eventually learned that Michael wanted to buy and control the rights to Vampirella, but that Jim Warren, who owned her, wasn't about to sell his "baby." Jim was willing to lend Vampirella to Carreras for three movie projects, but not to sell her outright.

The bottom line was that these two men were not willing to compromise, so they defeated their own purposes. The reason I was so mad at Michael was that I didn't blame Jim for not selling the merchandising rights. After all, Vampirella was *his* property. In addition, Carreras kept me hanging on for a year. He should have leveled with me and said up front that it would be in my best interest professionally and financially to look for other work, until a compromise could be worked out.

Nothing comes close to the disappointment and heartache that losing out on *Vampirella* brought to me.

Many years later, I learned that Jim had actually extended the *Vampirella* option to Michael for an additional period without further payment, so that he could pursue possible financing overseas. Indeed, in 1977 Michael approached another exotic brunette—British actress Caroline (*The Spy Who Loved Me*) Munro—about playing the part. As it turned out, however, he was unable to raise the money elsewhere.

Michael produced *The Lady Vanishes* in 1978, but it was a box-office flop. His most ambitious project, a $7 million fantasy epic about the Loch Ness Monster entitled *Nessie*, which he was co-producing with David Frost and Japan's Toho Films, collapsed during development. So severe were Hammer's financial woes by 1979 that Michael's creditors took the company—his family business—away from him, and subsequently sold it to two of his former employees. Following an unsuccessful attempt to reenter film production in the late 1980s, Michael Carreras died of cancer in 1994, at age 66.

Things worked out better with Jim Warren. Within a year, Warren Publishing featured me on eight of its *Vampirella* covers, (issues #67, 69, 71, 73, 74, 76, 77 and 78) immortalizing me forever as a part of her history. Twenty years later, I would be invited to appear at the Chiller Theatre Convention in New Jersey, as a celebrity guest as the "Original Vampirella." Numerous fans showed up to meet me, ask for my autograph and take my picture. Some of these people had seen me at the *Famous Monster* Convention in 1975 when they were kids. Now they came to Chiller with kids of their own. I was genuinely touched.

My Vampirella film may have died, but the character remains very much alive. Harris Comics eventually acquired the rights after Warren Publishing went bankrupt and has revived the property in several comic book mini-series, as well as reprints of the Warren material. Polygram Pictures owned the movie rights for several years, and director Jim Wynorski had hoped to star singer/dancer Paula Abdul in the title role. Finally, in 1996, Roger Corman produced a low budget version for Showtime—directed by Wynorski—which starred former model Talisa (*License to Kill*) Soto.

I still receive hundreds of letters a year from Vampirella fans—a true testament to her popularity. I will always be a part of Vampirella's legacy, and she remains a big part of who I am. In an unexpected way, Vampirella has finally paid off for me.

I can't ask for any more than that.

CHAPTER SEVENTEEN

After my major disappointment with *Vampirella*, I would go on to make three movies: *Swim Team*; *Mistress of the Apes* and *Seven*. I also continued with modeling and filming commercials.

In their January 1977 issue, *Playboy* published a second nude pictorial of me, entitled "Natural Leigh." After my first layout, Marilyn Grabowski and I became such close friends that we were like sisters. She was always aware of what was going on in my life, and she approached me when the time was right again. It was her idea for me to shoot with a different photographer, the sexy Phillip Dixon. By that time Charles Bush had gotten married, and his wife didn't want him to shoot nudes anymore, so it all worked out. I didn't feel as if I was letting Charles down.

This pictorial wasn't as ambitious as the first one. Phillip wanted to shoot it in black and white, which was fine with me. We only shot for four days in the summer of 1976, in private homes in Los Angeles and at the beach in Malibu. He didn't shoot nearly as many rolls of film as we did for "Indian."

Although I didn't have the same working relationship with Phillip that I had with Charles, we still worked well together. I let Phillip be the director, but I also contributed with my own ideas. For example, it was my idea to pose in wet sheets, and *Playboy* printed a few of those shots.

This time, I agreed to pose for full frontal nudes. I had a couple of glasses of champagne, and went with the flow. I tried to be creative. In the published pictorial, there is a shot of me being "naughty." I liked the contrast of showing me both naughty and nice.

I also didn't have as much control of the final layout as I had before. I didn't even get to see all of the photos, because I had only picture approval but wasn't involved with the editing process. *Playboy* retained all control. I agreed to that because I trusted Marilyn, and I felt that I looked good. I was shown the layout before publication, for my approval, and I liked it. I thought that the photos were quite beautiful.

Even though I had a ball making my last movie, *Seven*, in Hawaii, the bad experience with *Vampirella* took the wind out of my sails. The entertainment business has broken a lot of hearts and I was no exception. I had a few close calls when I was on the verge of the perfect role that might have catapulted me to stardom. Almost famous.

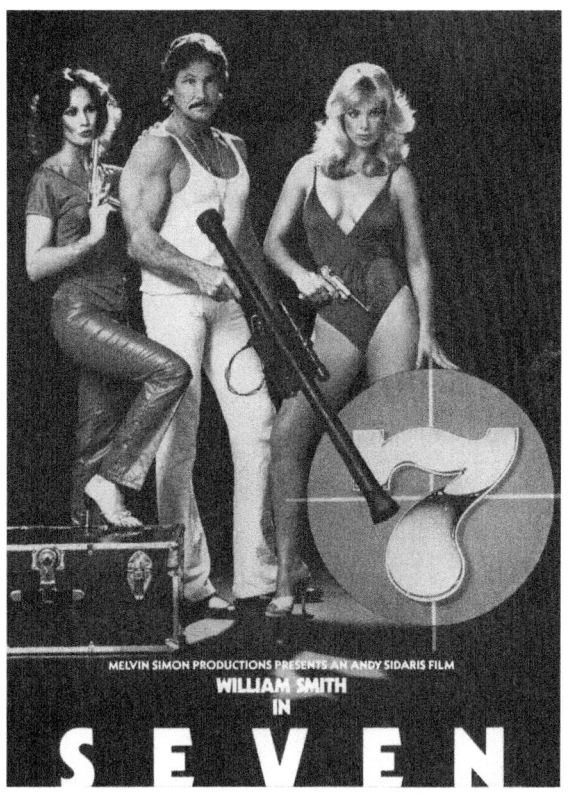

"Me in my last film, *Seven*, with William Smith and Susan Riger. Susan was also the playmate in the May 1977 *Playboy* layout." From the Barbara Leigh Collection.

I was set to co-star in Sidney J. Furie's *Sheila Levine Is Dead and Living in New York*, for Paramount Pictures. One of the film's producers told me that the star of the movie, Elaine May's daughter Jeannie (*The Heartbreak Kid*) Berlin, had seen my screen test and gotten scared. She refused to work with me, and wanted her friend, Rebecca Dianna Smith, to play the part of her girlfriend on screen.

I don't like to be unkind, but I'll never forgive Berlin for that—the studio bought out my contract, and paid me off. I was sad and depressed for a few weeks. The heartache that Hollywood can bring is often harsh.

While waiting for *Vampirella*, I was up for a leading role in a new television series for ABC. Michael Carreras left the decision up to me, and it was easy; I had grown up watching the classic horror films Hammer was known for, so I stayed with *Vampirella*. Bad decision. Jaclyn Smith went on to make television history in the part that could have been mine. The show was *Charlie's Angels*.

Because of *Vampirella*, I also turned down the second female lead in James Goldstone's *Swashbuckler*. The part eventually went to Anjelica Huston.

By the late 1970s, Hollywood was losing its glamour for me, and I was no longer so consumed with my career.

Life for Elvis Presley, Steve McQueen and James Aubrey began to pale as well.

The last time I saw Steve was in September 1976 at the Beverly Wilshire Hotel, while he was rehearsing for the film version of Arthur Miller's adaptation play of Henrik Ibsen's *An Enemy of the People*.

Steve and I hadn't had much contact since he and Ali MacGraw began their affair. We'd spoken a few times on the phone in the past five years. Somehow, he managed to get my phone number, and he'd find me even when I moved. Late one night I received a call from him, and he acted as if no time at all had passed.

"Hi, Barbara," said the voice on the other line.

"Steve!" I practically yelled, I was so happy to hear from him.

"How did you know it was me?" Steve asked in amazement.

"No one says Barbara quite like you do, Steve." We both laughed, because he knew I was pulling his leg. His voice was instantly recognizable.

"How would you like to have dinner with me?" he casually asked.

All kinds of thoughts ran through my head. Why, after all this time, did he want to have dinner with me? Where was his wife Ali? Why was he staying at the Beverly Wilshire Hotel, when he and Ali had a house on the beach in Malibu?

I didn't ask any questions, I simply said yes. He was my friend, and I thought it would be great to see his smiling face and catch up on our lives. If I could read between the lines, he seemed a little down. There was still a part of me that cared very deeply for Steve.

As I hung up the phone, I sat there wondering what Steve was up to. There had to be something going on, otherwise why would he call me? The camaraderie between us was one of trust and friendship. I didn't feel romantic toward him. He was with Ali, a sweet, classy lady who I thought was good for him.

I was a little apprehensive, but excited and even curious to see him after all this time. I knocked gently on his hotel room door and seconds later it flew open. The person on the other side of my stare was a stranger. I was unprepared for what I saw. He looked like a wild mountain man. His hair was long, shaggy and disheveled, and he sported a full beard that was scruffy looking at best.

"Hi," Steve said with a big smile. Those piercing baby blue eyes were still the same. He opened his arms and pulled me close to him, hugging me for a long time. It felt nice and comfortable—maybe we had missed each other a little. I walked into the suite. Movie scripts were piled to the ceiling, and motorcycle parts with grease all over them sat on the floor. *Same old Steve,* I thought. That's what I loved about him. He never tried to impress anyone. Steve's attitude was always, "Take me as I am, or leave me."

"Would you like a drink?" he graciously asked me.

"That sounds great, Steve. By the way, are we going out or are we ordering in?"

"Do you mind if we eat here?" he asked politely. He was going through his hermit phase, and didn't like to venture out in public.

"Fine with me. Is this your new look?" I asked, teasing and serious at the same time.

"It is for now. It's for my latest film project," and then he smiled. I thought his new look was awful, but he was proud of the fact that he could go out in public incognito. I also got the feeling that he liked shocking people with his new appearance.

Room service promptly arrived with our drinks, wine for me and a beer as usual for Steve. We toasted, both feeling pretty good about seeing each other again. We sat on the bed sipping our drinks and talking. After some time had passed, my curiosity got the best of me and so I finally asked Steve what was going on between him and Ali.

He drew a big breath and sighed. "Things aren't going too good with her, but I don't want to talk about her right now. I want to know about you!"

Oops! That wasn't a good sign at all. I instantly changed the topic of conversation. It was obvious that's what he wanted, too, and I didn't want to upset him by pressing him to talk about Ali.

I told him about *Vampirella* and my other projects. He had known for a long time that James and I had broken up. The only remark Steve ever made to me regarding James was that he didn't think he was good enough for me. In the end, I couldn't have agreed more.

One thing that I found amusing that evening was that Steve was caught up in brushing his hair a lot, even though it didn't look like it. He had discovered a new brush with soft rubber bristles, and had a large box filled with them. He grabbed one of the brushes and put it in my hand.

"Here, honey, try this," he ordered me.

I knew that it wasn't right for my long, baby fine hair, but I didn't want to hurt his feelings, so I took it and started brushing my hair. I smiled, thanking him. Secretly, I put it back in the bathroom before I left. How odd it was to see this little vanity in him now, because he'd had none when we were together years before. Back then, his idea of combing his hair was to run his fingers through it, like he did in a scene in *Bullitt*. Now, he had a box full of brushes. Quite a switch.

We had another round of drinks, and started to relax and feel more comfortable with each other. Some of the affection from the old days was beginning to surface. Steve produced a joint, but I declined. I didn't want to get into a compromising situation regarding sex, and I could feel it coming on.

Trying to change the mood, I said I was starving. He chuckled, knowing full well what I was doing, but gave in to me and ordered dinner from room service. Before our food arrived, he gently grabbed me and pulled me down on the bed into an embrace. It was nice to be in his arms, but I wasn't aroused whatsoever. He felt more like a brother, comfortable to be with.

"You feel good," he whispered into my ear, burying his face in my hair. "Ummm, you smell good, too."

"Thank you," I giggled, almost feeling embarrassed. I could sense his sadness, his need for female affection, but I didn't want to start anything I wasn't prepared to finish.

The doorbell to the suite chimed. Saved by the bell! It was room service. Steve wasn't interested in his food. I got the distinct feeling that it wasn't roasted chicken on the menu for tonight—it was me.

We sat down on the bed and ate dinner with our plates in front of us. It reminded me of eating on the bed with Elvis, which we often did while reciting scripture.

Steve wasn't going to give up his idea of romance. After we finished eating, he pushed the food cart into the hall and once again offered me a toke off his joint. This time I said yes. I was always in control with pot; it was liquor that I had a hard time controlling.

"Who's the man in your life now?" he brazenly inquired. That certainly took me by surprise.

I carefully thought about what I was going to say.

"Right now my concentration is on my career," I answered. "I really don't want or need a steady man in my life." It was just what Steve wanted to hear, and he was kissing me passionately before I knew it. Maybe I *could* feel something for him again; I wouldn't know until we tried. I let him kiss me, but to no avail. It just wasn't there for me. No bells, no tingles. I felt silly about letting things go as far as they did.

"Steve, maybe this isn't such a good idea," I said, slightly embarrassed. With that I sat up. He sat up, too.

"It's OK. I understand," he replied. He was a proud man, and I was happy to see that his ego was still intact. It made it much easier to bring the evening to a close. We got past the uncomfortable emotions, but still allowed ourselves a hug every now and then. As I sat talking with him, I couldn't help but think back to our *Junior Bonner* days when he has been so virile and handsome. The man with me now looked like Heidi's grandfather from the Swiss Alps. But then, his beauty was seen by my heart, if not by my eyes. The Steve McQueen mystique was gone.

His didn't look appealing to me, but he had the same beautiful, fragile spirit. I got the feeling that he was searching for something, some kind of happiness that had eluded him his whole life.

"Steve, it's getting late and I'd better go. I have an early call," I told him, breaking up our evening.

"I have an early call, too, baby," he said and we both laughed. We were both lying, but it was a polite way of leaving, blaming the reason on business. I headed for the door, and Steve made one last pass.

"Are you sure you won't stay, babe?" He was smiling, and gently nudging me in a playful way.

I smiled back, "I'd better go, or else we might get into trouble."

"I like trouble," he said with a laugh. He could be terribly charming, and for a split-second I considered the idea, but I knew that it wouldn't work out in the long run. There was no going back in time for either of us. I kissed his cheek gently and bid him farewell.

"Bye baby, I'll call you sometime," Steve promised. I started to walk away, knowing that he was still standing at the door.

"That would be nice," I replied. As I made my way toward the elevator, I turned to look at him one more time. It was my last glimpse of him alive.

I was living in New York City when Steve died. Like so many of his friends and fans, I was unaware of how ill he was because we hadn't spoken for so long. He had been diagnosed with a rare and deadly form of cancer called Mesothelioma for which there was and still is no cure. It wasn't fair.

After hearing his diagnosis, Steve decided that he wasn't going to lay down and die; he was going to fight. He sought treatment in Mexico when American doctors told him that he had three months to live. He would try to combat his cancer in a place where he was given hope, but unfortunately, he was criticized for taking a such a risky chance. I'm sure that from his viewpoint, he felt as if he had no other choice. A year after he was diagnosed, Steve died in Mexico on November 7, 1980, after an operation to remove a cancerous tumor. He fought for his life to the very end.

Steve became a born-again Christian in his last year, and met with the Reverend Billy Graham in his last days. His newfound religion brought great comfort to him. One thing I learned after his death that touched me deeply was that when he realized he was dying, he found the strength and the courage to locate those people he had wronged in the past, to ask for their forgiveness. He apologized to his first wife Neile for his years of unfaithfulness, for which she instantly forgave him. This act of contrition was a shining example of the real Steve McQueen.

When Steve died, I grieved for him. I still remember him as a vibrant, wild and unique human being. I felt blessed to have had the chance to know and love this true rebel. I only wish that I had been able to properly say goodbye.

After I began to write my book, I read Marshall Terrill's biography, *Steve McQueen: Portrait of an American Rebel* and Steve's memory came alive for me. I was deeply touched by what I learned concerning his less than idyllic boyhood, what had happened to him in his movie career, and how gallantly he handled his impending death.

One night after I began writing the section of this book that describes my time with Steve on *Junior Bonner*, I had a dream about him. I was standing in the checkout line of a supermarket. I got a strong feeling that someone was staring at me. I turned around to see who it was and there he was, standing behind me, looking just like he did the last time I saw him: full beard and mustache, wavy long hair and granny glasses.

Steve's spirit seemed more gentle. He was smiling at me. Our faces lit up; we were happy to see each other again. We greeted each other with a warm hug and a kiss on the cheek. A feeling of serenity and peace thoroughly embraced me. It felt as if nothing had changed, as if we were still young. That dream, that experience, or whatever you want to call it, overwhelmed me.

There was an aura of love, a feeling of happiness that consumed my heart and brought to the surface many memories of our time together. The two of us stood talking in that checkout line as if time didn't exist.

The dream allowed me to tap into my deepest feelings and most loving memories of him. The whole experience left me with a longing for and closeness to Steve. The next morning I awoke, feeling so good. I'd like to believe that Steve visited me in my dream to let me know that it was okay to write about our relationship, and to remember the wild and fun times we shared together. I remember him for the unique person he was: a devoted father, a wonderful actor, a loyal friend and an energetic lover.

I'll always have those memories to visit when I miss him. In a way, he's forever with me.

* * * * *

The last time I saw Elvis was in December 1976. Sadly, our busy schedules prevented us from getting together again in private. A group of friends and I went to Las Vegas to watch Elvis perform at the International Hilton. Elvis graciously picked up the tab for all of us and Joe Esposito took care of all the details. Like before, he was taking care of business.

The minute Elvis took to the stage, it was evident that The King was in trouble. He was now at his heaviest, tipping the scales at a hefty 260 pounds, almost 100 pounds overweight. Poor Elvis was beyond anyone's help.

Even though I was a huge fan of Elvis', his performance suffered that night. He would often forget the lyrics to his most familiar songs. It was devastating to see how much he had aged. He must have agonized over it. It brought tears to my eyes to see him this way. On the other hand, I admired his courage to let the show go on and not to worry about his physical appearance. Because Elvis was such a vain man when I knew him, this must have been especially frustrating for him. Even in his own misery, Elvis didn't want to let his fans down by allowing his ego to rule him. His fans were his first priority, and he did everything in his power to give them a great show.

At the end of the performance my girlfriends and I tried to show our support by yelling out, "Elvis, we *love* you!" Others cheered for him too, but I doubt if he could hear us because of the din of the crowd. Elvis knew I was in the audience that evening, but we couldn't meet because Ginger Alden, his latest girlfriend, was right there by E's side after his performance.

Physically, Ginger looked a lot like Priscilla—beautiful brown hair and piercing blue eyes. She was barely 20 at the time. Ginger's sister, Terry, was the current Miss Tennessee and Ginger herself was a former Miss Mid-South.

"Ginger, you're burning a hole through me," were Elvis' first words to her. They remained together until his death. Looking back, I feel sad for Ginger and the way she has been treated by certain people after E died. Somehow, it doesn't seem fair.

When the show was over, Elvis walked to the front of the stage, took a bow and blew kisses to the audience. That was my last glimpse of Elvis.

The last years of Elvis' life have been recounted many times, and the stories all tell of the disintegration of a man who had been such a vibrant human being. I don't think it's fair to judge Elvis based on his last years, because he had so many more good years than bad ones. Besides, Elvis wasn't meant to grow old; he possessed the soul of a young man. Elvis never had any illusions about life getting easier as you got older, and I don't think he looked forward to his "golden years." It takes a strong person to accept mortality.

Elvis didn't like aging, because so much of who he was was based on his handsome and sexy looks. All the world knows he was gifted with a beautiful voice. When both of those were starting to go, it was easy to lose faith in himself. He began to look for answers in other ways—drugs, meditation and food. People who do drugs don't think of growing old, they live for the now. Elvis wasn't thinking about the future at the end of his life—I believe he was looking for a way out. Maybe, a way to God.

I will always remember Elvis the way he was when I first met him in August 1970: beautiful, healthy and happy. His one-of-a-kind voice, his sexy smile, his full pouty lips, his crazy sense of humor, combined with his special love for people are permanently etched in my mind, my soul and my heart.

* * * * *

It had been many years since I had last seen James Aubrey, although my relationship with his daughter, Skye, blossomed into true friendship. Skye had married Ilya Salkind, a movie producer, and moved to Europe in the late 1970s. We saw each other frequently in London years later after I dated her dad. I always knew that James and I would run into each other eventually, but when we did, I was completely shocked. He was older and had drastically changed. It appeared as if his life force had been sapped and was the complete opposite from the once powerful man I knew.

By 1973, James and MGM's love affair came to an abrupt end. In his four year tenure at the studio, he managed to reduce

MGM's $80 million bank debt to $22 million. In the end, he walked away from life at the top because "he just didn't want to do it anymore."

James also stated for the record that expectations for movies, unlike television, were much too unrealistic.

"Every picture is supposed to be a smash and when it isn't, the executive becomes the heavy," he observed.

By the late 1980s, James had hit hard times. He was broke and living with Skye and her two children, Anastasia and Sebastian, in Beverly Hills. Skye and Ilya had divorced, and she had moved back to Southern California. Living with their grandfather gave Skye's children a chance to get to know him more intimately. When I visited Skye, his presence didn't bother me. In fact, it gave me the chance to observe him as a father and grandfather. I finally got to know the "real" James Aubrey. He had a hard time showing emotions, even to his grandchildren. He was pretty much the same to them as he was to his children: distant, cold and completely self-centered. With this perspective, he lost my respect. He was a hard man to figure out. Somewhere he had feelings, but they were locked away, the key long lost.

He wasn't the normal family member. He was more like a boarder in their home, doing things only for himself. I didn't get a sense that he was particularly broken up about it. The way I figure it, he was the one who lost out.

One evening when we found ourselves alone together in the kitchen James made an interesting remark to me.

"Indian, you were the best thing that ever happened to me, and I blew it!" he confessed. I probably should have been flattered by the compliment and a little sad at the way we ended, but I wasn't. I had become cynical. My only thought was to wonder how many times he had said those same words to other women.

The last years of James' life were hard. His professional career was basically over once he left MGM in 1973. He tried to make a comeback, partnering with his son, Jay, in their own production company. They had several exciting projects in the works, but James had made a lot of enemies along the way, and none of his business ventures got off the ground. When you're on top, everybody loves you, but when you're down, no one cares.

On a personal level, he no longer had a beautiful girlfriend on his arm, and his relationships with his children and grandchildren were strained. It was an ending not befitting a handsome, well educated and one-time powerful movie mogul. His selfish and controlling ways had caught up with the legendary Smiling Cobra.

In the end, James died alone in his apartment in Westwood on September 3, 1994, of an apparent heart attack. Thinking he was having an asthma attack, he used his inhaler, which only made it worse. The paramedics arrived on the scene, but they were unable to revive him.

The old saying, "familiarity breeds contempt," best describes my feelings for the once great love of my life. I love his children and grand kids, and believe he left the best of himself through them. Sometimes in life there are relationships that can never be fully reconciled. That's the way it was for James and me.

* * * * *

Even though Warren Publishing had featured me on the covers of eight issues of *Vampirella*, I was never paid for any of them. This led to a falling out with Jim Warren. We ended our dispute with my settling for a small amount of money, and receiving three of the eight original photos back. Jim said the other five original photos would follow, but they never have.

By 1979, I needed to move forward and put *Vampirella* in the past. One good thing happened from the quarrel with Jim Warren—the lawyer who represented me became my husband. Through Peter Schmidt's love and support, I made the decision to retire from films. Peter handled the settlement in an orderly fashion, and urged me to put it behind me and get on with my life, which is exactly what I did.

Peter was a bright, energetic, fun, sophisticated Park Avenue lawyer who specialized in European and corporate law. He grew up in a middle-class section of the Bronx, with a strict mother and father. There wasn't much love in his family. He had little to say about his childhood or his life growing up.

Although Peter was divorced, he was still a wonderful father, showering all the love on his four daughters that he had missed growing up. They were a priority in his life. He made sure that they were all well educated in the best private schools, and instilled in them the value of self-esteem. In the end, it was this trait that saved them from the hurt and embarrassment that came with his brief downfall.

"Peter Schmidt, my ex-husband and me in South Hampton in the early 1980s."
From the Barbara Leigh Collection.

After Peter and I were married in London on October 25, 1984, we shared a grand life together, with a posh Manhattan apartment, a weekend place in the Hamptons, and lived part-time in London. Peter was also a part owner in Xenon, a famous and trendy Manhatton nightspot. He was a trendsetter. Everyone looked up to him.

My life changed for the better and I began focusing on my husband, my son Gerry; and Peter's daughters. We were busy with our family, along with travel and social obligations. I found Peter's family to be very loving, and treated them as if they were my own. I even came to adore Peter's first wife, Dina. We were a happy family for several years. My life with Peter was a fairy tale, but one without a happy ever-after ending.

The nightmare began on a cold Wednesday afternoon in February 1988. Peter phoned me at our home in Manhattan, asking me to meet him at Melon's, a popular hamburger restaurant on Third Avenue.

He ordered a couple of beers, and appeared more nervous than usual. He definitely was agitated about something. Before I knew it, he was telling me a story that would change our lives forever. Peter was in a serious dilemma and owed a client money. He didn't mention the exact figure, but it was in the seven-figure range and large enough that he feared penal repercussions. The only solution he could come up with was to run. In short, he panicked.

Peter needed time to think about the predicament he was, in and how he could pull himself out of this financial fiasco, so he escaped New York to the safety of my mother's home in Miami.

The initial plan was for him to go to Miami, to find a way for us to proceed with our lives. As it turned out, it was the last time I would see my husband for seven years.

It didn't take long before I saw the big picture. Peter was in deep trouble, not only financially, but legally, as well. Although he had asked me to come with him, I declined. Life on the run might have looked glamorouns on the silver screen, but it didn't hold any romance for me.

I drove Peter to the airport on that dreary day, without the slightest suspicion that it would be our last day together. Everything had happened so suddenly. One day we were a blissfully happy family. The next day, he vanished.

In the beginning, I tried to be a supportive wife via long-distance. I didn't realize the severity of Peter's story until I was enlightened by the FBI, who paid me several visits.

It took me a couple of months to realize that I was on my own. Even though I loved Peter dearly, how could I continue to be married to a man who could so easily desert his wife and children?

Several New York newspapers soon picked up the story, and a 15-page article in Clay Felker's *Manhattan Inc.* magazine dubbed Peter "the Cary Grant of Park Avenue." The article was an inaccurate account of Peter's demise, and it was hurtful and overly dramatic. The writer dug low to build a story about Peter's rise and fall, even going so far as to print several pictures from my *Playboy* pictorial, hinting that I was a glamorous home wrecker. It didn't work, because anyone who knew us as a couple knew that the Schmidt family got along well and loved each other.

After four years on the lam, Peter was apprehended in Miami and spent two years behind bars. He also lost his license to practice law.

Peter fell into a pit, and was unable to pull himself out. He suffered a nervous breakdown as a result. I believed then, and still do, that he always intended to pay all his debts: circumstances just got out of hand. Peter was popular, doing many favors for his clients worldwide. Ironically, none of them were there for him when he needed a favor in return.

On a happier note, Peter has bounced back. He's produced a web site for legal advice and dispenses information to lawyers and we're the best of friends today. Even as I write these words, I still feel a part of his extended family. I especially missed watching the girls growing up and all of the family events.

Once again, I had the horrible feeling of being lost. With Peter gone, I did the only thing I could think of; I headed for Los Angeles.

Even though I haven't written of Hollywood in glowing terms, it was a town I was familiar with, and most of my friends were already living there. It was home.

Shortly after my arrival back in Los Angeles, my close friend Marilyn Grabowski got me a job interview for a position as the

Social and Membership Director of the St. James Club. The Club was housed in the landmark Sunset Towers on Sunset Boulevard, one-time home to the famous and infamous alike, including Marilyn Monroe, John Wayne and the flamboyant mobster Benjamin "Bugsy" Siegel.

I got the job, which included mingling with the Los Angeles elite, hosting all of the membership parties and events. It was a blast!

Sadly, the St. James Club closed in June 1994. A small private hotel called The Argyle is there now—still a romantic place to stay and dine.

I had studied Commercial Real Estate Development in Los Angeles for a year in the '80s , and I next put those skills to use. I got my real estate license only to discover that it's a tough business that takes years to build up a clientele. It also change's people, and I didn't like what it took to be successful. Although I enjoyed the challenges of selling real estate, a more exciting opportunity presented itself.

In June of 1997, Marilyn Grabowski invited me to formally become a member of the *Playboy* Magazine family. Marilyn has been with *Playboy* for almost 40 years, and is currently Vice President, West Coast Photo Editor for the magazine. She offered me a job as her assistant and Photo Projects Coordinator. She is one of my dearest friends, and has taught me a lot. Her advice has been some of the best I've ever been given—and I always come out on top when I'm smart enough to take it.

"Me and Marilyn Grabowski partying it up at a reception at Nicky Blair's in the 1970s." From the Barbara Leigh Collection.

Working for *Playboy* is another chapter in my life, one that is very interesting and challenging. If someone had told me when I shot my celebrity pictorials back in the '70s, that I'd be working for the legendary Hugh Hefner and his magazine a quarter of a century later, I wouldn't have believed it.

Every day at *Playboy* is an exciting one. What we do at *Playboy* Studio West is to produce all the gatefolds (Playmate centerfolds), celebrity pictorials, covers for the magazine and special layouts. As I see it, our office is the soul of the magazine because what we produce is what *Playboy* is all about—beautiful women.

To see how a Playmate is created from beginning to end is fascinating. To witness firsthand so many young girls' dreams come true, and to observe them develop into fine young women who are able to further their careers, travel extensively and enjoy wonderful life experiences and opportunities, is greatly rewarding.

These days the *Playboy* mansion is in full swing. Hef, one of the true icons of the last century, has made me feel at home. I feel lucky to be a part of *Playboy* family, and to work within it's kingdom of feminine fantasy and the Hugh Hefner empire.

Living in Los Angeles in the last decade has been an experience, to say the least. The city went through major changes while I lived in New York—more than I could have imagined. The population exploded, traffic worsened—as if it could get any worse than it already was—and the entertainment industry was taken over by college educated Yuppies. A lot of my friends have moved to more relaxed and enchanting environments, like Montana, Colorado and New Mexico. But despite its problems, the City of Angels is a hard town to beat.

As a hobby, I work with homeless animals. My Persian cat, "Bear," was partly responsible for my personal crusade on behalf of abandoned pets. His love and devotion has sensitized me to the needs of animals. He died in June of 2000. I own several cats, and feed countless others in the neighborhood. I consider each and every one of them to be members of my family.

I have also helped with community activities, and have volunteered my time to the Starlight Children's Foundation, as well as to the A.I.D.S. Health Care Foundation.

My involvement with A.I.D.S. stems from personal experience: my beloved son Gerry died of the disease on February 29, 1994. He was 29.

Gerry was one of the sweetest and nicest souls I have ever had the pleasure to know. He was truly a kind person, who adored me as much as I adored him. He was proud of me and my accomplishments, and was my biggest fan and supporter. I know that he would have enjoyed reading this book and poking fun at me at the same time.

Gerry and I finally got our wish of living together when he came to live with me in Los Angeles for six months. Unfortunately, the circumstances were very sad, but we were able to spend the Christmas of 1993 together, and were able to share some wonderful times.

His father and I were at his side as he took his last breath. The death of a child, no matter what age, is an indescribable pain and heartache. I miss Gerry terribly and I grieve for him every day, but he lives in my heart forever.

His dying changed my attitude toward death. I no longer fear it, but look at it as another step toward the Creator. On his headstone in a tiny cemetery in Chattanooga, Tennessee, is written: "We will see you again."

And I believe it!

Marilyn Grabowski once said that I'm more famous than I should be, considering the amount of work I did. The fact that *Vampirella* has come back into my life is a bonus. I think I deserve it!

Whenever I can spare the time, I appear as "the Original Vampirella" at celebrity autograph signings and horror conventions. I relish the interaction with fans who want to talk about *Vampirella*, and other movie and television projects I have done over the years. Their enthusiasm almost matches mine.

Fans can stay in touch with me through the Internet, on my Web site **www.barbaraleigh.com** or write to me at P.O. Box 246, Los Angeles, California, 90028-0246. I always answer everyone's letters and e-mails at baralee16@aol.com.

The fans who write to me, and who see me at my convention appearances, have always had a very positive reaction to my *Playboy* pictorials. Some of the fans from foreign countries, as well as from America, send me the actual pages torn out of the magazines, for my signature. Others bring the issues for me to sign at the conventions, tell me stories about how they've saved the issues for so many years. They're very sweet and endearing, and it's all done in good fun. I take it as sincere flattery, and never feel insulted.

My life seems to have worked out the way it was meant to be. Coincidentally, I am now the same age that James Aubrey was when I was with him. Yet, I still feel young at heart, which wasn't true of him. In my 20s, I thought that people in their 30s were old. When I saw Ali MacGraw in *Love Story*, I thought that she looked great for her age—and she was only 31. I remember that reaction when I turned 30, and it was a big awakening for me. It was the first time that I became aware of my age. But, the toughest birthday for me was turning 29, because I loved my 20s, and I knew that I would never be that age again. After that, no birthday has fazed me.

As you can see, my life is an open book. The truth is the truth. If I had it to do over again, I would make many different choices. Getting an education would have been my main goal because knowledge is the gift of life. For example, archeology is a subject dear to my heart because I love to explore. But because of my upbringing, and of having to constantly be in "survival mode," I never had the luxury of a great education or knew the importance of having one.

I wish I had taken the art of acting more seriously than I did. I wasted a lot of time on my relationships with men, instead of concentrating on myself. That kept me from being a more goal-oriented actress, and I was never very good at promoting myself. I wasted a lot of time having fun.

Yes, I have some regrets, but I also have rewards. The bottom line for me is that I finally know myself. Where I am today is the best place I've ever been. I've had more money, more luxuries and more free time, but never as much self-esteem as I have today.

I certainly believe that with age comes wisdom and peace. If you are happy in your heart, then that's all that matters.

I feel that I could live anywhere and be happy because of who I am. I am finally at a place where I want to live out my life in a quiet and mature manner, without feeling the need to be famous or recognized, although it is nice when it does happen.

So many famous people I have known were unhappy, unfulfilled and didn't have the fairytale ending they wanted.

As each of my life experiences becomes more vivid, I get a better sense of who I am —and I'm pleased about that. Today I keep a much lower profile, and I look forward to what each new year will bring.

I'm not afraid to take advice or criticism. I've learned that to look forward in the most positive way is the best guide through life. I hope I will be remembered as a caring and loving person who has lived an exciting life. To me, success is when one takes responsibility for one's choices.

I'm more aware of what life is all about—what I do and how it affects others, and vice versa. I try to focus on what I can to do to make a difference in the lives of the people around me.

To me, the best part of getting older is the wisdom that comes with it. Unfortunately, some of us grow up late in life. I am one of the "late ones." Most definitely I wasn't ready for stardom when I was in my 20s. If my acting career had taken off, and had I become a major movie or TV star, I don't think I could have handled it at that time. I didn't have any validation of my own identity. "Youth is wasted on the young," is an old cliché that rings true in my life. If only we could live our lives twice.

It has taken me a long time to reach where I am today. None of my past experiences—regardless of how glamorous they may have been—compares to the level of awareness and feeling of being centered that I have now. Each day is a blessing, because I learn something new.

The reality of mortality can be scary, yet I can see it as a friend. For the first time in my life, I feel satisfied.

The few years I've chosen to write about were wonderful, glamorous and what I call the fantasy years. I've tried to tell my story of a time when life was fast and exciting, a time when a young girl was pursued by the three most powerful men in that era of Hollywood. However, they weren't the best years of my life. The best years are yet to come!

Some might say I've come a long way for a little girl from Georgia.

BARBARA LEIGH

"Me today, enjoying life to the fullest." From the Barbara Leigh Collection.

FILMOGRAPHY

The Christian Licorice Store (1969)
National General Pictures
Director: James Frawley
Cast: Beau Bridges, Maud Adams, Gilbert Roland, Allen Arbus, McLean Stevenson, Jean Renoir, Monte Hellman

A young tennis champion falls victim to the pitfalls of Hollywood, commercialism and public adulation.
I had a very minor role, and portrayed a Hollywood starlet. My scene was shot at The Monkees' house. Maud Adams was my favorite model growing up, and it was interesting to watch her work and to get to know her. The film received only a limited release, which was delayed until 1971.

Love Is A Funny Thing (aka Un Homme Qui Me Plait/A Man I Like)
United Artists (1969)
Director: Claude Lelouch
Cast: Jean-Paul Belmondo, Annie Girardot, Kaz Garas, Peter Bergman, Farrah Fawcett, Bill Quinn

I had only one scene, at the front desk of a hotel, where I played a receptionist. Farrah Fawcett and I shared the same agent, the legendary Dick Clayton. She had a cute little part. Farrah always had a smile on her face. She was sweet, shy and unpretentious. We worked together on a few television commercials and print ads in the early 1970s.

The Student Nurses (1970)
(New World Pictures)
Director: Stephanie Rothman
Cast: Elaine Giftos, Karen Carlson, Brioni Farrell, Reni Santoni, Richard Rust

The title says it all—the trials and tribulations of student nurses and handsome interns.

This movie—the first one ever made by Roger Corman's independent company New World Pictures—was co-written and directed by Stephanie Rothman, one of the few female directors working in the exploitation field. She gave me a big break when she chose me to play Priscilla, a hippie student nurse who became pregnant and had an illegal abortion performed by one of the interns. It was my first big part.

Stephanie saw an innocence about me, which she liked. When she interviewed me, she asked me to expose my breasts, so she could see if they were worth photographing. I learned a lot about lighting, hitting my marks and the jobs of everyone on the set. My most memorable scene was when I was nude on the beach with actor Richard Rust. In it, he gave me orange juice laced with acid. In reality, he did just that—Richard put Sunshine Acid in my juice, and I was very stoned on camera.

The Student Nurses was very successful, and put New World Pictures on the map. It led Roger Corman to produce four sequels about sexy young nurses, as well as two similar films about sexy young teachers.

Pretty Maids All in a Row (1971)
MGM
Director: Roger Vadim
Cast: Rock Hudson, Angie Dickinson, Telly Savalas, John David Carson, Roddy McDowall, Keenan Wynn, James Doohan

At a Southern California high school, a rash of murders of young and nubile campus coeds threatens to get in the way of a football game. Rock Hudson starred as my husband, a lecherous guidance counselor/coach in this black comedy written and produced by *Star Trek*'s Gene Roddenberry.

I was walking on the beach at Malibu when I was spotted by famed French director Roger (*And God Created Woman*) Vadim, who discovered Brigitte Bardot. Running from his home, he asked me if I would like to audition for Jean, Rock's wife in the movie. After the test, Vadim was convinced that I was perfect for the part, and ended his search without auditioning any other actresses. Later, when we were in Paris, he offered me a role in a film starring opposite Brigitte Bardot, *Mrs. Don Juan*, but I was homesick for America. Thinking Vadim would hold the part for me, I opted to take a brief trip back to the States, and lost it to actress Jane Birkin. C'est la vie!

Junior Bonner (1972)
ABC Pictures
Director: Sam Peckinpah
Cast: Steve McQueen, Robert Preston, Ida Lupino, Ben Johnson, Joe Don Baker, Mary Murphy, Dub Taylor

An aging rodeo star, Steve McQueen, returns to his hometown of Prescott, Arizona, in hopes of winning the championship one more time.

I enjoyed this the most of all of my films. It was a dream shoot. The cast were seasoned actors, who were fun both on and off the set. Playing romantic scenes opposite Steve McQueen was exciting, and working with the controversial director Sam Peckinpah was unforgettable. Sam was a real pistol. He was a little man, and liked to tip the bottle and raise hell. He had a bad temper, and screamed constantly. But, when we wrapped, he apologized for being so mean to me. He told me that I was one of the sweetest actresses with whom he had ever worked, because I didn't give him back any shit. The truth is, I was petrified by him.

Terminal Island (1973)
Dimension Pictures

Director: Stephanie Rothman
Cast: Tom Selleck, Phyllis Davis, Don Marshall, Roger E. Mosley, Marta Kristen, Jo Morrow

In the near future, male and female prisoners are incarcerated together on a remote island, and try to survive as best as they can.

Stephanie Rothman cast me as Bunny, a catatonic who stabbed her parents to death with an ice pick. This was a low-budget film—shot during TV hiatus, when everyone needed work, including Tom Selleck. I knew him from working together on Brackens World, at Twentieth Century-Fox, and later on a British Sterling cologne commercial, in which I played a dark-haired woman riding a horse. Tom was always fun to work with, and was a genuinely good guy. The film was re-released a decade later to capitalize on the TV success of three cast members: Selleck and Mosley on *Magnum P.I.* and Davis on *Vega$*.

Boss Man (1975)
Dimension Pictures

Director: Jack Arnold
Cast: Fred Williamson, D'Urville Martin, R.G. Armstrong, William Smith

Between 1971 and 1975, more than 200 "Blaxploitation" films were made in this country. This film was an attempt at making a black western. After a dozen sheriffs meet their untimely deaths, the townspeople figure they have nothing to lose when Fred "The

Hammer" Williamson appoints himself "boss," killing off the bad guys one by one.

The movie was shot in Santa Fe, New Mexico, where I fell madly in love with the city. I portrayed a schoolteacher in the town. Cult director Jack (*The Creature From The Black Lagoon*) Arnold was absolutely horrid to me. He had wanted his daughter to play the part. It was Fred who wanted me, because he had a romantic interest in me. Fred was a true gentleman, who made me feel comfortable throughout the shoot, and mediated between Arnold and myself. I had recently had surgery, and shouldn't have been on a horse, so Fred wrote that scene out for me.

Swim Team (1979)
Director: James Polakof
Cast: James Daughton, Stephen Furst, Buster Crabbe

The Whalers school swim team hold a record of zero wins in seven years. Their team captain is a drunk, the star swimmer is practicing her stroke on the coach, and the team mascot is belly up on the beach. It's a case of sink or swim for the new coach, who wants to transform this group into a real swim team.

I played the part of a recreation teacher who taught the team how to swim. I basically pointed, blew a whistle and screamed a lot. Yes it's true: teachers are seriously underpaid!

Mistress of the Apes (1979)
Cine-World
Director: Larry Buchanan
Cast: Jenny Neumann, Garth Pillsbury, Walt Robin, Stuart Lancaster, Suzy Mandel

A woman searches for her missing husband in Africa with a group of scientists. She discovers a tribe of near-men who may be the missing link and becomes its queen. I played Laura, a member of the group and Jenny Neumman played the title role.

The notorious bad Larry (*Mars Needs Women*) Buchanan had watched me in acting class, and hired me to play the heavy. The movie was shot in the Thousand Oaks area of California, which doubled for Africa. After the shooting was finished, we had to do some "looping," to get rid of the background noises. I kept waiting for them to give me a recording date, but they wouldn't. I wanted to visit my ex-husband, Joe Lewis, who was shooting *Jaguar Lives!* in Spain. After I bought non-refundable plane tickets, they finally called me for the looping, so I couldn't do it. Larry never forgave me. It was only a small amount of looping, but he had *all* of my lines dubbed by another actress. I later ran into him at the Cannes Film Festival, where he was selling the movie on my name. He completely ignored me.

The best thing about this turkey is the beautiful painting on the front of the video box, by acclaimed fantasy artist Boris Vallejo.

Seven (1979)
American International Pictures
Director: Andy Sidaris
Cast: William Smith, Guich Koock, Martin Kove, Art Metrano, Susan Kiger

The U.S. government hires seven mercenaries to slaughter seven professional criminals. I played a spy who was supposed to hunt down and kill a murderer and woman torturer. This fast paced action film contains an abundance of tongue-in-cheek humor. That, combined with the location filming in Hawaii, made the experience quite enjoyable. I had a lot of fun flying helicopters on my days off. Andy Sidaris had been a director for ABC-TV sports, and became famous for shooting beautiful girls in the stands. Character actor Bill Smith, who usually portrayed villains, had a rare chance to play the hero. He was very modest, and kept saying that he wasn't well known, but I assured him that he had a cult following. This was my last feature film.

Television Movies

The Ballad of Andy Crocker
ABC—November 18, 1969

Director: George McCowan
Cast: Lee Majors, Joey Heatherton, Jimmy Dean, Agnes Moorhead, Marvin Gaye, Jill Haworth, Pat Hingle

In my first acting role, I played a hippie rolling joints in an alleyway. The script was written by actor Stuart Margolin, who went on to fame as "Angel," James Garner's troublesome friend on *The Rockford Files*.

Lee Majors, who was also under contract to Dick Clayton, struck up a friendship with me. Lee was a nice southern charmer who was just beginning to date his future wife, Farah Fawcett.

The President's Plane Is Missing
ABC—October 23, 1973

Director: Daryl Duke
Cast: Buddy Ebsen, Peter Graves, Arthur Kennedy, Rip Torn, Raymond Massey, Mercedes McCambridge, Dabney Coleman

Although this movie, based on Robert Serling's best-selling novel, was shot in 1971, ABC delayed its broadcast for two years, because the subject matter—about a Red Chinese plot to overthrow the U.S. Government—was considered too "politically sensitive." I played an officer in the Air Force along with Peter Graves, a lovely man, whom I adored as an actor. One night, a couple of cast members took me to a topless bar on Century Boulevard. Being naive, I had never been inside such an establishment, but I tried to play it cool. It was very hard to keep my composure when a stripper took a liking to me, and danced provocatively for me in front of my fellow actors. Every time I pass that location, (which is still there after 25 years) it always brings back the memory of that movie, and a smile to my face.

Smile, Jenny, You're Dead
ABC—February 3, 1974

Director: Jerry Thorpe
Cast: David Janssen, Andrea Marcovicci, John Anderson, Howard da Silva, Martin Gabel, Clu Gulager, Zalman King, Jodie Foster

David Janssen played private detective Harry Orwell, who lived on Paradise Cove beach in this pilot for his *Harry O* series. I played the "girl next door," who kept popping over to his place in a bikini. It was a small part, but it was a reoccurring role in the series. He was a very good friend, and we stayed in touch until his death. We shot my last episode after I was cast for *Vampirella*. When I told David that I was off to make the movie that would make me a star, he asked, "Who's Vampirella?" When I told him that it was the part of a female vampire, David smiled and wise-cracked, "Barbara, you can bite my neck anytime!"

Television Appearances

Bracken's World (NBC)
Most Deadly Game: "Witches Sabbath" (ABC)
Dan August (ABC)
Harry O: "The Acolyte" and "Mayday" (ABC)
The Price Is Right: hostess (CBS)
Baretta (ABC)
C.H.I.P.S. (NBC)
W.E.B. (NBC)
The Rockford Files (NBC)
The Incredible Hulk: "Killer Instinct" (CBS)

Printed in Great Britain
by Amazon